SAINT
OF THE
DAY

Revised Edition

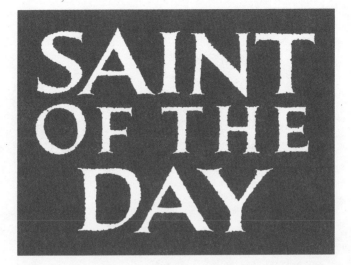

Lives and Lessons
for Saints and Feasts
of the New Missal

Leonard Foley, O.F.M., Editor

St. Anthony Messenger Press

CINCINNATI, OHIO

Nihil Obstat: Rev. Thomas Richstatter, O.F.M.
Rev. Robert J. Buschmiller

Imprimi Potest: Rev. John Bok, O.F.M.
Provincial

Imprimatur: +James H. Garland, V.G.
Archdiocese of Cincinnati
May 31, 1990

The *nihil obstat* and *imprimatur* are a declaration that a book is considered to be free from doctrinal or moral error. It is not implied that those who have granted the *nihil obstat* and *imprimatur* agree with the contents, opinions or statements expressed.

Scripture citations are taken from *The New American Bible With Revised New Testament*, copyright ©1986 by the Confraternity of Christian Doctrine, and are used by permission. All rights reserved.

Book design by Julie Lonneman
Cover calligraphy by Patti Paulus

ISBN 0-86716-318-6

Contents

MAY

JUNE

Introduction

A loving God offers us friendship, and the result of that gracious act is our holiness.

God alone is holy: to be God is to be holy. Not to be God is not to be holy. It is not "right" or "natural" for us to live the life of God. But God creates God's own life in us, and makes it "right" for God to love us. When God finds divine life and love in us, it becomes "natural" for us to live "supernatural" or divine lives.

This was God's eternal plan: "[God] chose us in [Christ], before the foundation of the world, to be holy and without blemish before him" (Ephesians 1:4). "I am the vine, you are the branches. Whoever remains in me and I in him will bear much fruit, because without me you can do nothing" (John 15:5).

With faith, all this is obvious. Without faith, it contradicts obvious human experience. A prime heresy of all ages has been the one that says holiness is what we create by our own efforts.

It seems so evident that it is *my* strength of character that refuses to take revenge; *my* hard-won decision to remain faithful that sustains my marriage; *my* endurance that brings me to Mass every Sunday; *my* devotion that prompts me to fast twice a week and give tithes of all I possess. Why shouldn't I thank God that I'm not like the rest of the world—at least many people?

Faith is the answer.

Faith is not a naive abandonment of reason to certain mysterious truths, or a feverish scrambling to put together a respectable life of good works. Faith is the gift whereby we are able to receive a gift. We are able to open ourselves to God's friendship, communion, oneness. Our freedom becomes total freedom when we let Christ enfold it in his own.

It is true that we must "work" at being holy—keeping the commandments, being on the alert for others' need, disciplining ourselves. But even this effort is God's gift, and the more we realize that the more we will use the gift. We have absolutely nothing to give God—except himself. One Eucharistic Prayer for weekdays says, "Our desire to thank you is itself your gift."

The supreme example of human holiness is that which Jesus received—*as truly human*—from his Father. His heart was totally open to the gift of his Father's love, and by his death and resurrection he is the living source whereby the Holy Spirit flows into us and through us.

The saints whose lives are described in this book are *special* signs of God's activity. Their surrender to God's love was so generous an approach to the total surrender of Jesus that the Church recognized them as heroes and heroines worthy to be held up for our inspiration. They remind us that the Church *is* holy, can never stop being holy and is called to show the holiness of God by living the life of Christ.

Our holiness is the same as theirs—God's holiness. Their lives were indeed conditioned by the culture and history of their own day; their expression of holiness is partly different from what it would be in the 20th century. But the essence is the same: They received God's gift with joy. They call to us to do likewise: "Do you not know that you are the temple of God, and that the Spirit of God dwells in you? If anyone destroys God's temple, God will destroy that person; for the temple of God, which you are, is holy" (1 Corinthians 3:16-17).

Legends and Facts

There are two kinds of saints' biography. First, there is *practical* hagiography (from *hagios*—"holy"—and *graphein*—"to write"). From earliest times lists of martyrs were drawn up so that their anniversaries could be remembered. Narratives of martyrdom were also written by their contemporaries. Finally, later writers wrote accounts to edify or to satisfy curiosity. Collections were made, finally developing into what were called *legendaries*.

Scientific hagiography began in the 17th century. A Jesuit, Rosweyde, first conceived the project of a collection of the lives of the saints. The project was actually carried out by J. Bollandus (hence the name Bollandists). As much as the state of historical science then permitted, the material of the lives of the saints was subjected to severe critical analysis. Later, with the development in archaeology, philology and paleography, greater advances were made in determining the factual content of saints' biographies.

In this book we clearly label legend as such. We have included the legendary material because it is part of the tradition (small "t") of the Church. Ages previous to ours were not blessed (or afflicted) with our passion for scientific historical accuracy. Whether this saint actually walked on the water or not, whether the sacred Host flew from the hands of the priest to the saint's heart or not was of no real concern. God had worked infinitely greater miracles of grace in the lives of these heroes and heroines of Christ. If what we call legendary is not factually true, it is often true to the character and spirit of the saint involved. In short, if it didn't happen, it easily could have.

We have kept and identified some of these legends, therefore, as the quaint and human poetry of countless ordinary Christians whose imaginations knew no bounds when divine friendship with God's holy ones was involved.

Other Celebrations

This revised edition of *Saint of the Day* includes other commemorations on the Roman calendar. For the first time, we have included the solemnities of Jesus which claim no Sunday or holy day as their own, the feasts of the premier saint, Mary, and celebrations which commemorate the dedication of key churches and honoring the angels. Last but by no means least, we have included the days which honor the whole galaxy of unnamed stars among God's people: All Saints and All Souls.

The highest class of liturgical celebration is the *solemnity*. There are three that honor specific saints: Joseph, Peter and Paul, John the Baptist; two are solemnities of the Lord; and two honor Mary.

The next class consists of *feasts*. Saints whose commemorations are ranked as feasts are those of the apostles, Paul, Mark, Luke, Stephen, Lawrence and the Holy Innocents. Other feasts include the Visitation, the Transfiguration and the Triumph of the Cross, Mary's birthday and the Dedication of St. John Lateran.

Memorials are divided into two classes. About one third of the saints' days are *obligatory* memorials, that is, they must be celebrated unless superseded by a higher ranking celebration (for example, a day of Lent). The other celebrations of saints' days are *optional*.

Authors

This book is the result of a cooperative effort of Franciscan friars of St. John the Baptist Province and the staff of the St. Anthony Messenger Press. Contributors include Franciscan friars John Bach, Murray Bodo, John Boehman, Leander Blumlein, Robert Buescher, Timothy Carmody, Bede Clancy, Steve Connair, George Darling, Berard Doerger, Roy Effler, Austin Ernstes, William Faber, William Farris, Aldric Heidlage, Alan Hirt, Jerome Kaelin, Christopher Kerr, Jerome Kircher, Cletus Kistner, Hilarion Kistner, Lawrence Landini, William Linesch, Nicholas Lohkamp, Patrick McCloskey, George Miller, Pio O'Connor, Norbert Oldegeering, Anthony Panozzo, Peter Poppleton, Joseph Ricchini, Peter Ricke, Gary Sabourin, Boniface Sack, Jeffrey Scheeler, Anthony Walter and Michael Wohler.

Contributing members of the St. Anthony Messenger Press staff are: Lisa Biedenbach, Leonard Foley, Jeremy Harrington, Carol Luebering, Norman Perry, Mary Lynne Rapien and Jack Wintz.

Mary, Mother of God

Mary's divine motherhood broadens the Christmas spotlight.
Mary has an important role to play in the Incarnation of the
Second Person of the Blessed Trinity. She consents to God's
invitation conveyed by the angel (Luke 1:26-38). Elizabeth
proclaims: "Most blessed are you among women and blessed is *the
fruit of your womb*. And how does this happen to me, that *the
mother of my Lord* should come to me?" (Luke 1:42-43, emphasis
added). Mary's role as mother of God places her in a unique
position in God's redemptive plan.

Without naming Mary, Paul asserts that "God sent his Son,
born of a woman, born under the law" (Galatians 4:4). Paul's
further statement that "God sent the spirit of his Son into our
hearts, crying out 'Abba, Father!' " helps us realize that Mary is
mother to all the brothers and sisters of Jesus.

Some theologians also insist that Mary's motherhood of
Jesus is an important element in God's creative plan. God's "first"
thought in creating was Jesus. Jesus, the incarnate Word, is the
one who could give God perfect love and worship on behalf of all
creation. As Jesus was "first" in God's mind, Mary was "second"
insofar as she was chosen from all eternity to be his mother.

The precise title "Mother of God" goes back at least to the
third or fourth century. In the Greek form *Theotokos* (God-
bearer), it became the touchstone of the Church's teaching about
the Incarnation. The Council of Ephesus in 431 insisted that the
holy Fathers were right in calling the holy virgin *Theotokos*. At
the end of this particular session crowds of people marched
through the street shouting: "Praised be the *Theotokos*!" The
tradition reaches to our own day. In its chapter on Mary's role in
the Church, Vatican II's *Constitution on the Church* calls Mary
"Mother of God" 12 times.

COMMENT: Other themes come together at today's celebration. It is the Octave of Christmas: Our remembrance of Mary's divine motherhood injects a further note of Christmas joy. It is a day of prayer for world peace: Mary is the mother of the Prince of Peace. It is the first day of a new year: Mary continues to bring new life to her children—who are also God's children.

QUOTE: "The Blessed Virgin was eternally predestined, in conjunction with the incarnation of the divine Word, to be the Mother of God. By decree of divine Providence, she served on earth as the loving mother of the divine Redeemer, an associate of unique nobility, and the Lord's humble handmaid. She conceived, brought forth, and nourished Christ" (*Constitution on the Church*, 61).

Basil the Great and Gregory Nazianzen

Bishops and Doctors

Basil the Great (329-379). Basil was on his way to becoming a famous teacher when he decided to begin a religious life of gospel poverty. After studying various modes of religious life, he founded what was probably the first monastery in Asia Minor. He is to monks of the East what St. Benedict is to the West, and his principles influence Eastern monasticism today.

He was ordained priest, assisted the Archbishop of Caesarea (now southeastern Turkey), and ultimately became archbishop himself, in spite of opposition from some of his suffragan bishops, probably because they foresaw coming reforms.

One of the most damaging heresies in the history of the Church, Arianism, which denied the divinity of Christ, was at its height. The emperor Valens persecuted the orthodox, and put great pressure on Basil to remain silent and admit the heretics to communion. Basil remained firm, and Valens backed down. But trouble remained. When the great St. Anthanasius died, the mantle of defender of the faith against Arianism fell upon Basil. He strove mightily to unite and rally his fellow Catholics who were crushed by tyranny and torn by internal dissension. He was misunderstood, misrepresented, accused of heresy and ambition. Even appeals to the pope brought no response. "For my sins I seem to be unsuccessful in everything."

He was tireless in pastoral care. He preached twice a day to huge crowds, built a hospital that was called a wonder of the world (as a youth he had organized famine relief and worked in a soup kitchen himself) and fought the white slave market.

Basil was best known as an orator. His writings, though not recognized greatly in his lifetime, rightly place him among the great teachers of the Church. Seventy-two years after his death the Council of Chalcedon described him as "the great Basil, minister of grace who has expounded the truth to the whole earth."

COMMENT: As the French say, "The more things change, the more they remain the same." Basil faced the same problems as modern Christians. Sainthood meant trying to preserve the spirit of Christ in such perplexing and painful problems as reform, organization, fighting for the poor, maintaining balance and peace in misunderstanding.

QUOTE: St. Basil said: "The bread which you do not use is the bread of the hungry; the garment hanging in your wardrobe is the garment of him who is naked; the shoes that you do not wear are the shoes of the one who is barefoot; the money that you keep locked away is the money of the poor; the acts of charity that you do not perform are so many injustices that you commit."

Gregory Nazianzen (329-390). Gregory gladly accepted his friend Basil's invitation to join him in a newly founded monastery after his baptism at 30. The solitude was broken when his father, a bishop, needed help in his diocese and estate. Gregory, it seems, was ordained priest practically by force, and only reluctantly accepted the responsibility. He was skillful in avoiding a schism that threatened because his own father made compromises with Arianism. At 41, he was chosen suffragan bishop of Caesarea and at once came into conflict with Valens, the emperor, who was supporting the Arians. An unfortunate by-product of the battle was the cooling of the friendship of two saints. Basil, his archbishop, sent him to a miserable and unhealthy town on the border of unjustly created divisions in his diocese. Basil reproached Gregory for not going to his see.

When protection for Arianism ended with the death of Valens, Gregory was called to rebuild the faith in the great see of Constantinople which had been under Arian teachers for three decades. Retiring and sensitive, he dreaded being drawn into the whirlpool of corruption and violence. He first stayed at a friend's home, which became the only orthodox church in the city. In such surroundings, he began giving the great sermons on the Trinity for which he is famous. In time, he did rebuild the faith in the city, but at the cost of great suffering, slander, insults and even personal violence. An interloper even tried to take over his bishopric.

His last days were spent in solitude and austerity. He wrote religious poetry, some of it autobiographical, of great depth and beauty. He was acclaimed simply as "the Theologian."

COMMENT: It may be small comfort, but the present turmoil of change in the Church is a mild storm compared to the devastation caused by the Arian heresy, a trauma the Church has never forgotten. Christ did not promise the kind of peace we would love to have—no problems, no opposition, no pain. In one way or another, holiness is always the way of the cross.

QUOTE: "God accepts our desires as though they were a great value. He longs ardently for us to desire and love him. He accepts our petitions for benefits as though we were doing him a favor. His joy in giving is greater than ours in receiving. So let us not be apathetic in our asking, nor set too narrow bounds to our requests; nor ask for frivolous things unworthy of God's greatness."

JANUARY 4   MEMORIAL (U.S.A.)

Elizabeth Ann Seton
Religious (1774-1821)

Mother Seton is one of the keystones of the American Catholic Church. She founded the first native American religious community for women, the Sisters of Charity, opened the first American parish school and established the first American Catholic orphanage. All this she did in the span of 46 years while raising her five children.

Elizabeth Ann Bayley Seton is a true daughter of the American Revolution, born August 28, 1774, just two years before the Declaration of Independence. By birth and marriage, she was linked to the first families of New York and enjoyed the fruits of high society. Reared a staunch Episcopalian by her mother and stepmother, she learned the value of prayer, Scripture and a nightly examination of conscience. Her father, Dr. Richard Bayley, did not have much use for churches but was a great humanitarian, teaching his daughter to love and serve others.

The early deaths of her mother in 1777 and her baby sister in 1778 gave Elizabeth a feel for eternity and the temporariness of

9

the pilgrim life on earth. Far from being brooding and sullen, she faced each new "holocaust," as she put it, with hopeful cheerfulness.

At 19, Elizabeth was the belle of New York and married a handsome, wealthy businessman, William Magee Seton. They had five children before his business failed and he died of tuberculosis. At 30, Elizabeth was widowed, penniless, with five small children to support.

While in Italy with her dying husband, Elizabeth witnessed Catholicity in action through family friends. Three basic points led her to become a Catholic: belief in the real presence, devotion to the Blessed Mother and conviction that the Catholic Church led back to the apostles and to Christ. Many of her family and friends rejected her when she became a Catholic in March 1805.

To support her children, she opened a school in Baltimore. From the beginning, her group followed the lines of a religious community, which was officially founded in 1809.

The thousand or more letters of Mother Seton reveal the development of her spiritual life from ordinary goodness to heroic sanctity. She suffered great trials of sickness, misunderstanding, the death of loved ones (her husband and two young daughters) and the heartache of a wayward son. She died January 4, 1821, and on March 17, 1963, Pope John XXIII proclaimed her the first American-born citizen to be beatified. She was canonized September 24, 1975.

COMMENT: Elizabeth Seton had no extraordinary gifts. She was not a mystic or stigmatic. She did not prophesy or speak in tongues. She had two great devotions: abandonment to the will of God and an ardent love for the Blessed Sacrament. She wrote to a friend, Julia Scott, that she would prefer to exchange the world for a "cave or a desert." "But God has given me a great deal to do, and I have always and hope always to prefer his will to every wish of my own." Her brand of sanctity is open to all if we love God and do his will.

QUOTE: Elizabeth Seton told her sisters, "The first end I propose in our daily work is to do the will of God; secondly, to do it in the manner he wills it; and thirdly, to do it because it is his will."

John Neumann
Bishop (1811-1860)

Perhaps because the United States got a later start in the history of the world, it has relatively few canonized saints, but their number is increasing.

Blessed John Neumann was born in what is now Czechoslovakia. After studying in Prague, he came to New York at 25 and was ordained a priest. He did missionary work in New York until he was 29, when he joined the Redemptorists and became the first of this order to profess vows in the United States. He continued missionary work in Maryland, Virginia and Ohio, where he became popular with the Germans.

At 41, as bishop of Philadelphia, he organized the parochial school system into a diocesan one, increasing the number of pupils almost twentyfold within a short time.

Gifted with outstanding organizing ability, he drew into the city many teaching orders of sisters and the Christian Brothers. During his brief assignment as vice provincial for the Redemptorists, he placed them in the forefront of the parochial movement.

Well-known for his holiness and learning, spiritual writing and preaching, on October 13, 1963, he became the first American bishop to be beatified. He was canonized June 19, 1977.

COMMENT: Neumann took seriously our Lord's words, "Go and teach all nations." From Christ he received his instructions and the power to carry them out. For Christ does not give a mission without supplying the means to accomplish it. The Father's gift in Christ to John Neumann was his exceptional organizing ability, which he used to spread the Good News.

Today the Church is in dire need of men and women to continue in our times the teaching of the Good News. The obstacles and inconveniences are real and costly. Yet if Christians would approach Christ, he would supply the necessary talents to answer today's needs. The Spirit of Christ will continue his work through the instrumentality of generous Christians.

QUOTE: "Since every man of whatever race, condition, and age is endowed with the dignity of a person, he has an inalienable right to an education corresponding to his proper destiny and suited to his native talents, his sex, his cultural background and his ancestral heritage. At the same time, this education should pave the way to brotherly association with other peoples, so that genuine unity and peace on earth may be promoted. For a true education aims at the formation of the human person with respect to the good of those societies of which, as a man, he is a member, and in whose responsibilities, as an adult, he will share" (*Declaration on Christian Education*, 1).

Andre Bessette

Religious (1845-1937)

Brother Andre expressed a saint's faith by a lifelong devotion to St. Joseph.

Sickness and weakness dogged him from his birth. He was the eighth of 12 children born to a French Canadian couple near Montreal. Adopted at 12, when both parents had died, he became a farmhand. Various trades followed: shoemaker, baker, blacksmith— all failures. He was a factory worker in the United States during the boom times of the Civil War.

At 25, he applied for entrance into the Congregation of the Holy Cross. After a year's novitiate, he was not admitted because of his weak health. But with an extension and the urging of Bishop Bourget (see Marie-Rose Durocher, October 6) he was finally received. He was given the humble job of doorkeeper at Notre Dame College in Montreal, with additional duties as sacristan, laundry worker and messenger. "When I joined this community, the superiors showed me the door, and I remained 40 years."

In his little room near the door, he spent much of the night on his knees. On his windowsill, facing Mount Royal, was a small statue of St. Joseph, to whom he had been devoted since childhood. When asked about it he said, "Some day, St. Joseph is going to be honored in a very special way on Mount Royal!"

When he heard someone was ill, he visited to bring cheer and to pray with the sick person. He would rub the sick person lightly with oil taken from a lamp burning in the college chapel. Word of healing powers began to spread.

When an epidemic broke out at a nearby college, Andre volunteered to nurse. Not one person died. The trickle of sick people to his door became a flood. His superiors were uneasy;

diocesan authorities were suspicious; doctors called him a quack. "I do not cure," he said again and again. "St. Joseph cures." In the end he needed four secretaries to handle the 80,000 letters he received each year.

For many years the Holy Cross authorities had tried to buy land on Mount Royal. Brother Andre and others climbed the steep hill and planted medals of St. Joseph. Suddenly, the owners yielded. Andre collected 200 dollars to build a small chapel and began receiving visitors there—smiling through long hours of listening, applying St. Joseph's oil. Some were cured, some not. The pile of crutches, canes and braces grew.

The chapel also grew. By 1931 there were gleaming walls, but money ran out. "Put a statue of St. Joseph in the middle. If he wants a roof over his head, he'll get it." The magnificent Oratory on Mount Royal took 50 years to build. The sickly boy who could not hold a job died at 92.

COMMENT: Rubbing ailing limbs with oil or a medal? Planting a medal to buy land? Isn't this superstition? Aren't we long past that?

Superstitious people rely *only* on the "magic" of a word or action. Brother Andre's oil and medals were authentic sacramentals of a simple, total faith in the Father who lets his saints help him bless his children.

QUOTE: "It is with the smallest brushes that the artist paints the most exquisitely beautiful pictures."

Raymond of Penyafort

Priest (1175-1275)

Since Raymond lived into his 100th year, he had a chance to do many things. As a member of the Spanish nobility, he had the resources and the education to get a good start in life.

By the time he was 20 he was teaching philosophy. In his early 30's he earned a doctorate in both canon and civil law. At 47 he became a Dominican. Pope Gregory IX called him to Rome to work for him and to be his confessor. One of the things the pope asked him to do was to gather together all the decrees of popes and councils that had been made in 80 years since a similar collection by Gratian. Raymond compiled five books called the "Decretals." They were looked upon as one of the best organized collections of Church law until the 1917 codification of canon law.

Earlier, Raymond had written for confessors a book of cases. It was called *Summa de casibus poenitentiae*. More than just a list of sins and penances, it discussed pertinent doctrines and laws of the Church that pertained to the problem or case brought to the confessor.

When Raymond was 60 he was appointed Archbishop of Tarragona, the capital of Aragon. He didn't like the honor at all and ended up getting sick and resigning in two years.

He didn't get to enjoy his peace long, however, because when he was 63 he was elected by his fellow Dominicans to be the head of the whole order, the second man to follow St. Dominic himself. Raymond worked hard, visited on foot all the Dominicans, reorganized their constitutions and managed to put through a provision that a master general be allowed to resign. When the new constitutions were accepted, Raymond, then 65, resigned.

He still had 35 years to oppose heresy and work for the conversion of the Moors in Spain. He got St. Thomas Aquinas to write his work *Against the Gentiles.*

In his 100th year the Lord let Raymond retire.

COMMENT: Raymond was a lawyer, a canonist. Legalism is one of the things that the Church tried to rid herself of at Vatican II. It is too great a preoccupation with the letter of the law to the neglect of the spirit and purpose of the law. The law can become an end in itself, so that the value the law was intended to promote is overlooked. But we must guard against going to the opposite extreme and seeing law as useless or something to be lightly regarded. Laws ideally state those things that are for the best interests of everyone and make sure the rights of all are safeguarded. From Raymond, we can learn a respect for law as a means of serving the common good.

QUOTE: "He who hates the law is without wisdom,/and is tossed about like a boat in a storm" (Sirach 33:2).

Hilary

Bishop and Doctor (315?-368)

This staunch defender of the divinity of Christ was a gentle and courteous man, devoted to writing some of the greatest theology on the Trinity, and was like his Master in being labeled a "disturber of the peace." In a very troubled period in the Church, his holiness was lived out in both scholarship and controversy.

Raised a pagan, he was converted to Christianity when he met his God of nature in the Scriptures. His wife was still living when he was chosen, against his will, to be the bishop of Poitiers in France. He was soon taken up with battling what became the scourge of the fourth century, Arianism, which denied the divinity of Christ.

The heresy spread rapidly. St. Jerome said "The world groaned and marveled to find that it was Arian." When the emperor Constantius ordered all the bishops of the West to sign a condemnation of Athanasius, the great defender of the faith in the East, Hilary refused and was banished from France to far off Phrygia (the day would come when he would be called the "Athanasius of the West"). While in exile, writing, he was invited by some semi-Arians (hoping for reconciliation) to a council the emperor called to counteract the council of Niceas. But Hilary predictably defended the Church, and when he sought public debate with the heretical bishop who had exiled him, the Arians, dreading the meeting and its outcome, pleaded with the emperor to send this troublemaker back home. Hilary was welcomed by his people.

COMMENT: Christ said his coming would bring not peace but a sword (see Matthew 10:34). The Gospels offer no support for us if we fantasize about a sunlit holiness that knows no problems. Christ did *not* escape at the last moment, though he did live happily ever after—after a life of controversy, problems, pain and frustration. Hilary, like all saints, simply had more of the same.

STORY: This immovable defender of orthodoxy was very gentle in reconciling the bishops of France who, in fear or ignorance, had accepted the Arian creed. And while he wrote a blistering indictment of the emperor for sponsoring heresy, he could also point out, calmly, that sometimes the difference between heretical and orthodox doctrines was in the words rather than the ideas. He counseled bishops of the West, therefore, to be reserved in their condemnation. And this, of course, won him new enemies.

Anthony
Abbot (251-356)

The life of Anthony will remind many of the life of St. Francis of Assisi. At 20, he was so moved by the Gospel message, "Go, sell what you have, and give to [the] poor" (Mark 10:21b), that he actually did just that with his rich inheritance. He is different from Francis in that most of his life was spent in solitude. He saw the world completely covered with snares, and gave the Church and the world the witness of solitary asceticism, great personal mortification and prayer. But no saint is antisocial, and Anthony drew many people to himself for spiritual healing and guidance.

At 54, he responded to many requests and founded a sort of monastery of scattered cells. Again like Francis, he had great fear of "stately buildings and well-laden tables."

At 60, he hoped to be a martyr in the renewed Roman persecution of 311, fearlessly exposing himself to danger while giving moral and material support to those in prison. At 88, he was fighting the Arian heresy, that massive trauma from which it took the Church centuries to recover. "The mule kicking over the altar" denied the divinity of Christ.

Anthony is associated in art with a T-shaped cross, a pig and a book. The pig and the cross are symbols of his valiant warfare with the devil—the cross his constant means of power over evil spirits, the pig a symbol of the devil himself. The book recalls his preference for "the book of nature" over the printed word.

Anthony died in solitude at 105.

COMMENT: In an age that smiles at the notion of devils and angels, a person known for having power over evil spirits must at least make us pause. And in a day when people speak of life as a "rat race," one who devotes a whole life to solitude and prayer points to an essential of the Christian life in all ages. Anthony's hermit life reminds us of the absoluteness of our break with sin and the totalness of our commitment to Christ. Even in God's good world there is another world whose false values constantly tempt us.

STORY: Lest we be misled by the awesomeness of Anthony's asceticism, we have a statement from his biographer that presses the meaning and result of all Christian life: "Strangers knew him from among his disciples by the joy on his face."

Even the great emperor Constantine wrote to him, asking for his prayers. Anthony told his friends, "Don't be surprised that the emperor writes to me—he's just another man, as I am. But be astounded that God should have written to us, and that he has spoken to us by his Son."

Fabian

Pope and Martyr (c. 250)

Fabian was a Roman layman who came into the city from his farm one day as clergy and people were preparing to elect a new pope. Eusebius, a Church historian, says a dove flew in and settled on the head of Fabian. This sign united the votes of clergy and laity and he was chosen unanimously.

He led the Church for 14 years and died a martyr's death during the persecution of Decius in A.D. 250. St. Cyprian wrote to his successor that he was an "incomparable" man whose glory in death matched the holiness and purity of his life.

In the catacombs of St. Callistus, the stone that covered Fabian's grave may still be seen, broken into four pieces, bearing the Greek words, "Fabian, bishop, martyr."

COMMENT: We can go confidently into the future and accept the change that growth demands only if we have firm roots in the past, in a living tradition. A few pieces of stone in Rome are a reminder to us that we are bearers of 20 centuries of a living tradition of faith and courage in living the life of Christ and showing it to the world. We have brothers and sisters who have "gone before us marked with the sign of faith," as the First Eucharistic Prayer puts it, to light the way for us.

QUOTE: "The blood of the martyrs is the seed of the Church" (Tertullian).

JANUARY 20   OPTIONAL

Sebastian

Martyr (257?-288?)

Nothing is historically certain about St. Sebastian except that he was a Roman martyr, was venerated in Milan even in the time of St. Ambrose and was buried on the Appian Way, probably near the present Basilica of St. Sebastian. Devotion to him spread rapidly, and he is mentioned in several martyrologies as early as A.D. 350.

The *legend* of St. Sebastian is important in art, and there is a vast iconography. What scholars now agree is a pious fable has Sebastian entering the Roman army only because in that position he could assist the martyrs without arousing suspicion. Finally he was found out, hailed before Emperor Diocletian and delivered to Mauritanian archers to be shot to death. His body was pierced with arrows, and he was left for dead. But he was found still alive by those who came to bury him. He recovered, but refused to flee. One day he took up a position near where the emperor was to pass. He accosted the emperor, denouncing him for his cruelty to Christians. This time the sentence of death was carried out. Sebastian was beaten to death with clubs.

COMMENT: The fact that many of the early saints made such a tremendous impression on the Church—awakening widespread devotion and great praise from the greatest writers of the Church—is proof of the heroism of their lives. As has been said, legends are by definition not true. Yet they may express the very substance of the faith and courage evident in the lives of these heroes and heroines of Christ.

STORY: Another legend describes Sebastian's effectiveness in bolstering the courage of those in prison. Two men under sentence of death seemed about to give in to their captors. Sebastian made such an impassioned exhortation to constancy that it not only confirmed the two in their original convictions but won over many other prisoners in the jail. Again, this particular story may not be true. But it is true of the lives of all saints.

Agnes

Virgin and Martyr (d. 258?)

Almost nothing is known of this saint except that she was very young—12 or 13—when she was martyred in the last half of the third century. Various modes of death have been suggested— beheading, burning, strangling.

Legend has it she was a beautiful girl whom many young men wanted to marry. Among those she refused, one reported her to the authorities as being a Christian. She was arrested and confined to a house of prostitution. The legend continues that one who looked upon her lustfully lost his sight and had it restored by her prayer. She was condemned, executed and buried near Rome in a catacomb that eventually was named after her. The daughter of Constantine built a basilica in her honor.

COMMENT: Like that of modern Maria Goretti, the martyrdom of a virginal young girl made a deep impression on a society enslaved to a materialistic outlook. Like Agatha, who died in similar circumstances, Agnes is a symbol that holiness does not depend on length of years, experience or human effort. It is a gift God offers to all.

QUOTE: "This is a virgin's birthday; let us follow the example of her chastity. It is a martyr's birthday; let us offer sacrifices; it is the birthday of holy Agnes: let men be filled with wonder, little ones with hope, married women with awe, and the unmarried with emulation. It seems to me that this child, holy beyond her years and courageous beyond human nature, received the name of Agnes (Greek: pure) not as an earthly designation but as a revelation from God of what she was to be" (from St. Ambrose's discourse on virginity).

Vincent

Deacon and Martyr (d. 304)

When Jesus deliberately began his "journey" to death, Luke says that he "set his face" to go to Jerusalem. It is this quality of rocklike courage that distinguishes the martyrs.

Most of what we know about this saint comes from the poet Prudentius. His "acts" have been rather freely colored by the imagination of their compiler. But St. Augustine, in one of his sermons on St. Vincent, speaks of having the acts of his martyrdom before him. We are at least sure of his name, his being a deacon, the place of his death and burial.

According to the story we have (and as with some of the other early martyrs the unusual devotion he inspired must have had a basis in a very heroic life), Vincent was ordained deacon by his friend St. Valerius of Saragossa in Spain. The Roman emperors had published their edicts against the clergy in 303, and the following year against the laity. Vincent and his bishop were imprisoned in Valencia. Hunger and torture failed to break them. Like the youths in the fiery furnace, they seemed to thrive on suffering.

Valerius was sent into exile, and Dacian now turned the full force of his fury on Vincent. Tortures that sound like those of World War II were tried. But their main effect was the progressive disintegration of Dacian himself. He had the torturers beaten because they failed.

Finally he suggested a compromise: Would Vincent at least give up the sacred books to be burned according to the emperor's edict? He would not. Torture on the gridiron continued, the prisoner remaining courageous, the torturer losing control of himself. Vincent was thrown into a filthy prison cell—and converted the jailer. Dacian wept with rage, but strangely enough, ordered the prisoner to be given some rest.

Friends among the faithful came to visit him, but he was to have no earthly rest. When they finally settled him on a comfortable bed, he went to his eternal rest.

COMMENT: The martyrs are heroic examples of what God's power can do. It is humanly impossible, we realize, for someone to go through tortures such as Vincent had and remain faithful. But it is equally true that by human power alone no one can remain faithful even *without* torture or suffering. God does not come to our rescue at isolated, "special" moments. God is supporting the supercruisers as well as children's toy boats.

QUOTE: "Wherever it was that Christians were put to death, their executions did not bear the semblance of a triumph. Exteriorly they did not differ in the least from the executions of common criminals. But the moral grandeur of a martyr is essentially the same, whether he preserved his constancy in the arena before thousands of raving spectators or whether he perfected his martyrdom forsaken by all upon a pitiless flayer's field" (*The Roman Catacombs*, Hertling-Kirschbaum).

Francis de Sales

Bishop and Doctor (1567-1622)

Francis was destined by his father to be a lawyer so that the young man could eventually take his elder's place as a senator from the Province of Savoy in France. For this reason Francis was sent to Padua to study law. After receiving his doctorate, he returned home and, in due time, told his parents he wished to enter the priesthood. His father strongly opposed Francis in this, and only after much patient persuasiveness on the part of the gentle Francis did he finally consent. Francis was ordained and elected provost of the diocese of Geneva, then a center for the heretical Calvinists. Francis set out to convert them, especially in the district of Chablais. By preaching and distributing the little pamphlets he wrote to explain true Catholic doctrine he had remarkable success.

At 35 he became bishop of Geneva. While administering his

diocese he continued to preach, hear confessions and catechize the children. His gentle character was a great asset in winning souls. He practiced his own axiom: "A spoonful of honey attracts more flies than a barrelful of vinegar."

Besides his two well-known books, *The Introduction to the Devout Life* and *A Treatise on the Love of God*, he wrote many pamphlets and carried on a vast correspondence. For his writings, he has been named patron of the Catholic Press. His writings, filled with his characteristic gentle spirit, are addressed to lay people. He wants to make them understand that they too are called to be saints. As he wrote in *The Introduction to the Devout Life*: "It is an error, or rather a heresy, to say devotion is incompatible with the life of a soldier, a tradesman, a prince, or a married woman....It has happened that many have lost perfection in the desert who had preserved it in the world."

In spite of his busy and comparatively short life, he had time to collaborate with another saint, Jane Frances de Chantal, in the work of establishing the Sisters of the Visitation. These women were to practice the virtues exemplified in Mary's visit to Elizabeth: humility, piety and mutual charity. They at first engaged to a limited degree in works of mercy for the poor and the sick. Today, while some communities conduct schools, others live a strictly contemplative life.

COMMENT: Francis de Sales took seriously the words of Christ "Learn of me for I am meek and humble of heart." As he said himself, it took him 20 years to conquer his quick temper, but no one ever suspected he had such a problem, so overflowing with good nature and kindness was his usual manner of acting. His perennial meekness and sunny disposition won for him the title of "Gentleman Saint."

QUOTE: Francis tells us: "The person who possesses Christian meekness is affectionate and tender towards everyone: he is disposed to forgive and excuse the frailties of others; the goodness of his heart appears in a sweet affability that influences his words and actions, presents every object to his view in the most charitable and pleasing light."

Conversion of Paul

Apostle

Paul's entire life can be explained in terms of one experience—his meeting with Jesus on the road to Damascus. In an instant, he saw that all the zeal of his dynamic personality was being wasted, like the strength of a boxer swinging wildly. Perhaps he had never seen Jesus, though he was only some years older. But he had acquired a zealot's hatred of all Jesus stood for, as he began to harass the Church: "...entering house after house and dragging out men and women, he handed them over for imprisonment" (Acts 8:3b). Now he himself was "entered," possessed, all his energy harnessed to one goal—being a slave of Christ in the ministry of reconciliation, an instrument to help others experience the one Savior.

One sentence determined his theology: "I am Jesus, whom you are persecuting" (Acts 9:5b). Jesus was mysteriously identified with people—the loving group of people Saul had been running down like criminals. Jesus, he saw, was the mysterious fulfillment of all he had been blindly pursuing.

From then on, his only work was to "present everyone perfect in Christ. For this I labor and struggle, in accord with the exercise of his power working within me" (Colossians 2:28b-29). "For our gospel did not come to you in word alone, but also in power and in the Holy Spirit and [with] much conviction" (1 Thessalonians 1:5a).

Paul's life became a tireless proclaiming and living out of the message of the cross: Christians die baptismally to sin and are buried with Christ; they are dead to all that is sinful and unredeemed in the world. They are made into a new creation, already sharing Christ's victory and someday to rise from the dead like him. Through this risen Christ the Father pours out the Spirit on them, making them completely new.

So Paul's great message to the world was: You are saved entirely by God, not by anything you can do. Saving faith is the gift of total, free, personal and loving commitment to Christ, a commitment that then bears fruit in more "works" than the Law could ever contemplate.

COMMENT: Paul is undoubtedly hard to understand. His style often reflects the rabbinical style of argument of his day, and often his thought skips on mountaintops while we plod below. But perhaps our problems are accentuated by the fact that so many beautiful jewels have become part of the everyday coin in our Christian language (see Quote, below).

QUOTE: "Love is patient, love is kind. It is not jealous, [love] is not pompous, it is not inflated, it is not rude, it does not seek its own interests, it is not quick-tempered, it does not brood over injury, it does not rejoice over wrongdoing but rejoices with the truth. It bears all things, believes all things, hopes all things, endures all things" (1 Corinthians 13:4-7).

Timothy and Titus

Bishops

Timothy (d. 97?). What we know from the New Testament of Timothy's life makes it sound like that of a modern harried bishop. He had the honor of being a fellow apostle with Paul, both sharing the privilege of preaching the gospel and suffering for it.

Timothy had a Greek father and a Jewish mother named Eunice. Being the product of a "mixed" marriage, he was considered illegitimate by the Jews. It was his grandmother, Lois, who first became Christian. Timothy was a convert of Paul around the year 47 and later joined him in his apostolic work. He was with Paul at the founding of the Church in Corinth. During the 15 years he worked with Paul, he became one of his most faithful and trusted friends. He was sent on difficult missions by Paul—often in the face of great disturbance in Churches Paul had founded.

Timothy was with Paul in Rome during the latter's house arrest. At some period Timothy himself was in prison (Hebrews 13:23). Paul installed him as his representative at the Church of Ephesus.

Timothy was comparatively young for the work he was doing. ("Let no one have contempt for your youth," Paul writes in 1 Timothy 4:12a.) Several references seem to indicate that he was timid. And one of Paul's frequently quoted lines was addressed to him: "Stop drinking only water, but have a little wine for the sake of your stomach and your frequent illnesses" (1 Timothy 5:23).

COMMENT: Nostalgia for the good old days in the Church— especially the early Church—should not blind us to the fact that the servants have never been greater than the Master. Their holiness was lived out in day-to-day perplexities, sufferings and apparent failure. The world is not saved by what we do, but by what God does through the life he creates for us.

QUOTE: Paul writes, "...I remind you to stir into flame the gift of God that you have through the imposition of my hands. For God did not give us a spirit of cowardice but rather of power and love and self-control. So do not be ashamed of your testimony to our Lord, nor of me, a prisoner for his sake; but bear your share of hardship for the gospel with the strength that comes from God" (2 Timothy 1:6-8).

Titus, bishop (d. 94?). Titus has the distinction of being a close friend and disciple of Paul as well as a fellow missionary. He was a Greek, apparently from Antioch. In spite of his being a Gentile, Paul would not let him be forced to undergo circumcision at Jerusalem. Titus is seen as a peacemaker, administrator, great friend. Paul's second letter to Corinth affords an insight into the depth of his friendship with Titus, and the great fellowship they had in preaching the gospel: "When I went to Troas...I had no relief in my spirit because I did not find my brother Titus. So I took leave of them and went on to Macedonia....For even when we came into Macedonia, our flesh had no rest, but we were afflicted in every way—external conflicts, internal fears. But God, who encourages the downcast, encouraged us by the arrival of Titus..." (2 Corinthians 2:12a, 13; 7:5-6).

When Paul was having trouble with the community at Corinth, Titus was the bearer of Paul's severe letter and was successful in smoothing things out. Paul writes he was strengthened not only by the arrival of Titus but also "by the encouragement with which he was encouraged in regard to you, as he told us of your yearning, your lament, your zeal for me, so that I rejoiced even more....And his heart goes out to you all the more, as he remembers the obedience of all of you, when you received him with fear and trembling" (2 Corinthians 7:7a, 15).

In the Letter to Titus, Titus is seen to be administrator of the Christian community on the island of Crete, charged with organizing it, correcting abuses and appointing presbyter-bishops.

COMMENT: In Titus we get another glimpse of life in the early Church: great zeal in the apostolate, great communion in Christ, great friendship. Yet always there is the problem of human nature and the unglamorous details of daily life: the need for charity and patience in "quarrels with others, fears within myself," as Paul says. Through it all, the love of Christ sustained them. At the end of this letter to Titus, Paul says that when the temporary substitute comes, "hurry to me."

QUOTE: "But when the kindness and generous love
            of God our Savior appeared,
        not because of any righteous deeds we had done
            but because of his mercy,
        he saved us through the bath of rebirth
            and renewal by the holy Spirit,
        whom he richly poured out on us
            through Jesus Christ our savior,
        so that we might be justified by his grace
            and become heirs in hope of eternal life.
        This saying is trustworthy." (Titus 3:4-8)

Angela Merici

Virgin (1470?-1540)

Angela has the double distinction of founding the first teaching order of women in the Church and what is now called a "secular institute" of religious women.

As a young woman she became a member of the Third Order of St. Francis, and lived a life of great austerity, wishing, like St. Francis, to own nothing, not even a bed. Early in life she was appalled at the ignorance among poorer children, whose parents could not or would not teach them the elements of religion. Angela's charming manner and good looks complemented her natural qualities of leadership. Others joined her in giving regular instruction to the little girls of their neighborhood.

She was invited to live with a family in Brescia (where, she had been told in a vision, she would one day found a religious community). Her work continued and became well known. She became the center of a group of people with similar ideals.

She eagerly took the opportunity for a trip to the Holy Land. When they had gotten as far as Crete, she was struck with blindness. Her friends wanted to return home, but she insisted on going through with the pilgrimage, and visited the sacred shrines with as much devotion and enthusiasm as if she had her sight. On the way back, while praying before a crucifix, her sight was restored at the same place where it had been lost.

At 57, she organized a group of 12 girls to help her in catechetical work. Four years later the group had increased to 28. She formed them into the Company of St. Ursula (patroness of medieval universities and venerated as a leader of women) for the purpose of re-Christianizing family life through solid Christian education of future wives and mothers. The members continued to live at home, had no special habit and took no formal vows, though the early rule prescribed the practice of virginity, poverty and obedience. The idea of a teaching order of women was new and took time to develop. The community thus existed as a "secular institute" until some years after Angela's death.

COMMENT: As with so many saints, history is mostly concerned with their activities. But we must always presume deep Christian faith and love in one whose courage lasts a lifetime, and who can take bold new steps when human need demands.

QUOTE: In a time when change is problematic to many, it may be helpful to recall a statement this great leader made to her sisters: "If according to times and needs you should be obliged to make fresh rules and change certain things, do it with prudence and good advice."

Thomas Aquinas
Priest and Doctor (1225-1274)

By universal consent Thomas Aquinas is the preeminent spokesman of the Catholic tradition of reason and of divine revelation. He is one of the great teachers of the medieval Catholic Church, honored with the titles Doctor of the Church and Angelic Doctor.

At five he was given to the Benedictine monastery at Monte Cassino in his parents' hopes that he would choose that way of life and later become abbot. In 1239 he was sent to Naples to complete his studies. It was here that he was first attracted to Aristotle's philosophy.

By 1243, Thomas abandoned his family's plans for him and

joined the Dominicans, much to his mother's dismay. On her order, Thomas was captured by his brother and kept at home for over a year.

Once free, he went to Paris and then to Cologne, where he finished his studies with Albert the Great. He held two professorships at Paris, lived at the court of Pope Urban IV, directed the Dominican school at Rome and Viterbo, combated adversaries of the Mendicants and Averroists and argued with some Franciscans about Aristotelianism.

His greatest contribution to the Catholic Church is his writings. The unity, harmony and continuity of faith and reason, of revealed and natural human knowledge, pervades his writings. One might expect Thomas, as a man of the gospel, to be an ardent defender of revealed truth. But he was broad enough, deep enough, to see the whole natural order as coming from God the Creator, and to see reason as a divine gift to be highly cherished.

The *Summa Theologica*, his last and, unfortunately, uncompleted work, deals with the whole of Catholic theology. He stopped work on it after celebrating Mass on December 6, 1273. When asked why he stopped writing, he replied, "I cannot go on...All that I have written seems to me like so much straw compared to what I have seen and what has been revealed to me." He died March 7, 1274.

COMMENT: We can look to Thomas Aquinas as a towering example of Catholicism in the sense of broadness, universality and inclusiveness. We should be determined anew to exercise the divine gift of reason in us, our power to know, learn and understand. At the same time we should thank God for the gift of his revelation, especially in Jesus Christ.

QUOTE: "Hence we must say that for the knowledge of any truth whatsoever man needs divine help, that the intellect may be moved by God to its act. But he does not need a new light added to his natural light, in order to know the truth in all things, but only in some that surpasses his natural knowledge" (*Summa Theologica*, 1-2, 109, 1).

John Bosco
Priest (1815-1888)

John Bosco's theory of education could well be used in today's schools. It was a preventive system, rejecting corporal punishment and placing students in surroundings removed from the likelihood of committing sin. He advocated frequent reception of the sacraments of Penance and Holy Communion. He combined catechetical training and fatherly guidance, seeking to unite the spiritual life with one's work, study and play.

Encouraged during his youth to become a priest so he could work with young boys, John was ordained in 1841. His service to youths started when he met a poor orphan and instructed him in preparation for receiving Holy Communion. He then gathered young apprentices and taught them catechism.

After serving as chaplain in a hospice for working girls, John opened the Oratory of St. Francis de Sales for boys. Several wealthy and powerful patrons contributed money, enabling him to provide two workshops for the boys, shoemaking and tailoring.

By 1856, the institution had grown to 150 boys and had added a printing press for publication of religious and catechetical pamphlets. His interest in vocational education and publishing justify him as patron of young apprentices and Catholic publishers.

John's preaching fame spread and by 1850 he had trained his own helpers because of difficulties in retaining young priests. In 1854 he and his followers informally banded together under

St. Francis de Sales.

With Pope Pius IX's encouragement, John gathered 17 men and founded the Salesians in 1859. Their activity concentrated on education and mission work. Later, he organized a group of Salesian Sisters to assist girls.

COMMENT: John Bosco educated the whole person—body and soul united. He believed that Christ's love and our faith in that love should pervade everything we do—work, study, play. For John Bosco, being a Christian was a full-time effort, not a once-a-week, Mass-on-Sunday experience. It is searching and finding God and Jesus in everything we do, letting their love lead us. Yet, John realized the importance of job-training and the self-worth and pride that comes with talent and ability so he trained his students in the trade crafts, too.

QUOTE: "Every education teaches a philosophy; if not by dogma then by suggestion, by implication, by atmosphere. Every part of that education has a connection with every other part. If it does not all combine to convey some general view of life, it is not education at all" (G.K. Chesterton, *The Common Man*).

Presentation of the Lord

At the end of the fourth century a woman named Etheria made a pilgrimage to Jerusalem. Her journal, discovered in 1887, gives an unprecedented glimpse of liturgical life there. Among the celebrations she describes is the Epiphany (January 6), the observance of Christ's birth and the gala procession in honor of his Presentation in the Temple 40 days later—February 15. (Under the Mosaic Law, a woman was ritually "unclean" for 40 days after childbirth, when she was to present herself to the priests and offer sacrifice—her "purification." Contact with anyone who had brushed against mystery—birth or death—excluded a person from Jewish worship.)

The observance spread throughout the Western Church in the fifth and sixth centuries. But the Church in the West celebrated Jesus' birth on December 25, so the Presentation was moved to February 2, 40 days after Christmas.

At the beginning of the eighth century, Pope Sergius inaugurated a candlelight procession; at the end of the same century the blessing and distribution of candles which continues to this day became part of the celebration, giving the feast its popular name: Candlemas.

COMMENT: In Luke's account, Jesus was welcomed in the temple by two elderly people, Simeon and the widow Anna. They embody Israel in their patient expectation; they acknowledge the infant Jesus as the long-awaited Messiah. Early references to the Roman feast dub it the feast of St. Simeon, the old man who burst into a song of joy which the Church still sings at day's end.

QUOTE: "Christ himself says, 'I am the light of the world.' And we are the light, we ourselves, if we receive it from him....But how do we receive it, how do we make it shine? ...[T]he candle tells us: by burning, and being consumed in the burning. A spark of fire, a ray of love, an inevitable immolation are celebrated over that pure, straight candle, as, pouring forth its gift of light, it exhausts itself in silent sacrifice" (Paul VI).

Blase

Bishop and Martyr (d. 316)

We know more about the devotion to St. Blase by Christians around the world than we know about the saint himself. His feast is observed as a holy day in the Eastern Church. The Council of Oxford, in 1222, prohibited servile labor in England on Blase's feast day. The Germans and Slavs hold him in special honor and for decades most United States Catholics yearly have sought the blessing of St. Blase for their throats.

We know that Bishop Blase was martyred in his episcopal city of Sebastea, Armenia, in 316. The *legendary* "acts" of St. Blase were written 400 years later. According to them Blase was a good bishop, working hard to encourage the spiritual and physical health of his people. Although the Edict of Toleration, 311, granting freedom of worship in the Roman Empire was already five years old, persecution still raged in Armenia. Blase was apparently forced to flee to the back country. There he lived as a hermit in solitude and prayer, but made friends with the wild animals. One day a group of hunters seeking wild animals for the amphitheater stumbled upon Blase's cave. They were first surprised and then frightened. The bishop was kneeling in prayer surrounded by patiently waiting wolves, lions and bears.

As the hunters hauled Blase off to prison, the legend has it, a mother came with her young son who had a fish bone lodged in his throat. At Blase's command the child was able to cough up the bone.

Agricolaus, governor of Cappadocia, tried to persuade Blase to sacrifice to pagan idols. The first time he refused, he was beaten. The next time he was suspended from a tree and his flesh torn with iron combs or rakes. (English wool combers, who used similar iron combs, took Blase as their patron. They could easily appreciate the agony the saint underwent.) Finally he was beheaded.

COMMENT: Four centuries give ample opportunity for fiction to creep in with fact. Who can be sure how accurate Blase's biographer was? But biographical details are not essential. Blase is seen as one more example of the power those have who give themselves entirely to Jesus. As Jesus told his apostles at the Last Supper, "If you remain in me and my words remain in you, ask for whatever you want and it will be done for you" (John 15:7). With faith we can follow the lead of the Church in asking for Blase's protection.

QUOTE: "Through the intercession of St. Blase, bishop and martyr, may God deliver you from ailments of the throat and from every other evil. In the name of the Father, and of the Son and of the Holy Spirit" (Blessing of St. Blase).

Ansgar

Bishop (801-865)

The "apostle of the north" (Scandinavia) had enough frustrations
to become a saint—and he did. He became a Benedictine at
Corbie, where he had been educated. Three years later, when the
king of Denmark became a convert, he went to that country for
three years of missionary work, without noticeable success.
Sweden asked for Christian missionaries, and Ansgar went there,
suffering capture by pirates and other hardships on the way. Less
than two years later he was recalled, to become abbot of New
Corbie (Corvey) and bishop of Hamburg. The Pope made him
legate for the Scandinavian missions. Funds for the northern
apostolate stopped with the emperor Louis' death. After 13 years'
work in Hamburg, Ansgar saw it burned to the ground by
invading Northmen; Sweden and Denmark returned to
paganism.

   He directed new apostolic activities in the North, himself
traveling to Denmark and being instrumental in the conversion
of another king. By the strange device of casting lots, the King of
Sweden allowed the Christian missionaries to return.

   Ansgar's biographers remark that he was an extraordinary
preacher, a humble and ascetical priest. He was devoted to the
poor and the sick, imitating the Lord in washing their feet and
waiting on them at table. He died peacefully at Bremen,
Germany, without achieving his wish to be a martyr.

   Sweden became pagan again after his death, and remained
so until the coming of missionaries two centuries later.

COMMENT: History records what people do, rather than what they
are. Yet the courage and perseverance of men and women like
Ansgar can only come from a solid base of union with the original

courageous and persevering Missionary. Ansgar's life is another reminder that God writes straight with crooked lines. Christ takes care of the effects of the apostolate in his own way; he is first concerned about the purity of the apostles themselves.

STORY: One of his followers was bragging about all the miracles the saint had wrought. Ansgar rebuked him by saying "If I were worthy of such a favor from my God, I would ask that he grant me this one miracle: that by his grace he would make of me a good man."

Agatha

Virgin and Martyr (d. 251?)

As in the case of Agnes, another virgin-martyr of the early Church, almost nothing is historically certain about this saint except that she was martyred in Sicily during the persecution of the Roman emperor Decius in 251.

Legend has it that Agatha, like Agnes, was arrested as a Christian, tortured and sent to a house of prostitution to be mistreated. She was preserved from being violated, and was later put to death.

She is claimed as the patroness of both Palermo and Catania. The year after her death, the stilling of an eruption of Mt. Etna was attributed to her intercession. As a result, apparently, people continued to ask her prayers for protection against fire.

COMMENT: The scientific modern mind winces at the thought of a volcano's might being contained by God because of the prayers of a Sicilian girl. Still less welcome, probably, is the notion of that saint being the patroness of such varied professions as those of foundrymen, nurses, miners and Alpine guides. Yet, in our historical precision, have we lost an essential human quality of wonder and poetry, and even our belief that we come to God by helping each other, both in action and prayer?

QUOTE: When Agatha was arrested, the legend says, she prayed: "Jesus Christ, Lord of all things! You see my heart, you know my desires. Possess all that I am—you alone. I am your sheep; make me worthy to overcome the devil." And in prison: "Lord, my creator, you have protected me since I was in the cradle. You have taken me from the love of the world and given me patience to suffer. Now receive my spirit."

Paul Miki and Companions

Martyrs (d. 1597)

Nagasaki, Japan, is familiar to Americans as the city on which the second atomic bomb was dropped, killing hundreds of thousands. Three and a half centuries before, 26 martyrs of Japan were crucified on a hill, now known as the Holy Mountain, overlooking Nagasaki. Among them were priests, brothers and laymen, Franciscans, Jesuits and members of the Third Order of St. Francis; there were catechists, doctors, simple artisans and servants, old men and innocent children—all united in a common faith and love for Jesus and his Church.

Brother Paul Miki, a Jesuit and a native of Japan, has become the best known among the martyrs of Japan. While hanging upon a cross Paul Miki preached to the people gathered for the execution: "The sentence of judgment says these men came to

Japan from the Philippines, but I did not come from any other country. I am a true Japanese. The only reason for my being killed is that I have taught the doctrine of Christ. I certainly did teach the doctrine of Christ. I thank God it is for this reason I die. I believe that I am telling only the truth before I die. I know you believe me and I want to say to you all once again: Ask Christ to help you to become happy. I obey Christ. After Christ's example I forgive my persecutors. I do not hate them. I ask God to have pity on all, and I hope my blood will fall on my fellow men as a fruitful rain."

When missionaries returned to Japan in the 1860's they at first found no trace of Christianity. But after establishing themselves they found that thousands of Christians lived around Nagasaki and that they had secretly preserved the faith. Beatified in 1627, the martyrs of Japan were finally canonized in 1862.

COMMENT: Today a new era has come for the Church in Japan. Although the number of Catholics is not large, the Church is respected and has total religious freedom. The spread of Christianity in the Far East is slow and difficult. Faith such as that of the 26 martyrs is needed today as much as in 1597.

QUOTE: "Since Jesus, the Son of God, manifested his charity to laying down his life for us, no one has greater love than he who lays down his life for Christ and his brothers. From the earliest times, then, some Christians have been called upon—and some will always be called upon—to give this supreme testimony of love to all men, but especially to persecutors. The Church, therefore, considers martyrdom as an exceptional gift and as the highest proof of love.

"Though few are presented with such an opportunity, nevertheless, all must be prepared to confess Christ before men, and to follow him along the way of the cross through the persecutions which the Church will never fail to suffer" (*Constitution on the Church*, 42).

Jerome Emiliani
(1481-1537)

A careless and irreligious soldier for the city-state of Venice, Jerome was captured in a skirmish at an outpost town and chained in a dungeon. In prison Jerome had a lot of time to think, and he gradually learned how to pray. When he escaped, he returned to Venice where he took charge of the education of his nephews— and began his own studies for the priesthood.

In the years after his ordination events again called Jerome to a decision and a new life-style. Plague and famine swept northern Italy. Jerome began caring for the sick and feeding the hungry at his own expense. In his service to the sick and the poor he soon resolved to devote himself and his property solely to others, particularly to abandoned children. He founded three orphanages, a shelter for penitent prostitutes and a hospital.

Around 1532 Jerome and two other priests established a congregation dedicated to the care of orphans and the education of youth. Jerome died in 1537 from a disease he caught while tending the sick. In 1928 Pius XI named him the patron of orphans and abandoned children.

COMMENT: Very often in our lives it seems to take some kind of "imprisonment" to free us from the shackles of our self-centeredness. When we're "caught" in some situation we don't want to be in, we finally come to know the liberating power of Another. Only then can we become another for "the imprisoned" and "the orphaned" all around us.

QUOTE: " 'The father of orphans and the defender of widows is God in his holy dwelling. God gives a home to the forsaken; he leads forth prisoners to prosperity; only rebels remain in the parched land' (Psalm 68)....We should not forget the growing number of persons who are often abandoned by their families and by the community: the old, orphans, the sick and all kinds of people who are rejected...We must be prepared to take on new functions and new duties in every sector of human activity and especially in the sector of world society, if justice is really to be put into practice. Our action is to be directed above all at those men and nations which, because of various forms of oppression and because of the present character of our society, are silent, indeed voiceless, victims of injustice" (*Justice in the World*, 1971 World Synod of Bishops).

Scholastica

Virgin (480-542?)

Twins often share the same interests and ideas with an equal intensity. Therefore, it is no surprise that Scholastica and her twin brother, Benedict, both established religious communities within a few miles from each other.

Born in 480 of wealthy parents, Scholastica and Benedict were brought up together until he left for Rome to continue his studies.

Little is known of Scholastica's early life. She founded a religious community for women near Monte Cassino at Plombariola, five miles from where her brother governed a monastery.

The twins visited each other once a year in a farmhouse because Scholastica was not permitted inside the monastery. They spent these times discussing spiritual matters.

According to the *Dialogues of St. Gregory the Great*, the

brother and sister spent their last day together in prayer and conversation. Scholastica sensed her death was close at hand and she begged Benedict to stay with her until the next day.

He refused her request because he did not want to spend a night outside the monastery, thus breaking his own rule. Scholastica asked God to let her brother remain and a severe thunderstorm broke out, preventing Benedict and his monks from returning to the abbey.

Benedict cried out, "God forgive you, Sister. What have you done?" Scholastica replied, "I asked a favor of you and you refused. I asked it of God and he granted it."

Brother and sister parted the next morning after their long discussion. Three days later, Benedict was praying in his monastery and saw the soul of his sister rising heavenward in the form of a white dove. Benedict then announced the death of his sister to the monks and later buried her in the tomb he had prepared for himself.

COMMENT: Scholastica and Benedict gave themselves totally to God and gave top priority to deepening their friendship with him through prayer. They sacrificed some of the opportunities they would have had to be together as brother and sister in order better to fulfill their vocation to the religious life. In coming closer to Christ, however, they found they were also closer to each other. In joining a religious community, they did not forget or forsake their family but rather found more brothers and sisters.

QUOTE: "All religious have the duty, each according to his proper vocation, of cooperating zealously and diligently in building up and increasing the whole Mystical Body of Christ and for the good of the particular churches....It is their duty to foster these objectives primarily by means of prayer, works of penance, and the example of their own life" (*Decree on the Bishops*, 33).

Our Lady of Lourdes

On December 8, 1854, Pope Pius IX proclaimed the dogma of the Immaculate Conception in the Constitution *Ineffabilis Deus*. A little more than three years later, on February 11, 1858, a young lady appeared to Bernadette Soubirous. This began a series of visions. During the apparition on March 24 the lady identified herself with the words: "I am the Immaculate Conception."

Bernadette was a sickly child of poor and unambitious parents. Their practice of the Catholic faith was scarcely more than lukewarm. Bernadette could pray the Our Father, the Hail Mary and the Creed. She also knew the prayer of the Miraculous Medal: "O Mary conceived without sin."

During interrogations Bernadette gave an account of what she saw. It was "something white in the shape of a girl." She used the word "Aquero," a dialect term meaning "this thing." It was "a pretty young girl with a rosary over her arm." Her white robe was encircled by a blue girdle. She wore a white veil. There was a yellow rose on each foot. A rosary was in her hand. Bernadette was also impressed by the fact that the lady did not use the informal form of address (*tu*), but the polite form (*vous*). The humble virgin appeared to a humble girl and treated her with dignity.

Through the humble girl Mary revitalized and continues to revitalize the faith of millions of people. People began to flock to Lourdes from other parts of France and from all over the world. In 1862 Church authorities confirmed the authenticity of the apparitions and authorized the cult of Our Lady of Lourdes for the diocese. The Feast of Our Lady of Lourdes became worldwide in 1907.

COMMENT: Lourdes has become a place of pilgrimage and healing, but even more of faith. Church authorities have recognized 64 miraculous cures, although there have probably been many more. To people of faith this is not surprising. It is a continuation of Jesus' healing miracles—now performed at the intercession of his mother.

Some would say that the greater miracles are hidden. Many who visit Lourdes return home with renewed faith and a readiness to serve God in their needy brothers and sisters. There still may be people who doubt the apparitions of Lourdes. Perhaps the best that can be said to them are the words that introduce the film *Song of Bernadette*: "For those who believe in God, no explanation is necessary. For those who do not believe, no explanation is possible."

QUOTE: "Lo! Mary is exempt from stain of sin,
Proclaims the Pontiff high;
And earth applauding celebrates with joy
Her triumph, far and high.

Unto a lowly timid maid she shows
Her form in beauty fair,
And the Immaculate Conception truth
Her sacred lips declare."
(Unattributed hymn from the *Roman Breviary*)

Cyril and Methodius

Monk (d. 869) and Bishop (d. 884)

Because their father was an officer in a part of Greece inhabited by many Slavs, these two Greek brothers ultimately became missionaries, teachers and patrons of the Slavic peoples.

After a brilliant course of studies, Cyril (called Constantine until he became a monk shortly before his death) refused the governorship of a district such as his brother had accepted among the Slavic-speaking population. He withdrew to a monastery where his brother Methodius had become a monk after some years in a governmental post.

A decisive change in their lives occurred when the Duke of Moravia (present-day Moravia or Slovakia) asked the Eastern Emperor Michael for political independence from German rule and ecclesiastical autonomy (having their own clergy and liturgy). Cyril and Methodius undertook the missionary task.

Cyril's first work was to invent an alphabet, probably still used in Yugoslavian liturgy. His followers probably formed the Cyrillic alphabet (for example, modern Russian) from Greek capital letters. Together they translated the Gospels, the Psalter, Paul and the liturgical books into Slavic, and composed a Slavic liturgy, highly irregular then.

That and their free use of the vernacular in preaching led to opposition from the German clergy. The bishop refused to consecrate Slavic bishops and priests, and Cyril was forced to appeal to Rome. On the visit to Rome, they had the joy of seeing their new liturgy approved by Pope Adrian II. Cyril, long an invalid, died in Rome 50 days after taking the monastic habit.

Methodius continued mission work for 16 more years. He was papal legate for all the Slavic peoples, consecrated bishop and then given an ancient see (in present Yugoslavia). When much of their former territory was removed from their jurisdiction, the Bavarian bishop retaliated with a violent storm of accusation against Methodius. As a result, Emperor Louis the German exiled Methodius for three years. Pope John VIII secured his release.

The Frankish clergy, still smarting, continued their accusations, and Methodius had to go to Rome to defend himself against charges of heresy and uphold his use of the Slavic liturgy. He was again vindicated.

Legend has it that in a feverish period of activity, Methodius translated the whole Bible into Slavic in eight months. He died on Tuesday of Holy Week, surrounded by his disciples, in his cathedral church.

Opposition continued after his death, and the work of the brothers in Moravia was brought to an end and their disciples scattered. But the expulsions had the beneficial effect of spreading the spiritual, liturgical and cultural work of the brothers to Bulgaria, Bohemia and southern Poland. Patrons of Moravia, and specially venerated by Catholic Czechs, Slovaks, Croatians, Orthodox Serbians and Bulgarians, Cyril and Methodius are eminently fitted to guard the long-desired unity of East and West.

COMMENT: Holiness means reacting to human life with God's love: human life *as it is*, crisscrossed with the political and the cultural, the beautiful and the ugly, the selfish and the saintly. For Cyril and Methodius much of their daily cross had to do with a problem familiar to us today: the language of the liturgy. They are not saints because they got the liturgy into Slavic, but because they did so with the courage and humility of Christ.

QUOTE: "Even in the liturgy, the Church has no wish to impose a rigid uniformity in matters which do not involve the faith or the good of the whole community. Rather she respects and fosters the spiritual adornments and gifts of the various races and peoples....Provided that the substantial unity of the Roman rite is maintained, the revision of liturgical books should allow for legitimate variations and adaptations to different groups, religions, and peoples, especially in mission lands" (*Constitution on the Liturgy*, 37, 38).

Seven Founders of the Order of Servites
(13th century)

Can you imagine seven prominent men of Boston or San Francisco banding together, leaving their homes and professions, and going into solitude for a life directly given to God? That is what happened in the cultured and prosperous city of Florence in the middle of the 13th century. The city was torn with political strife as well as the heresy of the Cathari. Morals were low and religion seemed meaningless.

In 1240 seven noblemen of Florence mutually decided to withdraw from the city to a solitary place for prayer and direct service of God. Their initial difficulty was providing for their dependents, since two were still married and two were widowers.

Their aim was to lead a life of penance and prayer, but they soon found themselves disturbed by constant visitors from Florence. They next withdrew to the deserted slopes of Monte Senario.

In 1244, under the direction of St. Peter of Verona, O.P., this small group adopted a religious habit similar to the Dominican habit, choosing to live under the rule of St. Augustine and adopting the name of the Servants of Mary. The new order took a form more like that of the mendicant friars than that of the older monastic orders.

Members of the community came to the United States from Austria in 1852 and settled in New York and later in Philadelphia. The two American provinces developed from the foundation made by Father Austin Morini in 1870 in Wisconsin.

Community members combined monastic life and active ministry. In the monastery, they led a life of prayer, work and silence while in the active apostolate they engaged in parochial work, teaching, preaching and other ministerial activities.

COMMENT: The time in which the seven Servite founders lived is very easily comparable to the situation in which we find ourselves today. It is "the best of times and the worst of times," as Dickens said. Some, perhaps many, feel called to a countercultural life, even in religion. All of us are faced in a new and urgent way with the challenge to make our lives *decisively* centered in Christ.

QUOTE: "Let all religious therefore spread throughout the whole world the good news of Christ by the integrity of their faith, their love for God and neighbor, their devotion to the Cross and their hope of future glory.... Thus, too, with the prayerful aid of that most loving Virgin Mary, God's Mother, 'Whose life is a rule of life for all,' religious communities will experience a daily growth in number, and will yield a richer harvest of fruits that bring salvation" (*Decree on Religious Life*, 25).

FEBRUARY 21   OPTIONAL

Peter Damian

Bishop and Doctor (1007-1072)

Maybe because he was orphaned and had been treated shabbily by one of his brothers, Peter Damian was very good to the poor. It was the ordinary thing for him to have a poor person or two with him at table and he liked to minister personally to their needs.

Peter had himself escaped poverty and the neglect of his own brother when his other brother, who was archpriest of Ravenna, took him under his wing. His brother sent him to good schools, and Peter became a professor.

Already in those days Peter was very strict with himself. He wore a hair shirt under his clothes, fasted rigorously and spent many hours in prayer. Soon, he decided to leave his teaching and give himself completely to prayer with the Benedictines of the reform of St. Romuald at Fonte Avellana. They lived two monks to a hermitage. Peter was so eager to pray and slept so little that he soon suffered from severe insomnia. He found he had to use some prudence in taking care of himself. When he was not praying, he studied the Bible.

The abbot commanded that when he died Peter should succeed him. As abbot Peter founded five other hermitages. He encouraged his brothers in a life of prayer and solitude and wanted nothing more for himself. The Holy See periodically called on him, however, to be a peacemaker or troubleshooter between two abbeys in dispute or a clergyman or government official in some disagreement with Rome.

Finally, Pope Stephen IX made Peter the cardinal-bishop of Ostia. He worked hard to wipe out simony, and encouraged his priests to observe celibacy and urged even the diocesan clergy to live together and maintain scheduled prayer and religious observance. He wished to restore primitive discipline among religious and priests, warning against needless travel, violations of poverty and too comfortable living. He even wrote to the Bishop of Besancon complaining that the canons there sat down when they were singing the psalms in the Divine Office.

He wrote many letters. Some 170 are extant. We also have 53 of his sermons and seven lives, or biographies, that he wrote. He preferred examples and stories rather than theory in his writings. The liturgical offices he wrote are evidence of his talent as a stylist in Latin.

He asked often to be allowed to retire as cardinal-bishop of Ostia, and finally Alexander II consented. Peter was happy to become once again just a monk, but he was still called to serve as a papal legate. When returning from such an assignment in Ravenna, he was overcome by a fever. With the monks gathered around him saying the Divine Office, he died on February 22, 1072.

In 1828 he was declared a doctor of the Church.

COMMENT: Peter was a reformer and if he were alive today would no doubt have encouraged the renewal started by Vatican II. He would also have applauded the greater emphasis on prayer that is shown by the growing number of prayer meetings attended by priests, religious and laypersons as well as the special houses of prayer recently established by many religious communities.

QUOTE: "...Let us faithfully transmit to posterity the example of virtue which we have received from our forefathers" (St. Peter Damian).

Chair of Peter

Apostle

This feast commemorates Christ's choosing Peter to sit in his place as the servant-authority of the whole Church (see June 29).

After the "lost weekend" of pain, doubt and self-torment, Peter hears the Good News. Angels at the tomb say to Magdalene, "The Lord has risen! Go, tell his disciples and Peter." John relates that when he and Peter ran to the tomb, the younger outraced the older, then waited for him. Peter entered, saw the wrappings on the ground, the headpiece rolled up in a place by itself. John saw and believed. But he adds a reminder: "...[T]hey did not yet understand the scripture that he had to rise from the dead" (John 20:9). They went home. There the slowly exploding, impossible idea became reality. Jesus appeared to them as they waited fearfully behind locked doors. "Peace be with you," he said (John 20:21b), and they rejoiced.

The Pentecostal event completed Peter's experience of the risen Christ. "...[T]hey were all filled with the holy Spirit" (Acts 2:4a) and began to express themselves in foreign tongues and make bold proclamation as the Spirit prompted them.

Only then can Peter fulfill the task Jesus had given him: "...[O]nce you have turned back, you must strengthen your brothers" (Luke 22:32). He at once becomes the spokesman for the Twelve about their experience of the Holy Spirit—before the civil authorities who wished to quash their preaching, before the council of Jerusalem, for the community in the problem of Ananias and Sapphira. He is the first to preach the Good News to the Gentiles. The healing power of Jesus in him is well attested: the raising of Tabitha from the dead, the cure of the crippled beggar. People carry the sick into the streets so that when Peter passed his shadow might fall on them.

Even a saint experiences difficulty in Christian living. When Peter stopped eating with Gentile converts because he did not want to wound the sensibilities of Jewish Christians, Paul says, "...I opposed him to his face because he clearly was wrong....[T]hey were not on the right road in line with the truth of the gospel..." (Galatians 2:11b, 14a).

At the end of John's Gospel, Jesus says to Peter, "Amen, amen, I say to you, when you were younger, you used to dress yourself and go where you wanted; but when you grow old, you will stretch out your hands, and someone else will dress you and lead you where you do not want to go" (John 21:18). What Jesus said indicated the sort of death by which Peter was to glorify God.

On Vatican Hill, in Rome, during the reign of Nero, Peter did glorify his Lord with a martyr's death, probably in the company of many Christians.

QUOTE: Peter described our Christian calling in the opening of his First Letter:

"Blessed be the God and Father of our Lord Jesus Christ, who in his great mercy gave us a new birth to a living hope through the resurrection of Jesus Christ from the dead..." (1 Peter 1:3a).

STORY: This saintly man's life is perhaps best summed up at his meeting with Jesus after the resurrection in the presence of the men Peter was to lead. In imitation of Peter's triple denial, Jesus asked him three times "Simon, son of John, do you love me?" (John 21:16b). Peter answered, "Yes, Lord, you know that I love you....Lord, you know everything; you know that I love you" (John 21:16-17b).

FEBRUARY 23   MEMORIAL

Polycarp
Bishop and Martyr (d. 156)

Polycarp, Bishop of Smyrna (modern Izmir, Turkey), disciple of St. John the Apostle and friend of St. Ignatius of Antioch was a revered Christian leader during the first half of the second century.

St. Ignatius, on his way to Rome to be martyred, visited Polycarp at Smyrna, and later at Troas wrote him a personal letter. The Asia Minor Churches recognized Polycarp's leadership by choosing him as a representative to discuss with Pope Anicetus the date of the Easter celebration in Rome—quite a controversy in the early Church.

Only one of the many letters written by Polycarp has been preserved, the one he wrote to the Church of Philippi, Macedonia.

At 86, Polycarp was led into the crowded Smyrna stadium to be burned alive. The flames did not harm him and he was finally killed by a dagger. The centurion ordered the saint's body burned. The "Acts" of Polycarp's martyrdom are the earliest preserved, fully reliable account of a Christian martyr's death. He died in 156.

COMMENT: Polycarp was recognized as a Christian leader by all Asia Minor Christians—a strong fortress of faith and loyalty to Jesus Christ. His own strength emerged from his trust in God, even when events contradicted this trust. Living among pagans and under a government opposed to the new religion, he led and fed his flock. Like the Good Shepherd, he laid down his life for his sheep and kept them from more persecution in Smyrna. He summarized his trust in God just before he died: "Father...I bless Thee, for having made me worthy of the day and hour..." (*Martyrdom*, Chapter 14).

QUOTE: "Stand fast, therefore, in this conduct and follow the example of the Lord, 'firm and unchangeable in faith, lovers of the brotherhood, loving each other, united in truth,' helping each other with the mildness of the Lord, despising no man" (Polycarp, *Letter to the Philippians*).

Katherine Drexel

Virgin (1858-1955)

If your father is an international banker and you ride in a private railroad car, you are not likely to be drawn to a life of voluntary poverty. But if your mother opens your home to the poor three days each week and your father spends half an hour each evening in prayer, it is not impossible that you will devote your life to the poor and give away 12 million dollars. Katherine Drexel did that.

She was born in Philadelphia in 1858. She had an excellent education and traveled widely. As a rich girl, she had a grand debut into society. But when she nursed her stepmother through a three-year terminal illness, she saw that all the Drexel money could not buy safety from pain or death, and her life took a profound turn.

She had always been interested in the plight of the Indians, having been appalled by reading Helen Hunt Jackson's *A Century of Dishonor*. While on a European tour, she met Pope Leo XIII and asked him to send more missionaries to Wyoming for her friend Bishop James O'Connor. The pope replied, "Why don't *you* become a missionary?" His answer shocked her into illness.

Back home, she visited the Dakotas, met Red Cloud the Sioux chief and began her systematic aid to Indian missions.

She could easily have married. But after much discussion with Bishop O'Connor, she wrote in 1889, "The feast of St. Joseph brought me the grace to give the remainder of my life to the Indians and Colored." Newspaper headlines screamed "Gives Up Seven Million!"

After three-and-a-half years of training, she and her first band of nuns (Sisters of the Blessed Sacrament for Indians and Colored) opened a boarding school in Santa Fe. A string of foundations followed. By 1942 she had a system of black Catholic schools in 13 states, plus 40 mission centers and 23 rural schools. Segregationists harassed her work, even burning a school in Pennsylvania. In all, she established 50 missions for Indians in 16 states.

Two saints met when she was advised by Mother Cabrini about the "politics" of getting her Order's rule approved in Rome. Her crowning achievement was the founding of Xavier University in New Orleans, the first university in the United States for blacks.

At 77, she suffered a heart attack and was forced to retire. Apparently her life was over. But now came almost 20 years of quiet, intense prayer from a small room overlooking the sanctuary. Small notebooks and slips of paper record her various prayers, ceaseless aspirations and meditation. She died at 96.

COMMENT: Saints have always said the same thing: Pray, be humble, accept the cross, love and forgive. But it is good to hear these things in the American idiom from one who, for instance, had her ears pierced as a teenager, who resolved to have "no cake, no preserves," who wore a watch, was interviewed by the press, traveled by train and could concern herself with the proper size of pipe for a new mission. These are obvious reminders that holiness can be lived in today's culture as well as in that of Jerusalem or Rome.

QUOTE: "The patient and humble endurance of the cross— whatever nature it may be—is the highest work we have to do." "Oh, how far I am at 84 years of age from being an image of Jesus in his sacred life on earth!" (Mother Katherine Drexel).

Casimir

(1458-1483)

A teenage conscientious objector is the patron saint of Poland and Lithuania. Casimir, born of kings and in line (third among 13 children) to be a king himself, was filled with exceptional values and learning by a great teacher, John Dlugosz. Even his critics could not say that his conscientious objection indicated softness. Even as a teenager, Casimir lived a highly disciplined, even severe life, sleeping on the ground, spending a great part of the night in prayer and dedicating himself to lifelong celibacy.

When nobles in Hungary became dissatisfied with their king, they prevailed upon Casimir's father, the king of Poland, to send his son to take over the country. Casimir obeyed his father, as many young men over the centuries have obeyed their government. The army he was supposed to lead was clearly outnumbered by the "enemy"; some of his troops were deserting because they were not paid. At the advice of his officers, Casimir decided to return home. His father was irked at the failure of his plans, and confined his 15-year-old son for three months. The lad made up his mind never again to become involved in the wars of his day, and no amount of persuasion could change his mind. He returned to prayer and study, maintaining his decision to remain celibate even under pressure to marry the emperor's daughter. He reigned briefly as King of Poland during his father's absence. He died of lung trouble at 23 while visiting Lithuania, of which he was also Grand Duke. He was buried in Vilna, Lithuania.

COMMENT: For many years Poland and Lithuania faded into the gray prison on the other side of the Iron Curtain. Despite repression, the Poles and Lithuanians remained firm in the faith which has become synonymous with their name. Their youthful patron offers them hope: Peace is not won by war; sometimes a comfortable peace is not even won by virtue, but Christ's peace can penetrate even iron curtains.

STORY: Casimir had great love of the Mother of God; in particular he loved the great Marian Latin hymn, *Omni die dic Mariae* (translated, not literally, as "Daily, daily, sing to Mary"). He asked that a copy of it be buried with him.

Perpetua and Felicity

Martyrs (d. 203?)

"When my father in his affection for me was trying to turn me from my purpose by arguments and thus weaken my faith, I said to him, 'Do you see this vessel—waterpot or whatever it may be? Can it be called by any other name than what it is?' 'No,' he replied. 'So also I cannot call myself by any other name than what I am—a Christian.' "

So writes Perpetua, young, beautiful, well educated, a noblewoman of Carthage, mother of an infant son and chronicler of the persecution of the Christians by the emperor Septimius Severus.

Despite threats of persecution and death, Perpetua, Felicity (a slavewoman and expectant mother) and three companions, Revocatus, Secundulus and Saturninus, refused to renounce their Christian faith. For their unwillingness, all were sent to the public games in the amphitheater. There, Perpetua and Felicity were beheaded, and the others killed by beasts.

Perpetua's mother was a Christian and her father a pagan. He continually pleaded with her to deny her faith. She refused and was imprisoned at 22.

In her diary, Perpetua describes her period of captivity: "What a day of horror! Terrible heat, owing to the crowds! Rough treatment by the soldiers! To crown all, I was tormented with anxiety for my baby....Such anxieties I suffered for many days, but I obtained leave for my baby to remain in the prison with me, and being relieved of my trouble and anxiety for him, I at once recovered my health, and my prison became a palace to me and I would rather have been there than anywhere else."

Felicity gave birth to a girl a few days before the games commenced.

Perpetua's record of her trial and imprisonment ends the day before the games. "Of what was done in the games themselves, let him write who will." The diary was finished by an eyewitness.

COMMENT: Persecution for religious beliefs is not confined to Christians in ancient times. Consider Anne Frank, the Jewish girl who, with her family, was forced into hiding and later died in one of Hitler's death camps during World War II. Anne, like Perpetua and Felicity, endured hardship and suffering and finally death because she committed herself to God. In her diary Anne writes, "It's twice as hard for us young ones to hold our ground, and maintain our opinions, in a time when all ideals are being shattered and destroyed, when people are showing their worst side, and do not know whether to believe in truth and right and God."

QUOTE: Perpetua, unwilling to renounce Christianity, comforted her father in his grief over her decision, "It shall happen as God shall choose, for assuredly we depend not on our own power but on the power of God."

John of God

Religious (1495-1550)

Having given up active Christian belief while a soldier, John was 40 before the depth of his sinfulness began to dawn on him. He decided to give the rest of his life to God's service, and headed at once for Africa, where he hoped to free captive Christians and, possibly, be martyred.

He was soon advised that his desire for martyrdom was not spiritually well based, and returned to Spain and the relatively prosaic activity of a religious goods store. Yet he was still not settled. Moved initially by a sermon of Blessed John of Avila, he one day engaged in a public beating of himself, begging mercy and wildly repenting for his past life.

Committed to a mental hospital for these actions, John was visited by Blessed John who advised him to be more actively involved in tending to the needs of others rather than in enduring personal hardships. John gained peace of heart, and shortly after left the hospital to begin work among the poor.

He established a house where he wisely tended to the needs of the sick poor, at first doing his own begging. But excited by the saint's great work and inspired by his devotion, many people began to back him up with money and provisions. Among them were the archbishop and marquis of Tarifa.

Behind John's outward acts of total concern and love for Christ's sick poor was a deep interior prayer life which was reflected in his spirit of humility. These qualities attracted helpers who, 20 years after John's death, formed the Brothers Hospitallers, now a worldwide religious order.

John became ill after 10 years of service but tried to disguise his ill health. He began to put the hospital's administrative work into order and appointed a leader for his helpers. He died under the care of a spiritual friend and admirer, Lady Anne Ossorio.

COMMENT: The utter humility of John of God, which led to a totally selfless dedication to others, is most impressive. Here is a man who realized his nothingness in the face of God. The Lord blessed him with the gifts of prudence, patience, courage, enthusiasm and the ability to influence and inspire others. He saw that in his early life he had turned away from the Lord, and, moved to receive his mercy, John began his new commitment to love others in openness to God's love.

STORY: The archbishop called John of God to him in response to a complaint that he was keeping tramps and immoral women in his hospital. In submission John fell on his knees and said: "The Son of Man came for sinners, and we are bound to seek their conversion. I am unfaithful to my vocation because I neglect this, but I confess that I know of no bad person in my hospital except myself alone, who am indeed unworthy to eat the bread of the poor." The archbishop could only trust in John's sincerity and humility, and dismissed him with deep respect.

Frances of Rome
Religious (1384-1440)

Frances' life combines aspects of secular and religious life. A devoted and loving wife, she longed for a life-style of prayer and service, so she organized a group of women to minister to the needs of Rome's poor.

Born of wealthy parents, Frances found herself attracted to the religious life during her youth. But her parents objected and a young nobleman was selected to be her husband.

As she became acquainted with her new relatives, Frances soon discovered that the wife of her husband's brother also wished to live a life of service and prayer. So the two, Frances and Vannozza, set out together—with their husbands' blessings—to help the poor.

Frances fell ill for a time, but this apparently only deepened her commitment to the suffering people she met. The years passed, and Frances gave birth to two sons and a daughter. With the new responsibilities of family life, the young mother turned her attention more to the needs of her own household. The family flourished under Frances' care, but within a few years a great plague began to sweep across Italy. It struck Rome with devastating cruelty and left Frances' second son dead. In an effort to help alleviate some of the suffering, Frances used all her money and sold her possessions to buy whatever the sick might possibly need. When all the resources had been exhausted, Frances and Vannozza went door to door begging. Later, Frances' daughter died, and the saint opened a section of her house as a hospital.

Frances became more and more convinced that this way of life was so necessary for the world, and it was not long before she requested and was given permission to found a society of women bound by no vows. They simply offered themselves to God and to the service of the poor. Once the society was established, Frances chose not to live at the community residence, but rather at home with her husband. She did this for seven years, until her husband passed away, and then came to live the remainder of her life with the society—serving the poorest of the poor.

COMMENT: Looking at the exemplary life of fidelity to God and devotion to her fellow human beings which Frances of Rome was blessed to lead, one cannot help but be reminded of Mother Teresa of Calcutta today. Mother Teresa sees this same vision of loving Jesus Christ in prayer and also in the poor. The life of Frances of Rome calls each of us not only to look deeply for God in prayer, but also to carry our devotion to Jesus living in the suffering of our world. Frances shows us that this life need not be restricted to those bound by vows.

QUOTE: In *Something Beautiful for God*, Mother Teresa says of the sisters in her community: "Let Christ radiate and live his life in her and through her in the slums. Let the poor seeing her be drawn to Christ and invite him to enter their homes and lives." Says Frances of Rome: "It is most laudable in a married woman to be devout, but she must never forget that she is a housewife. And sometimes she must leave God at the altar to find Him in her housekeeping" (*Butler's Lives of the Saints*).

MARCH 17   OPTIONAL

Patrick

Bishop (389?-461?)

Legends about Patrick abound; but truth is best served by our seeing two solid qualities in him: He was humble and he was courageous. The determination to accept suffering and success with equal indifference guided the life of God's instrument for winning most of Ireland for Christ.

Details of his life are uncertain. Patrick's birthplace is said to be either Dunbarton, Scotland, or Cumberland, England. He called himself both a Roman and a Briton. At 16, he and a large number of his father's slaves and vassals were captured by Irish raiders and sold as slaves in Ireland. Forced to work as a shepherd, he suffered greatly from hunger and cold.

After six years, Patrick escaped, probably to France, and later returned to Britain at the age of 22. His captivity had meant spiritual conversion. He may have studied at Lerins, off the

French coast; he spent years at Auxerre, and was consecrated bishop at the age of 43. His great desire was to proclaim the Good News to the Irish.

In a dream vision it seemed "all the children of Ireland from their mothers' wombs were stretching out their hands" to him. He understood the vision to be a call to do mission work in pagan Ireland. Despite opposition from those who felt his education had been defective, he was sent to carry out the task. He went to the west and north, where the faith had never been preached, obtained the protection of local kings and made numerous converts.

Because of the island's pagan background, Patrick was emphatic in encouraging widows to remain chaste and young women to consecrate their virginity to Christ. He ordained many priests, divided the country into dioceses, held Church councils, founded several monasteries and continually urged his people to greater holiness in Christ.

He suffered much opposition from pagan druids, and was criticized in both England and Ireland for the way he conducted his mission.

In a relatively short time the island had experienced deeply the Christian spirit, and was prepared to send out missionaries whose efforts were greatly responsible for Christianizing Europe.

Patrick was a man of action, with little inclination toward learning. He had a rocklike belief in his vocation, in the cause he had espoused.

One of the few certainly authentic writings is his *Confessio*, above all an act of homage to God for having called Patrick, unworthy sinner, to the apostolate.

There is hope rather than irony in the fact that his burial place is said to be in strife-torn Ulster, in County Down.

COMMENT: What distinguishes Patrick is the durability of his efforts. When one considers the state of Ireland when he began his mission work, the vast extent of his labors (all of Ireland) and how the seeds he planted continued to grow and flourish, one can only admire the kind of man Patrick must have been. The holiness of a person is known only by the fruits of his or her work.

QUOTE: "Christ shield me this day: Christ with me, Christ before me, Christ behind me, Christ in me, Christ beneath me, Christ above me, Christ on my right, Christ on my left, Christ when I lie down, Christ when I arise, Christ in the heart of every person who thinks of me, Christ in the eye that sees me, Christ in the ear that hears me" (from "The Breastplate of St. Patrick").

Cyril of Jerusalem
Bishop and Doctor (315?-386)

Problems in the Church today are minor compared with the reverberations of the Arian heresy that denied the divinity of Christ. Cyril was to be caught up in the controversy, accused (later) of Arianism by St. Jerome, and ultimately vindicated both by the men of his own time and by being declared a Doctor of the Church in 1822.

Raised in Jerusalem, well-educated, especially in the Scriptures, he was ordained priest by the bishop of Jerusalem and given the task of catechizing those preparing for Baptism (during Lent) and those newly baptized (during the weeks after Easter). His *Catecheses* remains valuable as examples of the ritual and theology of the Church in mid-fourth century.

There are conflicting reports about the circumstances of his becoming bishop of Jerusalem. It is certain that he was validly consecrated by bishops of the province. Since one of them was an Arian, Acacius, it may have been expected that his "cooperation" would follow. Conflict soon rose between Cyril and Acacius, bishop of the rival nearby see of Caeserea. Cyril was summoned to a council, accused of insubordination and of selling Church property to relieve the poor. Probably, however, a theological difference was also involved. He was condemned, driven from Jerusalem, and later vindicated, not without some association and help of Semi-Arians. Half his episcopate was spent in exile (his first experience was repeated twice). He finally returned to find Jerusalem torn with heresy, schism and strife, and racked with crime. Even St. Gregory of Nyssa, sent to help, left in despair.

They both went to the (second ecumenical) Council of Constantinople, where the amended form of the Nicene Creed was promulgated. Cyril accepted the word *consubstantial* (that is, of Christ and the Father). Some said it was an act of repentance, but the bishops of the Council praised him as a champion of orthodoxy against the Arians. Though not friendly with the greatest defender of orthodoxy against the Arians, Cyril may be counted among those whom Athanasius called "brothers, who mean what we mean, and differ only about the word [*consubstantial*]."

COMMENT: Those who fancy that the lives of saints are simple and placid, untouched by the vulgar breath of controversy, are rudely shocked by history. Yet it should be no surprise that saints, indeed all Christians, will experience the same difficulties as their Master. The definition of truth is an endless, complex pursuit, and good men and women have suffered the pain of both controversy and error. Intellectual, emotional and political roadblocks may slow up men like Cyril for a time. But their lives taken as a whole are monuments to honesty and courage.

QUOTE: "It is not only among us, who are marked with the name of Christ, that the dignity of faith is great; all the business of the world, even of those outside the Church, is accomplished by faith. By faith, marriage laws join in union persons who were strangers to one another. By faith, agriculture is sustained; for a man does not endure the toil involved unless he believes he will reap a harvest. By faith, seafaring men, entrusting themselves to a tiny wooden craft, exchange the solid element of the land for the unstable motion of the waves. Not only among us does this hold true but also, as I have said, among those outside the fold. For though they do not accept the Scriptures but advance certain doctrines of their own, yet even these they receive on faith" (*Catechesis* V).

Joseph

Husband of Mary

The Bible pays Joseph the highest compliment: he was a "just" man. The quality meant a lot more than faithfulness in paying debts.

When the Bible speaks of God "justifying" someone, it means that God, the all holy or "righteous" One, so transforms a person that the individual shares somehow in God's own holiness, and hence it is really "right" for God to love him or her. In other words, God is not playing games, acting as if we were lovable when we are not.

By saying Joseph was "just," the Bible means that he was one who was completely open to all that God wanted to do for him. He became holy by opening himself totally to God.

The rest we can easily surmise. Think of the kind of love with which he wooed and won Mary, and the depth of the love they shared during their marriage.

It is no contradiction of Joseph's manly holiness that he decided to divorce Mary when she was found to be with child.

The important words of the Bible are that he planned to do this "quietly" because he was "a righteous man, yet unwilling to expose her to shame" (Matthew 1:19).

The just man was simply, joyfully, wholeheartedly obedient to God—in marrying Mary, in naming Jesus, in shepherding the precious pair to Egypt, in bringing them to Nazareth, in the undetermined number of years of quiet faith and courage.

COMMENT: The Bible tells us nothing of Joseph in the years after the return to Nazareth except the incident of finding Jesus in the Temple (see Luke 2:41-51). Perhaps this can be taken to mean that God wants us to realize that the holiest family was like every other family, that the circumstances of life for the holiest family were like those of every family, so that when Jesus' mysterious nature began to appear, people couldn't believe that he came from such humble beginnings: "Is he not the carpenter's son? Is not his mother named Mary...?" (Matthew 13:55a). It was almost as indignant as "Can anything good come from Nazareth?" (John 1:46b).

QUOTE: "He was chosen by the eternal Father as the trustworthy guardian and protector of his greatest treasures, namely, his divine Son and Mary, Joseph's wife. He carried out this vocation with complete fidelity until at last God called him, saying: 'Good and faithful servant, enter into the joy of your Lord' " (St. Bernardine of Siena).

Turibius of Mogrovejo

Bishop (1538-1606)

Together with Rose of Lima, Turibius is the first known saint of the New World, serving the Lord in Peru, South America, for 26 years.

Born in Spain and educated for the law, he became so brilliant a scholar that he was made professor of law at the University of Salamanca and eventually became chief judge of the Inquisition at Granada. He succeeded too well. But he was not sharp enough a lawyer to prevent a surprising sequence of events.

When the archbishopric of Lima in Spain's Peruvian colony became vacant, it was decided that Turibius was the man needed to fill the post: He was the one person with the strength of character and holiness of spirit to heal the scandals that had infected that area.

He cited all the canons that forbade giving laymen ecclesiastical dignities, but he was overruled. He was ordained priest and bishop and sent to Peru, where he found colonialism at its worst. The Spanish conquerors were guilty of every sort of oppression of the native population. Abuses among the clergy were flagrant, and he devoted his energies (and suffering) to this area first.

He began the long and arduous visitation of an immense archdiocese, studying the language, staying two or three days in each place, often with neither bed nor food. He confessed every morning to his chaplain, and celebrated Mass with intense fervor. Among those to whom he gave the Sacrament of Confirmation was St. Rose of Lima, and possibly St. Martin de Porres. After 1590 he had the help of another great missionary, Francis Solanus.

His people, though very poor, were sensitive, dreading to accept public charity from others. Turibius solved the problem by helping them anonymously.

COMMENT: The Lord indeed writes straight with crooked lines. Against his will, and from the unlikely springboard of an Inquisition tribunal, this man became the Christlike shepherd of a poor and oppressed people. God gave him the gift of loving others as they needed it.

STORY: When Turibius undertook the reform of the clergy as well as unjust officials, he naturally suffered opposition. Some tried, in human fashion, to "explain" God's law in such a way as to sanction their accustomed way of life. He answered them in the words of Tertullian, "Christ said, 'I am the truth'; he did not say, 'I am the custom.' "

MARCH 25 SOLEMNITY

Annunciation of the Lord

The feast of the Annunciation goes back to the fourth or fifth century. Its central focus is the Incarnation: God has become one of us. From all eternity God had decided that the Second Person of the Blessed Trinity should become human. Now, as Luke 1:26-38 tells us, the decision is being realized. The God-Man embraces all humanity, indeed all creation, to bring it to God in one great act of love. Because human beings have rejected God, Jesus will accept a life of suffering and an agonizing death: "No one has greater love than this, to lay down one's life for one's friends" (John 15:13).

Mary has an important role to play in God's plan. From all

eternity God destined her to be the mother of Jesus and closely related to him in the creation and redemption of the world. We could say that God's decrees of creation and redemption are joined in the decree of Incarnation. As Mary is God's instrument in the Incarnation, she has a role to play with Jesus in creation and redemption. It is a God-given role. It is God's grace from beginning to end. Mary becomes the eminent figure she is only by God's grace. She is the empty space where God could act. Everything she is she owes to the Trinity.

She is the virgin-mother who fulfills Isaiah 7:14 in a way that Isaiah could not have imagined. She is united with her son in carrying out the will of God (Psalms 40:8-9; Hebrews 10:7-9; Luke 1:38).

Together with Jesus, the privileged and graced Mary is the link between heaven and earth. She is the human being who best, after Jesus, exemplifies the possibilities of human existence. She received into her lowliness the infinite love of God. She shows how an ordinary human being can reflect God in the ordinary circumstances of life. She exemplifies what the Church and every member of the Church is meant to become. She is the ultimate product of the creative and redemptive power of God. She manifests what the Incarnation is meant to accomplish for all of us.

COMMENT: Sometimes spiritual writers are accused of putting Mary on a pedestal and thereby discouraging ordinary humans from imitating her. Perhaps such an observation is misguided. God did put Mary on a pedestal and has put all human beings on a pedestal. We have scarcely begun to realize the magnificence of divine grace, the wonder of God's freely given love. The marvel of Mary—even in the midst of her very ordinary life—is God's shout to us to wake up to the marvelous creatures that we all are by divine design.

QUOTE: "Enriched from the first instant of her conception with the splendor of an entirely unique holiness, the virgin of Nazareth is hailed by the heralding angel, by divine command, as 'full of grace' (cf. Luke 1:28). To the heavenly messenger she replies: 'Behold the handmaid of the Lord; be it done to me according to thy word' (Luke 1:38). Thus the daughter of Adam, Mary, consenting to the word of God, became the Mother of Jesus. Committing herself wholeheartedly and impeded by no sin to God's saving will, she devoted herself totally, as a handmaid of the Lord, to the person and work of her Son, under and with him, serving the mystery of redemption, by the grace of Almighty God" (*Constitution on the Church*, 56).

Francis of Paola

Hermit (1416-1507)

Francis of Paola was a man who deeply loved contemplative solitude and wished only to be the "least in the household of God." Yet, when the Church called him to active service in the world, he became a miracle-worker and influenced the course of nations.

After accompanying his parents on a pilgrimage to Rome and Assisi, he began to live as a contemplative hermit in a remote cave on the seacoast near Paola. Before he was 20, he received the first followers who had come to imitate his way of life. Seventeen years later, when his disciples had grown in number, Francis established a rule for his austere community and sought Church approval. This was the founding of the Hermits of St. Francis of Assisi, who were approved by the Holy See in 1474.

In 1492, Francis changed the name of his community to "Minims" because he wanted them to be known as the least (*minimi*) in the household of God. Humility was to be the hallmark of the brothers as it had been in Francis' personal life. Besides the vows of poverty, chastity and obedience, Francis enjoined upon his followers the fourth obligation of a perpetual Lenten fast. He felt that heroic mortification was necessary as a means for spiritual growth.

It was Francis' desire to be a contemplative hermit, yet he believed that God was calling him to the apostolic life. He began to use the gifts he had received, such as the gifts of miracles and prophesy, to minister to the people of God. A defender of the poor and oppressed, Francis incurred the wrath of King Ferdinand of Naples for the admonitions he directed towards the king and his sons.

Following the request of Pope Sixtus IV, Francis traveled to

Paris to help Louis XI of France prepare for his death (see Story, below). While ministering to the king, Francis was able to influence the course of national politics. He helped to restore peace between France and Britanny by advising a marriage between the ruling families, and between France and Spain by persuading Louis XI to return some disputed land.

Francis died while at the French court.

COMMENT: The life of Francis of Paola speaks plainly to an overactive world. He was a contemplative man called to active ministry and must have felt keenly the tension between prayer and service. Yet in Francis' life it was a productive tension, for he clearly utilized the fruits of contemplation in his ministry, which came to involve the workings of nations. He responded so readily and so well to the call of the Church from a solid foundation in prayer and mortification. When he went out to the world, it was not he who worked but Christ working through him—"the least in the household of God."

STORY: The King of France, Louis XI, was slowly dying after an apoplectic seizure. He sent to Italy to beg Francis to come and heal him, making many promises to assist him and his order. Francis refused, until the king appealed to the pope, who ordered him to go. Louis fell on his knees and begged Francis to heal him. The saint replied that the lives of kings are in the hands of God and have their appointed limits: Prayer should be addressed to God.

Many meetings followed. Though Francis was an unlearned man, those who heard him have testified that his words were so full of wisdom that all present were convinced that the Holy Spirit was speaking through him. By prayer and example he brought about a change of heart in the king, who died peacefully in his arms.

Isidore of Seville

Bishop and Doctor (560?-636)

The 76 years of Isidore's life were a time of conflict and growth for the Church in Spain. The Visigoths had invaded the land a century and a half earlier and shortly before Isidore's birth they set up their own capital. They were Arians—Christians who said Christ was not God. Thus Spain was split in two: One people (Catholic Romans) struggled with another (Arian Goths).

Isidore reunited Spain, making it a center of culture and learning, a teacher and guide for other European countries whose culture was also threatened by barbarian invaders.

Born in Carthagena of a family that included three other saints, he was educated (severely) by his elder brother, whom he succeeded as bishop of Seville.

An amazingly learned man, he was sometimes called "The Schoolmaster of the Middle Ages" because the encyclopedia he wrote was used as a textbook for nine centuries. He required seminaries to be built in every diocese, wrote a rule for religious orders and founded schools that taught every branch of learning. Isidore wrote numerous books, including a dictionary, an encyclopedia, a history of Goths and a history of the world beginning with creation! He completed the Mozarabic liturgy which is still in use in Toledo, Spain.

He continued his austerities even as he approached 80. During the last six months of his life, he increased his charities so much that his house was crowded from morning till night with the poor of the countryside.

COMMENT: Our country can well use Isidore's spirit of combining learning and holiness. Loving, understanding knowledge can heal and bring a broken people back together. We are not barbarians like the invaders of Isidore's Spain. But people who are swamped by riches and overwhelmed by scientific and technological advances can lose much of their understanding love for one another.

STORY: Once, when Isidore was a boy, he ran away from home and from school. His brother Leander, some 20 years older than he, was his teacher, and a very demanding one. While Isidore sat by himself out in the woods, loafing, he watched some drops of water falling on a rock. Then he noticed that the dripping water had worn a hole in the hard rock! The thought came to him that he could do what the little drops of water did. Little by little, by sticking to it, he could learn all his brother demanded, and maybe even more.

Vincent Ferrer

Priest (1350?-1419)

The polarization in the Church today is a mild breeze compared with the tornado that ripped the Church apart during the lifetime of this saint. If any saint is a patron of reconciliation, Vincent Ferrer is.

Despite parental opposition, he entered the Dominican Order in his native Spain at 19. After brilliant studies, he was ordained priest by Cardinal Peter de Luna—who would figure tragically in his life.

Of a very ardent nature, he practiced the austerities of the order with great energy. He was chosen prior of the Dominican monastery in Valencia shortly after his ordination.

The Western Schism divided Christianity first between two,

then three, popes. Clement lived at Avignon in France, Urban in Rome. Vincent was convinced the election of Urban was invalid (though Catherine of Siena was just as devoted a supporter of the Roman pope). In the service of Cardinal de Luna, he worked to persuade Spaniards to follow Clement. When Clement died, Cardinal de Luna was elected at Avignon and became Benedict XIII.

Vincent worked for him as apostolic penitentiary and Master of the Sacred Palace. But the new pope did not resign as all candidates in the conclave had sworn to do. He remained stubborn despite being deserted by the French king and nearly all of the cardinals.

Vincent became disillusioned and very ill, but finally took up the work of simply "going through the world preaching Christ," though he felt that any renewal in the Church depended on healing the schism. An eloquent and fiery preacher, he spent the last 20 years of his life spreading the Good News in Spain, France, Switzerland, the Low Countries and Lombardy, stressing the need of repentance and the fear of coming judgment. (He became known as the "Angel of the Judgment.")

He tried, unsuccessfully, in 1408 and 1415, to persuade his former friend to resign. He finally concluded that Benedict was not the true pope. Though very ill, he mounted the pulpit before an assembly over which Benedict himself was presiding and thundered his denunciation of the man who had ordained him priest. Benedict fled for his life, abandoned by those who had formerly supported him. Strangely, Vincent had no part in the Council of Constance, which settled the schism.

COMMENT: The split in the Church at the time of Vincent Ferrer should have been fatal—36 long years of having two "heads." We cannot imagine what condition the Church today would be in if, for that length of time, half the world had followed a succession of Popes in Rome, and half, an equally "official" number of popes in, say, Rio de Janiero. It is an ongoing miracle that the Church has not long since been shipwrecked on the rocks of pride and ignorance, greed and ambition. Contrary to Lowell's words, "Truth forever on the scaffold, wrong forever on the throne," we believe that "truth is mighty, and it shall prevail"—but it sometimes takes a long time.

QUOTE: "Precious stone of virginity...
Flaming torch of charity...
Mirror of penance...
Trumpet of eternal salvation...
Flower of heavenly wisdom...
Vanquisher of demons."

(From the litanies of St. Vincent)

John Baptist de la Salle
Priest (1651-1719)

Complete dedication to what he saw as God's will for him dominates the life of John Baptist de la Salle. In 1950, Pope Pius XII named him patron of schoolteachers for his efforts in upgrading school instruction. As a young 17th-century Frenchman, John had everything going for him: scholarly bent, good looks, noble family background, money, refined upbringing. At the early age of 11, he received the tonsure and started preparation for the priesthood, to which he was ordained at 27. He seemed assured then of a life of dignified ease and a high position in the Church.

But God had other plans for John, which were gradually revealed to him in the next several years. During a chance meeting with M. Nyel of Raven, he became interested in the creation of schools for poor boys in Raven, where he was stationed. Though the work was extremely distasteful to him at first, he became more involved in working with the deprived youths.

Once convinced that this was his divinely appointed mission, John threw himself wholeheartedly into the work, left home and family, abandoned his position as canon at Rheims, gave away his fortune and reduced himself to the level of the poor to whom he devoted his entire life.

The remainder of his life was closely entwined with the community of religious men he founded, the Brothers of the Christian School (Christian Brothers). This community grew rapidly and was successful in educating boys of poor families using methods designed by John, preparing teachers in the first training college for teachers and also setting up homes and schools for young delinquents of wealthy families. The motivating element in all these endeavors was the desire to become a good Christian.

Yet even in his success, John did not escape experiencing many trials: heartrending disappointment and defections among his disciples, bitter opposition from the secular schoolmasters who resented his new and fruitful methods and persistent opposition from the Jansenists of his time, whose heretical doctrines John resisted vehemently all his life.

Afflicted with asthma and rheumatism in his last years, he died on Good Friday at 68 and was canonized in 1900.

COMMENT: Complete dedication to one's calling by God, whatever it may be, is a rare quality. Jesus asks us to "love the Lord your God with *all* your heart, with *all* your soul, with *all* your mind, and with *all* your strength" (Mark 12:30b, emphasis added). Paul gives similar advice: "Whatever you do, do from the heart..." (Colossians 3:23).

QUOTE: "What is nobler than to mold the character of the young? I consider that he who knows how to form the youthful mind is

truly greater than all painters, sculptors and all others of that sort"
(St. John Chrysostum).

Stanislaus

Bishop and Martyr (1030-1079)

Anyone who reads the history of Eastern Europe cannot help but
chance on the name of Stanislaus, the saintly but tragic Bishop of
Kraków, patron of Poland. He is remembered with Saints Thomas
More and Thomas Becket for vigorous opposition to the evils of
an unjust government.

Born in Szczepanow near Kraków on July 26, 1030, he was
ordained priest after being educated in the cathedral schools of
Gniezno, then capital of Poland, and at Paris. He was appointed
preacher and archdeacon to the bishop of Kraków, where his
eloquence and example brought about real conversion in many of
his penitents, both clergy and laity. He became bishop of Kraków
in 1072.

During an expedition against the Grand Duchy of Kiev,
Stanislaus became involved in the political situation of Poland.
Known for his outspokenness, he aimed his attacks at the evils of
the peasantry and the king, especially the unjust wars and
immoral acts of King Boleslaus II.

The king first excused himself, then made a show of
penance, then relapsed into his old ways. Stanislaus continued
his open opposition in spite of charges of treason and threats of
death, finally excommunicating the king. The latter, enraged,
ordered soldiers to kill the bishop. When they refused, the king
killed him with his own hands.

Forced to flee to Hungary, Boleslaus supposedly spent the

rest of his life as a penitent in the Benedictine Abbey in Osiak, Hungary.

COMMENT: John the Baptist, Thomas Becket, Thomas More and Stanislaus are a few of the prophets who dared to denounce corruption in high places. They follow in the footsteps of Jesus himself, who pointed the finger at the moral corruption in the religious leadership of his day. It is a risky business: "Let the one among you who is without sin be the first to throw a stone..." (John 8:7b).

QUOTE: "Men desire authority for its own sake that they may bear a rule, command and control other men, and live uncommanded and uncontrolled themselves" (St. Thomas More, A Dialogue of Comfort).

Martin I

Pope and Martyr (d. 655)

When Martin I became pope in 649, Constantinople was the capital of the Byzantine empire and the Patriarch of Constantinople was the most influential Church leader in the eastern Christian world. The struggles that existed within the Church at that time were magnified by the close cooperation of emperor and patriarch.

A teaching, strongly supported in the East, held that Christ had no human will. Twice emperors had officially favored this position, Heraclius by publishing a formula of faith and Constans II by silencing the issue of one or two wills in Christ.

Shortly after assuming the office of the papacy (which he did without first being confirmed by the emperor), Martin held a council at the Lateran in which the imperial documents were censured, and in which the patriarch of Constantinople and two of his predecessors were condemned. Constans II, in response, tried first to turn bishops and people against the pope.

Failing in this and in an attempt to kill the pope, the emperor sent troops to Rome to seize Martin and to bring him back to Constantinople. Martin, already in poor health, offered no resistance, returned with the exarch Calliopas and was then submitted to various imprisonments, tortures and hardships. Although condemned to death and with some of the torture imposed already carried out, Martin was saved from execution by the pleas of a repentant Paul, Patriarch of Constantinople, who himself was gravely ill.

Martin died shortly thereafter, tortures and cruel treatment having taken their toll. He is the last of the early popes to be venerated as a martyr.

COMMENT: The real significance of the word *martyr* comes not from the dying but from the witnessing, which the word means in its derivation. People who are willing to give up everything, their most precious possessions, their very lives, put a supreme value on the cause or belief for which they sacrifice. Martyrdom, dying for the faith, is an incidental extreme to which some have had to go to manifest their belief in Christ. A living faith, a life that exemplifies Christ's teaching throughout, and that in spite of difficulties, is required of all Christians. Martin I might have temporized; he might have sought means to ease his lot, to make some accommodations with the civil rulers.

QUOTE: The breviary of the Orthodox Church pays tribute to Martin: "Glorious definer of the Orthodox Faith...sacred chief of divine dogmas, unstained by error...true reprover of heresy...foundation of bishops, pillar of the Orthodox faith, teacher of religion...Thou didst adorn the divine see of Peter, and since from this divine Rock, thou didst immovably defend the Church, so now thou art glorified with him."

Anselm

Bishop and Doctor (1033-1109)

Indifferent toward religion as a young man, Anselm became one of the Church's greatest theologians and leaders. He received the title "Father of Scholasticism" for his attempt to analyze and illumine the truths of faith through the aid of reason.

At 15, Anselm wanted to enter a monastery, but was refused acceptance because of his father's opposition. Twelve years later, after careless disinterest in religion and years of worldly living, he finally fulfilled his desire to be a monk. He entered the monastery of Bec in Normandy, three years later was elected prior and 15 years later was unanimously chosen abbot.

Considered an original and independent thinker, Anselm was admired for his patience and gentleness and teaching skill. Under his leadership, the Abbey of Bec became a monastic school, influential in philosophical and theological studies.

During these years, at the community's request, Anselm began publishing his theological works, comparable to those of St. Augustine. His best-known work is the book *Cur Deus Homo* ("Why God Became Man").

At 60, against his will, Anselm was appointed Archbishop of Canterbury in 1093. His appointment was opposed at first by England's King William Rufus and later accepted. Rufus persistently refused to cooperate with efforts to reform the Church.

Anselm finally went into voluntary exile until Rufus died in

1100. He was then recalled to England by Rufus's brother and successor, Henry I. Disagreeing fearlessly with Henry over the king's right to invest England's bishops, Anselm spent another three years in exile in Rome.

His care and concern extended to the very poorest people and he was the first in the Church to oppose the slave trade. Anselm obtained from the National Council at Westminster the passage of a resolution prohibiting the sale of human beings.

COMMENT: Anselm, like every true follower of Christ, had to carry his cross, especially in the form of opposition and conflict with those in political control. Though personally a mild and gentle man and a lover of peace, he would not back off from conflict and persecution when principles were at stake.

QUOTE: "No one will have any other desire in heaven than what God wills; and the desire of one will be the desire of all; and the desire of all and of each one will also be the desire of God" (St. Anselm, *Opera Omnis*, Letter 112).

OPTIONAL

George

Martyr

If Mary Magdalene (July 22) was the victim of misunderstanding (see page 169), George is the object of a vast amount of imagination. There is every reason to believe that he was a real martyr who suffered at Lydda in Palestine, probably before the time of Constantine. The Church adheres to his memory, but not to the legends surrounding his life.

That he was willing to pay the supreme price to follow

Christ is what the Church believes. And it is enough.

The story of George's slaying the dragon, rescuing the king's daughter and converting Libya is a 12th-century Italian fable.

George was a favorite patron saint of crusaders, as well as of Eastern soldiers in earlier times. He is a patron saint of England, Portugal, Germany, Aragon, Genoa and Venice.

COMMENT: Human nature seems unable to be satisfied with mere cold historical data. Americans have Washington and Lincoln, but we somehow need Paul Bunyan, too. The life of St. Francis of Assisi is inspiring enough, but for centuries the Italians have found his spirit in the legends of the *Fioretti*, too. Santa Claus is the popular extension of the spirit of St. Nicholas. Both fact and legend are human ways of illumining the mysterious truth about the One who alone is holy.

QUOTE: "When we look at the lives of those who have faithfully followed Christ, we are inspired with a new reason for seeking the city which is to come" (*Constitution on the Church*, 50).

Fidelis of Sigmaringen
Priest and Martyr (1577-1622)

If a poor man needed some clothing, Fidelis would often give the man the clothes right off his back. Complete generosity to others characterized this saint's life.

Born in 1577, Mark Rey (Fidelis was his religious name) became a lawyer who constantly upheld the causes of the poor and oppressed people. Nicknamed "the poor man's lawyer," Fidelis soon grew disgusted with the corruption and injustice he saw among his colleagues. He dropped his law career to become a priest, joining his brother George as a Franciscan friar of the Capuchin order. His wealth was divided between needy seminarians and the poor.

As a follower of Francis, Fidelis continued his devotion to the weak and needy. Once, during a severe epidemic in a city where he was guardian of a friary, Fidelis cared for and cured many sick soldiers.

He was appointed head of a group of Capuchins sent to preach against the Calvinists and Zwinglians in Switzerland. Almost certain violence threatened. Those who observed the mission felt that success was more attributable to the prayer in which Fidelis spent his nights than to his sermons and instructions.

He was accused of being an opponent of the peasants' national aspirations for independence from Austria. While he was preaching at Seewis, to which he had gone against the advice of his friends, a gun was fired at him, but he escaped unharmed. A Protestant offered to shelter Fidelis, but he declined, saying his life was in God's hands. On the road back, he was set upon by a group of armed men and killed.

COMMENT: Fidelis's constant prayer was that he be kept completely faithful to God and not give in to any lukewarmness or apathy. He was often heard to exclaim, "Woe to me if I should prove myself but a halfhearted soldier in the service of my thorn-crowned Captain." His prayer against apathy, and his concern for the poor and weak make him a saint whose example is valuable today. The modern Church is calling us to follow the example of "the poor man's lawyer" by sharing ourselves and our talents with those less fortunate and by working for justice in the world.

QUOTE: "Action on behalf of justice and participation in the transformation of the world fully appear to us as a constitutive dimension of the preaching of the Gospel, or, in other words, of the Church's mission for the redemption of the human race and its liberation from every oppressive situation" ("Justice in the World," Synod of Bishops, 1971).

Mark

Evangelist

Most of what we know about Mark comes directly from the New Testament. He is usually identified with the Mark of Acts 12:12. (When Peter escaped from prison, he went to the home of Mark's mother.)

Paul and Barnabas took him along on the first missionary journey, but for some reason Mark returned alone to Jerusalem. It is evident, from Paul's refusal to let Mark accompany him on the second journey despite Barnabas' insistence, that Mark had displeased Paul. Later, Paul asks Mark to visit him in prison so we may assume the trouble did not last long.

The oldest and the shortest of the four Gospels, Mark emphasizes Jesus' rejection by humanity while being God's triumphant envoy. Probably written for Gentile converts in Rome—after the death of Peter and Paul sometime between A.D. 60 and 70—Mark's Gospel is the gradual manifestation of a "scandal": a crucified Messiah.

Evidently a friend of Mark (Peter called him "my son"), Peter is only one of the Gospel sources, others being the Church in Jerusalem (Jewish roots) and the Church at Antioch (largely Gentile).

Like one other Gospel writer, Luke, Mark was not one of the 12 apostles. We cannot be certain whether he knew Jesus personally. Some scholars feel that the evangelist is speaking of himself when describing the arrest of Jesus in Gethsemani: "Now a young man followed him wearing nothing but a linen cloth about his body. They seized him, but he left the cloth behind and ran off naked" (Mark 14:51-52).

Others hold Mark to be the first bishop of Alexandria, Egypt. Venice, famous for the Piazza San Marco, claims Mark as its patron saint; the large basilica there is believed to contain his remains.

A winged lion is Mark's symbol. The lion derives from Mark's description of John the Baptist as a "voice of one crying out in the desert" (Mark 1:3), which artists compared to a roaring lion. The wings come from the application of Ezekiel's vision of four winged creatures to the evangelists.

COMMENT: Mark fulfilled in his life what every Christian is called to do: proclaim to all men the Good News which is the source of salvation. In particular, Mark's way was by writing. Others may proclaim the Good News by music, drama, poetry or by teaching children around a family table.

QUOTE: There is very little in Mark which is not in the other Gospels—only four passages. One is: "...This is how it is with the kingdom of God; it is as if a man were to scatter seed on the land and would sleep and rise night and day and the seed would sprout and grow, he knows not how. Of its own accord the land yields fruit, first the blade, then the ear, then the full grain in the ear. And when the grain is ripe, he wields the sickle at once, for the harvest has come" (Mark 4:26-29).

Peter Chanel

Priest and Martyr (1803-1841)

Anyone who has worked in loneliness, with great adaptation required and with little apparent success, will find a kindred spirit in Peter Chanel.

As a young priest he revived a parish in a "bad" district by the simple method of showing great devotion to the sick. Wanting to be a missionary, he joined the Society of Mary (Marists) at 28. Obediently, he taught in the seminary for five years. Then, as superior of seven Marists, he traveled to Western Oceania where he was entrusted with a vicariate. The bishop accompanying the missionaries left Peter and a brother on Futuna Island in the New Hebrides, promising to return in six months. The interval lasted five years.

Meanwhile he struggled with the unknown language and mastered it, making the difficult adjustment to life with whalers, traders and warring natives. Despite little apparent success and severe want, he maintained a serene and gentle spirit and endless patience and courage. A few natives had been baptized, a few more were being instructed. When the chieftain's son asked to be baptized persecution by the chieftain reached a climax. Father Chanel was clubbed to death, his body cut to pieces.

Within two years after his death, the whole island became Catholic and has remained so. Peter Chanel is the first martyr of Oceania and its patron.

COMMENT: Suffering for Christ means suffering because we are like Christ. Very often the opposition we meet is the result of our own selfishness or imprudence. We are not martyrs when we are "persecuted" by those who merely treat us as we treat them. A Christian martyr is one who, like Christ, is simply a witness to

God's love, and brings out of human hearts the good or evil that is already there.

QUOTE: "No one is a martyr for a conclusion, no one is a martyr for an opinion; it is faith that makes martyrs" (Cardinal Newman, *Discourses to Mixed Congregations*).

Catherine of Siena

Virgin and Doctor (1347-1380)

The value Catherine makes central in her short life and which sounds clearly and consistently through her experience is complete surrender to Christ. What is most impressive about her is that she learns to view her surrender to her Lord as a goal to be reached through time.

She was the 23rd child of Jacopo and Lapa Benincasa and grew up as an intelligent, cheerful and intensely religious person. Catherine disappointed her mother by cutting off her hair as a protest against being overly encouraged to improve her appearance in order to attract a husband. Her father ordered her to be left in peace and she was given a room of her own for prayer and meditation.

She entered the Dominican Third Order at 18 and spent the next three years in seclusion, prayer and austerity. Gradually a group of followers gathered around her—men and women, priests and religious. An active public apostolate grew out of her contemplative life. Her letters, mostly for spiritual instruction and encouragement of her followers, began to take more and more note of public affairs. Opposition and slander resulted from her mixing fearlessly with the world and speaking with the candor and authority of one completely committed to Christ. She was cleared of all charges at the Dominican General Chapter of 1374.

Her public influence reached great heights because of her evident holiness, her membership in the Dominican Order, and the deep impression she made on the pope. She worked tirelessly for the crusade against the Turks and for peace between Florence and the pope.

In 1378, the Great Schism broke, splitting the allegiance of Christendom between two, then three, popes and putting even saints on opposing sides (see St. Vincent Ferrer, April 5). Catherine spent the last two years of her life in Rome, in prayer and pleading on behalf of the cause of Urban VI and the unity of the Church. She offered herself as a victim for the Church in its agony. She died surrounded by her "children."

Catherine ranks high among the mystics and spiritual writers of the Church. In 1970 Paul VI named her a doctor of the Church. She is the second woman (after Teresa of Avila) to bear that title. Her spiritual testament is found in *The Dialogue*.

COMMENT: Though she lived her life in a faith experience and spirituality far different from that of our own time, Catherine of Siena stands as a companion with us on the Christian journey in her undivided effort to invite the Lord to take flesh in her own life. Events which might make us wince or chuckle or even yawn fill her biographies: a mystical experience at six, childhood betrothal to Christ, stories of harsh asceticism, her frequent ecstatic visions. Still, Catherine lived in an age which did not know the rapid change of 20th-century mobile America. The value of her life for us today lies in her recognition of holiness as a goal to be sought over the course of a lifetime.

QUOTE: Catherine's book *Dialogue* contains four treatises—her testament of faith to the spiritual world. She wrote, "No one should judge that he has greater perfection because he performs great penances and gives himself in excess to the staying of the body than he who does less, inasmuch as neither virtue nor merit consists therein; for otherwise he would be an evil case, who for some legitimate reason was unable to do actual penance. Merit consists in the virtue of love alone, flavored with the light of true discretion, without which the soul is worth nothing."

Pius V

Pope (1504-1572)

This is the pope whose job was to implement the historic Council of Trent. If we think recent popes have had difficulties in implementing the Vatican Council II, Pius V had even greater problems after that historic council four centuries ago.

During his papacy, 1566-1572, Pius V was faced with the almost overwhelming responsibility of getting a shattered and scattered Church back on its feet. The family of God had been shaken by corruption, by the Reformation, by the constant threat of Turkish invasion and by the bloody bickering of the young nation-states. In 1545 a previous pope convened the Council of Trent in an attempt to deal with all these pressing problems. For 18 years the Church Fathers discussed, condemned, affirmed and decided upon a course of action. The Council closed in 1563.

Pius V was elected in 1566 and was charged with the task of implementing the sweeping reforms called for by the Council. He ordered the founding of seminaries for the proper training of priests. He published a new missal, a new breviary, a new catechism and established the Confraternity of Christian Doctrine (CCD) classes for the young. Pius zealously enforced legislation against abuses in the Church. He patiently served the sick and the poor by building hospitals, providing food for the hungry and giving money customarily used for the papal banquets to poor Roman converts.

In striving to reform both Church and state Pius encountered vehement opposition from England's Queen Elizabeth and the Roman Emperor Maximilian II. Problems in France and in the Netherlands also hindered Pius's hopes for a Europe united against the Turks. Only at the last minute was he able to organize a fleet which won a decisive victory in the Gulf of Lepanto, off Greece, on October 7, 1571.

Pius's ceaseless papal quest for a renewal of the Church was grounded in his personal life as a Dominican friar. He spent long hours with his God in prayer, fasted rigorously, deprived himself of many customary papal luxuries and faithfully observed the Dominican Rule and its spirit.

COMMENT: In their personal lives and in their actions as popes, Pius V and Paul VI both led the family of God in the process of interiorizing and implementing the new birth called for by the Spirit in major Councils. With zeal and patience Pius and Paul pursued the changes urged by the Council Fathers. Like Pius and Paul, we too are called to constant change of heart and life.

QUOTE: "In this universal assembly, in this privileged point of time and space, there converge together the past, the present, and the future. The past: for here, gathered in this spot, we have the Church of Christ with her tradition, her history, her Councils, her doctors, her saints; the present: we are taking leave of one another to go out toward the world of today with its miseries, its sufferings, its sins, but also with its prodigious accomplishments, values, and virtues; and the future is here in the urgent appeal of the peoples of the world for more justice, in their will for peace, in their conscious or unconscious thirst for a higher life, that life precisely which the Church of Christ can give and wishes to give to them" (from Pope Paul's closing message to the Council Fathers at Vatican II).

Joseph the Worker

Apparently in response to the "May Day" celebrations for workers sponsored by Communists, Pius XII instituted the feast of St. Joseph the Worker in 1955. But the relationship between Joseph and the cause of workers has a longer history.

In a constantly necessary effort to keep Jesus from being removed from ordinary human life, the Church has from the beginning proudly emphasized that Jesus was a carpenter, obviously trained by Joseph in both the satisfactions and the drudgery of that vocation. Humanity is like God not only in thinking and loving, but also in creating. Whether we make a table or a cathedral, we are called to bear fruit with our hands and mind, ultimately for the building up of the Body of Christ.

COMMENT: "The LORD God then took the man and settled him in the garden of Eden, to cultivate and care for it" (Genesis 2:15). The Father created all and asked humanity to continue the work of creation. We find our dignity in our work, in raising a family, in participating in the life of the Father's creation. Joseph the Worker was able to help participate in the deepest mystery of creation. Pius XII emphasized this when he said, "The spirit flows to you and to all men from the heart of the God-man, Savior of the world, but certainly, no worker was ever more completely and profoundly penetrated by it than the foster father of Jesus, who lived with Him in closest intimacy and community of family life and work. Thus, if you wish to be close to Christ, we again today repeat, 'Go to Joseph' " (see Genesis 41:44).

QUOTE: In *Brothers of Men*, René Voillaume of the Little Brothers of Jesus speaks about ordinary work and holiness: "Now this holiness (of Jesus) became a reality in the most ordinary circumstances of life, those of word, of the family and the social life of a village, and this is an emphatic affirmation of the fact that the most obscure and humdrum human activities are entirely compatible with the perfection of the Son of God....In relation to this mystery, involves *the conviction that the evangelical holiness proper to a child of God is possible in the ordinary circumstances of a man who is poor and obliged to work for his living.*"

Athanasius

Bishop and Doctor (295?-373)

Athanasius led a tumultuous but dedicated life of service to the Church. He was the great champion of the faith against the widespread heresy of Arianism. The vigor of his writings earned him the title of doctor of the Church.

Born of a Christian family in Alexandria and given a classical education, Athanasius entered the priesthood, became secretary to Alexander, the bishop of Alexandria, and eventually was elevated to bishop himself. His predecessor, Alexander, had been an outspoken critic of a new movement growing in the East—Arianism.

When Athanasius assumed his role as bishop of Alexandria, he continued the fight against Arianism. At first it seemed that the battle would be easily won and that Arianism would be condemned. Such, however, did not prove to be the case. The Council of Tyre was called and for several reasons which are still unclear, the Emperor Constantine exiled Athanasius to Northern Gaul. This was to be the first in a series of travels and exiles reminiscent of the life of St. Paul.

Constantine died, and his succeeding son restored

Athanasius as bishop. This only lasted a year, however, for he was deposed once again by a coalition of Arian bishops. Athanasius took his case to Rome, and Pope Julius I called a synod to review the case and other related matters.

Five times he was exiled for his defense of the doctrine of Christ's divinity. During one period of his life, he enjoyed 10 years of relative peace—reading, writing and promoting the Christian life along the lines of the monastic ideal to which he was greatly devoted.

His dogmatic and historical writings are almost all polemic, directed against every aspect of Arianism. Among his ascetical writings, his *Life of St. Anthony* achieved astonishing popularity and contributed greatly to the establishment of monastic life throughout the Western Christian world.

COMMENT: Athanasius suffered many trials while he was bishop of Alexandria. He was given the grace to remain strong against what probably seemed at times to be insurmountable opposition. Athanasius lived his office as bishop completely. He defended the true faith for his flock, regardless of the cost to himself. In today's world we are experiencing this same call to remain true to our faith no matter what.

QUOTE: The hardships Athanasius suffered in exile, hiding, fleeing from place to place remind us of what Paul said of his own life: "[O]n frequent journeys, in dangers from rivers, dangers from robbers, dangers from my own race, dangers from Gentiles, dangers in the city, dangers in the wilderness, dangers at sea, dangers among false brothers; in toil and hardship, through many sleepless nights, through hunger and thirst, through frequent fastings, through cold and exposure. And apart from these things, there is the daily pressure upon me of my anxiety for all the churches" (2 Corinthians 11:26-28).

Philip and James

Apostles

James, Son of Alphaeus. We know nothing of this man but his name, and of course the fact that Jesus chose him to be one of the 12 pillars of the New Israel, his Church. He is *not* the James of Acts, son of Clopas, "brother" of Jesus and later bishop of Jerusalem and the traditional author of the Epistle of James.

Philip. Philip came from the same town as Peter and Andrew, Bethsaida in Galilee. Jesus called him directly, whereupon he sought out Nathanael and told him of the "one about whom Moses wrote" (John 1:45).

Like the other apostles, Philip took a long time coming to realize who Jesus was. On one occasion, when Jesus saw the great multitude following him and wanted to give them food, he asked Philip where they should buy bread for the people to eat. St. John comments, "[Jesus] said this to test him, because he himself knew what he was going to do" (John 6:6). Philip answered, "Two hundred days' wages worth of food would not be enough for each of them to have a little [bit]" (John 6:7).

John's story is not a put-down of Philip. It was simply necessary for these men who were to be the foundation stones of the Church to see the clear distinction between humanity's total helplessness apart from God and the human ability to be a bearer of divine power by God's gift.

On another occasion, we can almost hear the exasperation in Jesus' voice. After Thomas had complained that they did not know where Jesus was going, Jesus said "I am the way....If you know me, then you will also know my Father. From now on you do know him and have seen him" (John 14:6a, 7). Then Philip said, "Master, show us the Father, and that will be enough for us"

(John 14:8). Enough! Jesus answered, "Have I been with you for so long a time and you still do not know me, Philip? Whoever has seen me has seen the Father" (John 14:9a).

Possibly because Philip bore a Greek name or because he was thought to be close to Jesus, some Gentile proselytes came to him and asked him to introduce them to Jesus. Philip went to Andrew, and Andrew went to Jesus. Jesus' reply in John's Gospel is indirect; Jesus says that now his "hour" has come, that in a short time he will give his life for Jew and Gentile alike.

COMMENT: As in the case of the other apostles, we see a very human man who became a foundation stone of the Church, and we are reminded again that holiness and its consequent apostolate are entirely the gift of God, not a matter of human achieving. All power is God's power, even the power of human freedom to accept his gifts. "You will be clothed with power from on high," Jesus told Philip and the others. Their first commission had been to expel unclean spirits, heal diseases, announce the kingdom. They learned, gradually, that these externals were sacraments of an even greater miracle inside their persons—the divine power to love like God.

QUOTE: "He sent them...so that as sharers in his power they might make all peoples his disciples, sanctifying and governing them....They were fully confirmed in this mission on the day of Pentecost (cf. Acts 2:1-26) in accordance with the Lord's promise: 'You shall receive power when the Holy Spirit comes upon you, and you shall be witnesses for me...even to the very ends of the earth' (Acts 1:8). By everywhere preaching the gospel (cf. Mark 16:20), which was accepted by their hearers under the influence of the Holy Spirit, the apostles gathered together the universal Church, which the Lord established on the apostles and built upon blessed Peter, their chief, Christ Jesus himself remaining the supreme cornerstone..." (*Constitution on the Church*, 19).

Nereus and Achilleus

Martyrs (first century?)

Devotion to these two saints goes back to the fourth century, though almost nothing is known of their lives. They were praetorian soldiers of the Roman army, became Christians and were removed to the island of Terracina, where they were martyred. Their bodies were buried in a family vault, later known as the cemetery of Domitilla. Excavations by De Rossi in 1896 resulted in the discovery of their empty tomb in the underground church built by Pope Siricius in 390.

Two hundred years after their death Pope Gregory the Great delivered his 28th homily on the occasion of their feast. "These saints, before whom we are assembled, despised the world and trampled it under their feet when peace, riches and health gave it charms."

COMMENT: As in the case of many early martyrs, the Church clings to its memories though the events are clouded in the mists of history. It is a heartening thing for all Christians to know that they have a noble heritage. Our brothers and sisters in Christ have stood in the same world in which we live—militarist, materialist, cruel and cynical—yet transfigured from within by the presence of the Living One. Our own courage is enlivened by the heroes and heroines who have gone before us marked by the sign of faith and the wounds of Christ.

QUOTE: Pope Damasus wrote an epitaph for Nereus and Achilleus in the fourth century. The text is known from travelers who read it while the slab was still entire, but the broken fragments found by De Rossi are sufficient to identify it: "The martyrs Nereus and Achilleus had enrolled themselves in the army and exercised the cruel office of carrying out the orders of the tyrant, being ever ready, through the constraint of fear, to obey his will. O miracle of faith! Suddenly they cease from their fury, they become converted, they fly from the camp of their wicked leader; they throw away their shields, their armor and their blood-stained javelins. Confessing the faith of Christ, they rejoice to bear testimony to its triumph. Learn now from the words of Damasus what great things the glory of Christ can accomplish."

Pancras

Martyr (d. 304?)

St. Pancras Railway Station in London got its name from an early Christian martyr about whom we have very little information. He is said to have been martyred at 14 during the persecution of Diocletian. He was buried in a cemetery which later was named after him. Gregory the Great built a monastery for Benedictines and, when Augustine of Canterbury (a Benedictine) came to England, he named the first church he erected after Pancras. Hence the name of the railway station.

Pancras (Pancratius) appears in fictionalized form in Cardinal Wiseman's novel *Fabiola*. German farmers had a saying that three saints whose names are similar—Pancras, Servatz and Bonifatz—were the "ice men" because it was unseasonably chilly on their feast days, May 12, 13, 14.

COMMENT: Again we have a saint about whom almost nothing is known, but whose life and death are cherished in the Church's memory. Details fall away or are mixed with the fantasy of legend. But a single, powerful fact remains: He died for Christ and his heroism sent a wave of inspiration through the Church of his day. It is good for us to share that feeling.

QUOTE: "[T]hey will seize and persecute you, they will hand you over to the synagogues and to prisons, and they will have you led before kings and governors because of my name. It will lead to your giving testimony. Remember, you are not to prepare your defense beforehand, for I myself shall give you a wisdom in speaking that all your adversaries will be powerless to resist or refute" (Luke 21:12-15).

Matthias

Apostle

According to Acts 1:15-26, during the days after the Ascension, Peter stood up in the midst of the brothers (about 120 of Jesus' followers). Now that Judas had betrayed his ministry, it was necessary, Peter said, to fulfill the scriptural recommendation: "May another take his office." "Therefore, it is necessary that one of the men who accompanied us the whole time the Lord Jesus came and went among us, beginning from the baptism of John until the day on which he was taken up from us, become with us a witness to his resurrection" (Acts 1:21-22).

They nominated two men: Joseph Barsabbas and Matthias. They prayed and drew lots. The choice fell upon Matthias, who was added to the Eleven.

Matthias is not mentioned by name anywhere else in the New Testament.

COMMENT: What was the holiness of Matthias? Obviously he was suited for apostleship by the experience of being with Jesus from his baptism to his ascension. He must also have been suited personally, or he would not have been nominated for so great a responsibility. Must we not remind ourselves that the fundamental holiness of Matthias was his receiving gladly the relationship with the Father offered him by Jesus and completed by the Holy Spirit? If the apostles are the foundations of our faith by their witness, they must also be reminders, if only implicitly, that holiness is entirely a matter of God's giving, and it is offered to all, in the everyday circumstances of life. We receive, and even for this God supplies the power of freedom.

QUOTE: Jesus speaks of the apostles' function of being judges, that is, rulers. He said, "Amen, I say to you that you who have followed me, in the new age, when the Son of Man is seated on his throne of glory, will yourselves sit on twelve thrones, judging the twelve tribes of Israel" (Matthew 19:28).

MAY 15   OPTIONAL (U.S.A.)

Isidore the Farmer
(1070-1130)

Isidore has become the patron of farmers and rural communities. In particular he is the patron of Madrid, Spain, and of the United States National Rural Life Conference.

When he was barely old enough to wield a hoe, Isidore entered the service of John de Vergas, a wealthy landowner from Madrid, and worked faithfully on his estate outside the city for the rest of his life. He married a young woman as simple and upright as himself who also became a saint—Maria de la Cabeza. They had one son, who died as a child.

Isidore had deep religious instincts. He rose early in the morning to go to church and spent many a holiday devoutly visiting the churches of Madrid and surrounding areas. All day long, as he walked behind the plow, he communed with God. His devotion, one might say, became a problem, for his fellow workers sometimes complained that he often showed up late because of lingering in church too long.

He was known for his love of the poor, and there are accounts of Isidore's supplying them miraculously with food. He had a great concern for the proper treatment of animals.

He died May 15, 1120, and was declared a saint in 1622 with Ignatius, Francis Xavier, Teresa and Philip Neri. Together, the group is known in Spain as "the five saints."

COMMENT: Many implications can be found in a simple laborer achieving sainthood: Physical labor has dignity; sainthood does not stem from status; contemplation does not depend on learning; the simple life is conducive to holiness and happiness. Legends about angel helpers and mysterious oxen indicate that his work was *not* neglected and his duties did *not* go unfulfilled. Perhaps the truth which emerges is this: If you have your spiritual self in order, your earthly commitments will fall into order also. "[S]eek first the kingdom [of God] and his righteousness," said the carpenter from Nazareth, "and all these things will be given you besides" (Matthew 6:33).

QUOTE: "God blessed them, saying: 'Be fertile and multiply; fill the earth and subdue it....See, I give you every seed-bearing plant all over the earth and every tree that has seed-bearing fruit on it to be your food; and to all the animals of the land, all the birds of the air, and all the living creatures that crawl on the ground, I give all the green plants for food'" (Genesis 1:28a, 29-30a).

John I

Pope and Martyr (d. 526)

Pope John I inherited the Arian heresy, which denied the divinity of Christ. Italy had been ruled for 30 years by an emperor who espoused the heresy, though he treated the Catholics of the empire with toleration. His policy changed at about the time the young John was elected pope.

When the eastern emperor began imposing severe measures on the Arians of his area, the western emperor forced John to head a delegation to the East to soften the measures against the heretics. Little is known of the manner or outcome of the negotiations—designed to secure continued toleration of Catholics in the West.

When John returned to Rome, he found that the emperor had begun to suspect his friendship with his eastern rival.

On his way home, John was imprisoned when he reached Ravenna because the emperor suspected a conspiracy against his throne. Shortly after his imprisonment, John died, apparently from the treatment he had received.

COMMENT: We cannot choose the issues for which we have to suffer and perhaps die. John I suffered because of a power-conscious emperor. Jesus suffered because of the suspicions of those who were threatened by his freedom, openness and powerlessness. "If you find that the world hates you, know it has hated me before you."

QUOTE: "By martyrdom a disciple is transformed into an image of his Master, who freely accepted death on behalf of the world's salvation; he perfects that image even to the shedding of blood. Though few are presented with such an opportunity, nevertheless all must be prepared to confess Christ before men, and to follow him along the way of the cross through the persecutions which the Church will never fail to suffer" (*Constitution on the Church*, 42).

Bernardine of Siena
Priest (1380-1444)

Most of the saints suffer great personal opposition, even persecution. Bernardine, by contrast, seems more like a human dynamo who simply took on the needs of the world.

He was the greatest preacher of his time, journeying across Italy, calming strife-torn cities, attacking the paganism he found rampant, attracting crowds of 30,000, following St. Francis' admonition to preach about "vice and virtue, punishment and glory."

Compared with St. Paul by the pope, Bernardine had a keen intuition of the needs of the time, along with solid holiness and boundless energy and joy. He accomplished all this despite having a very weak and hoarse voice, miraculously improved later because of his devotion to Mary.

When he was 20, the plague was at its height in his hometown, Siena. Sometimes as many as 20 people died in one day at the hospital. Bernardine offered to run the entire establishment and, with the help of other young men, nursed patients there for four months. He escaped the plague but was so exhausted that a fever confined him for several months. He spent another year caring for a beloved aunt (her parents had died when he was a child) and at her death began to fast and pray to know God's will for him.

At 22, he entered the Franciscan Order and was ordained two years later. For almost a dozen years he lived in solitude and prayer, but his gifts ultimately caused him to be sent to preach. He always traveled on foot, sometimes speaking for hours in one place, then doing the same in another town.

Especially known for his devotion to the Holy Name of Jesus, Bernardine devised a symbol—*IHS*, the first three letters of the name of Jesus in Greek, in Gothic letters on a blazing sun. This was to displace the superstitious symbols of the day, as well as the insignia of factions (for example, Guelphs and Ghibellines). The devotion spread, and the symbol began to appear in churches, homes and public buildings. Opposition arose from those who thought it a dangerous innovation. Three attempts were made to have the pope take action against him, but Bernardine's holiness, orthodoxy and intelligence were evidence of his faithfulness.

General of a branch of the Franciscans, the Friars of the Strict Observance, he strongly emphasized scholarship and further study of theology and canon law. When he started there were 300 friars in the community; when he died there were 4,000. He returned to preaching the last two years of his life, dying "on the road."

COMMENT: Another dynamic saint once said, "...I will not be a burden, for I want not what is yours, but you....I will most gladly spend and be utterly spent for your sakes" (2 Corinthians 12:14). There is danger that we see only the whirlwind of activity in the Bernardines of faith—taking care of the sick, preaching, studying, administering, always driving—and forget the source of their energy. We should not say that Bernardine *could* have been a great contemplative if he had had the chance. He had the chance, every day, and he took it.

STORY: At Bologna, Bernardine preached mightily against the evils of gambling. As was the custom, a huge bonfire was made in the public square, to be a holocaust consuming all the instruments of the vice—playing cards, dice and the like. A manufacturer of playing cards complained that Bernardine was taking away his livelihood. The saint told him to start making the symbol *IHS* and he made more money than ever before.

Venerable Bede

Priest and Doctor (672?-735)

Bede is one of the few saints who was honored as such even during his lifetime. His writings were filled with such faith and learning that even while he was still alive, a Church council ordered them to be read publicly in the churches.

At an early age Bede was entrusted to the care of the abbot of the monastery of St. Paul, Jarrow. The happy combination of genius and the instruction of scholarly, saintly monks produced a saint and an extraordinary scholar, perhaps the most outstanding of his time. He was deeply versed in all the sciences of his times: natural philosophy, the philosophical principles of Aristotle, astronomy, arithmetic, grammar, ecclesiastical history, the lives of the saints and, especially, Holy Scripture.

From the time of his ordination to the priesthood at 30 (he had been ordained deacon at 19) till his death, he was ever occupied with learning, writing and teaching. Besides the many books that he copied, he composed 45 of his own, of which 30 were devoted to commentary on the Bible.

Although eagerly sought by kings and other notables, even Pope Sergius, Bede managed to remain in his own monastery till his death. Only once did he leave for a few months in order to teach in the school of the archbishop of York.

Bede died in 735 praying his favorite prayer: "Glory be to the Father, and to the Son, and to the Holy Spirit. As in the beginning, so now, and forever."

His *Ecclesiastical History of the English People* is commonly regarded as of decisive importance in the art and science of writing history. A golden age was coming to an end at the time of Bede's death: It had fulfilled its purpose of preparing Western Christianity to assimilate the non-Roman barbarian North. Bede recognized the opening to a new day in the life of the Church even as it was happening.

COMMENT: Though his *History* is the greatest legacy Bede has left us, his work in all the sciences (especially in Scripture) should not be overlooked. During his last Lent, he worked on a translation of the Gospel of St. John into English, completing it the day he died. But of this work "to break the word to the poor and unlearned" nothing remains today.

QUOTE: "We have not, it seems to me, amid all our discoveries, invented as yet anything better than the Christian life which Bede lived, and the Christian death which he died" (C. Plummer, editor of Bede's *Ecclesiastical History*).

Gregory VII
Pope (1020-1085)

The 10th century and the first half of the 11th were dark days for the Church, partly because the papacy was the pawn of various Roman families. In 1049, things began to change when Pope Leo IX, a reformer, was elected. He brought a young monk named

Hildebrand to Rome as his counselor and special representative on important missions. He was to become Gregory VII.

Three evils plagued the Church then: simony (the buying and selling of sacred offices and things), the unlawful marriage of the clergy and lay investiture (kings and nobles controlling the appointment of Church officials). To all of these Hildebrand directed his reformer's attention, first as counselor to the popes and later (1073-1085) as pope himself.

Gregory's papal letters stress the role of bishop of Rome as the vicar of Christ and the visible center of unity in the Church. He is well known for his long dispute with Holy Roman Emperor Henry IV over who should control the selection of bishops and abbots.

Gregory fiercely resisted any attack on the liberty of the Church. For this he suffered and finally died in exile. He said, "I have loved justice and hated iniquity; therefore I die in exile." Thirty years later the Church finally won its struggle against lay investiture.

COMMENT: The Gregorian Reform, a milestone in the history of Christ's Church, was named after this man who tried to extricate the papacy and the whole Church from undue control by civil rulers. Against an unhealthy Church nationalism in some areas, Gregory reasserted the unity of the whole Church based on Christ and expressed in the Bishop of Rome, the successor of St. Peter.

QUOTE: Gregory has much to say to our age in which civil or national religion is making subtle demands: "In every country, even the poorest of women is permitted to take a lawful husband according to the law of the land and by her own choice; but, through the desires and evil practices of the wicked, Holy Church, the bride of God and mother of us all, is not permitted lawfully to cling to her spouse on earth in accordance with divine law and her own will" (*A Call to the Faithful*).

. . . .

Mary Magdalene de Pazzi

Virgin (1566-1607)

Mystical ecstasy is the elevation of the spirit to God in such a way that the person is aware of this union with God and both internal and external senses are detached from the sensible world. Mary Magdalene de Pazzi was so generously given this special gift of God that she is called the "ecstatic saint."

She was born into a noble family in Florence in 1566, when Florence was a great city and its first families had influence. The normal course would have been for Catherine de Pazzi to have married nobly and enjoyed comfort. But she hardly followed the normal course. At nine she learned to meditate from the family confessor. She made her First Communion at the then early age of 10 and made a vow of virginity one month later. When 16, she entered the Carmelite convent in Florence because she could receive Communion daily there.

Catherine had taken the name Mary Magdalene and had been a novice for a year when she became critically ill. Death seemed near so her superiors let her make her profession of vows from a cot in the chapel in a private ceremony. Immediately after, she fell into an ecstasy that lasted about two hours. This was repeated after Communion on the following 40 mornings. These ecstasies were rich experiences of union with God and contained marvelous insights into divine truths.

As a safeguard against deception and to preserve the revelations, her confessor asked Mary Magdalene to dictate her experiences to sister secretaries. Over the next six years, five large volumes were filled. The first three books record ecstasies from May 27, 1584, through Pentecost week of 1585. This week was a preparation for a severe five-year trial. The fourth book records that trial and the fifth is a collection of letters concerning reform and renewal. Another book, *Admonitions*, is a collection of her sayings arising from her experiences in the formation of religious.

The extraordinary was ordinary for this saint. She read the thoughts of others and predicted future events. During her lifetime, she appeared to several persons in distant places and cured a number of sick people.

It would be easy to dwell on the ecstasies and pretend that Mary Magdalene only had spiritual highs. This is far from true. It seems that God permitted her this special closeness to prepare her for the five years of desolation that followed when she experienced spiritual dryness. She was plunged into a state of darkness in which she saw nothing but what was horrible in herself and all around her. She had violent temptations and endured great physical suffering. She died in 1607 at 41 and was canonized in 1669. Over 350 years later, her body is uncorrupt.

COMMENT: Intimate union, God's gift to mystics, is a reminder to all of us of the eternal happiness of union he wishes to give us. The cause of mystical ecstasy in this life is the Holy Spirit, working through spiritual gifts. The ecstasy occurs because of the weakness of the body and its powers to withstand the divine illumination, but as the body is purified and strengthened, ecstasy no longer occurs. On various aspects of ecstasy, see Teresa of Avila, *Interior Castle*, "Sixth Mansion," Chapter 5, and John of the Cross, *Dark Night of the Soul*, 2:1-2.

QUOTE: There are many people today who see no purpose in suffering. Mary Magdalene de Pazzi discovered saving grace in suffering. When she entered religious life she was filled with a desire to suffer during the rest of her life for Christ. The more she suffered, the greater grew her desire for it. Her dying words to her fellow sisters were: "The last thing I ask of you—and I ask it in the name of our Lord Jesus Christ—is that you love him alone, that you trust implicitly in him and that you encourage one another continually to suffer for the love of him."

Philip Neri
Priest (1515-1595)

Philip Neri was a sign of contradiction, combining popularity
with piety against the background of a corrupt Rome and a
disinterested clergy, the whole post-Renaissance malaise.

At an early age, he abandoned the chance to become a
businessman, moved to Rome from Florence and devoted his life
and individuality to God. After three years of philosophy and
theology he gave up any thought of ordination. The next 13 years
were spent in a vocation unusual at the time—that of a layperson
actively engaged in prayer and the apostolate.

As the Council of Trent was reforming the Church on a
doctrinal level, Philip's appealing personality was winning him
friends from all levels of society, from beggars to cardinals. He
rapidly gathered around himself a group of laypersons won over by
his audacious spirituality. Initially they met as an informal prayer
and discussion group, and also served the needy of Rome.

At the urging of his confessor, he was ordained priest and
soon became an outstanding confessor, gifted with the knack of
piercing the pretenses and illusions of others, though always in a
charitable manner and often with a joke. He arranged talks,
discussions and prayers for his penitents in a room above the
church. He sometimes led "excursions" to other churches, often
with music and a picnic on the way.

Some of his followers became priests and lived together in
community. This was the beginning of the Oratory, the religious
institute he founded. A feature of their life was a daily afternoon
service of four informal talks, with vernacular hymns and prayers.
Palestrina was one of Philip's followers, and composed music for
the services.

The Oratory was finally approved after suffering through a

period of accusations of being an assembly of heretics, where laypersons preached and sang vernacular hymns! (Cardinal Newman founded the first English-speaking house of the Oratory.)

Philip's advice was sought by many of the prominent figures of his day. He is one of the influential figures of the Counter-Reformation, mainly for converting to personal holiness many of the influential people within the Church itself. His characteristic virtues were humility and gaiety.

COMMENT: Many people wrongly feel that such an attractive and jocular personality as Philip's cannot be combined with an intense spirituality. Philip's life melts our rigid, narrow views of piety. His approach to sanctity was truly catholic, all-embracing and accompanied by a good laugh. Philip always wanted his followers to become not less but more human through their striving for holiness.

QUOTE: Philip Neri prayed, "Let me get through today, and I shall not fear tomorrow."

Augustine of Canterbury

Bishop (d. 605?)

In the year 596 a small party of some 30 monks set out from Rome to evangelize the Anglo-Saxons in England. Leading the group was Augustine, the prior of their monastery in Rome. Hardly had he and his men reached Gaul (France) when they heard stories of the ferocity of the Anglo-Saxons and of the treacherous waters of the English Channel. Augustine returned to Rome and to the pope who had sent them—St. Gregory the Great—only to be assured by him that their fears were groundless.

Augustine again set out and this time the group crossed the channel and landed in the territory of Kent, ruled by King Ethelbert, a pagan married to a Christian. Ethelbert received them kindly, set up a residence for them in Canterbury and within the year, on Pentecost Sunday, 597, was himself baptized. After being consecrated a bishop in France, Augustine returned to Canterbury, where he founded his see. He constructed a church and monastery on the site where the present cathedral, begun in 1070, now stands. As the faith spread, additional sees were established at London and Rochester.

Work was sometimes slow and Augustine did not always meet with success. Attempts to reconcile the Anglo-Saxon Christians with the original Briton Christians (who had been driven into western England by Anglo-Saxon invaders) ended in dismal failure. Augustine failed to convince the Britons to give up certain Celtic customs at variance with Rome and to forget their bitterness, helping him evangelize their Anglo-Saxon conquerors.

Laboring patiently, Augustine wisely heeded the missionary principles—quite enlightened for the times—suggested by Pope Gregory the Great: purify rather than destroy pagan temples and customs; let pagan rites and festivals be taken over into Christian feasts; retain local customs as far as possible. The limited success Augustine achieved in England before his death in 605, a short eight years after he arrived in England, would eventually bear fruit long after in the conversion of England. Truly Augustine of Canterbury can be called the "apostle of England."

COMMENT: Augustine of Canterbury comes across today as a very human saint, one who could suffer like many of us from a failure of nerve. For example, his first venture to England ended in a big U-turn back to Rome. He made mistakes and met failure in his peacemaking attempts with the Briton Christians. He often wrote to Rome for decisions on matters he could have decided on his own had he been more self-assured. He even received mild warnings against pride from Pope Gregory who cautioned him to "fear lest, amidst the wonders that are done, the weak mind be puffed up by self-esteem." Augustine's perseverance amidst obstacles and only partial success teaches today's apostles and pioneers to struggle on despite frustrations and be satisfied with gradual advances.

QUOTE: In a letter to Augustine, Pope Gregory the Great wrote: "He who would climb to a lofty height must go by steps, not leaps."

Visitation

This is a fairly late feast, going back only to the 13th or 14th century. It was established widely throughout the Church to pray for unity. The present date of celebration was recently fixed in order to follow the Annunciation of the Lord (March 25) and precede the Birthday of John the Baptist (June 24).

Like most feasts of Mary, it is closely connected with Jesus and his saving work. The more visible actors in the visitation drama (see Luke 1:39-45) are Mary and Elizabeth. However, Jesus and John the Baptist steal the scene in a hidden way. Jesus makes John leap with joy—the joy of messianic salvation. Elizabeth, in turn, is filled with the Holy Spirit and addresses words of praise to Mary—words that echo down through the ages.

It is helpful to recall that we do not have a journalist's account of this meeting. Rather, Luke, speaking for the Church, gives a prayerful poet's rendition of the scene. Elizabeth's praise of

Mary as "the mother of my Lord" can be viewed as the earliest Church's devotion to Mary. As all authentic devotion to Mary, Elizabeth's (the Church's) words first praise God for what God has done to Mary. Only secondly does she praise Mary for trusting God's words.

Then comes the Magnificat. Here Mary herself (like the Church) traces all her greatness to God.

COMMENT: One of the invocations in Mary's litany is "Ark of the Covenant." Like the Ark of the Covenant of old, Mary brings God's presence into the lives of other people. As David danced before the Ark, John the Baptist leaps for joy. As the Ark helped to unite the 12 tribes of Israel by being placed in David's capital, so Mary has the power to unite all Christians in her Son. At times, devotion to Mary may have occasioned some divisiveness, but it is to be hoped that authentic devotion will lead all to Christ and therefore to one another.

QUOTE: "Moved by charity, therefore, Mary goes to the house of her kinswoman....While every word of Elizabeth's is filled with meaning, her final words would seem to have a fundamental importance: 'And blessed is she who believed that there would be a fulfillment of what had been spoken to her from the Lord' (Luke 1:45). These words can be linked with the title 'full of grace' of the angel's greeting. Both of these texts reveal an essential Mariological content, namely the truth about Mary, who has become really present in the mystery of Christ precisely because she 'has believed.' The fullness of grace announced by the angel means the gift of God himself. Mary's faith, proclaimed by Elizabeth at the visitation, indicates how the Virgin of Nazareth responded to this gift" (Pope John Paul II, *The Mother of the Redeemer*, 12).

Sacred Heart

Devotion to the heart pierced on Calvary is nearly as old as
Christianity, but it has undergone many changes over the
centuries.

Patristic writers saw in the blood and water issuing from the
crucified Lord's side (John 19:34) the fulfillment of his promise to
give living water (John 4:13-14; 7:37), the fountain from which
the Spirit flows upon the Church. Medieval piety placed less
emphasis on Jesus' heart as the source of grace and moved toward
more personal and sentimental devotion.

The public cult celebrated today began in the 17th century,
when St. John Eudes pressed for a liturgy (Mass and Office) of the
Sacred Heart. Toward the end of that century St. Mary Margaret
Alacoque received visions of the Lord exposing his heart and
urging public devotion. Her apparitions gave impetus to the
devotion and shape to its purpose: to offer reparation for human
ingratitude, especially indifference to the Blessed Sacrament.

Pius VI saw the devotion as a means of refuting the Jansenist
heresy, which rejected the doctrine that Christ died for all.
Clement XIII first granted the petition for a liturgical observance
to the Polish bishops and the Roman Archconfraternity of the
Sacred Heart in 1765. Pius IX extended the observance to the
universal Church in 1856 and late in the 19th century Leo XIII
raised its rank to a feast.

Popular devotion includes the nine First Fridays and the
enthronement of an image of the Sacred Heart in homes as a sign
that love is the Christian way of life.

COMMENT: A Jewish midrash on the Exodus account of Moses'
encounter with God compares the burning bush to the human
heart: the only created thing which can burn without being

consumed. Yet nothing seems to be harder for human beings to believe in than unconditional love—love which is neither deserved nor earned. The Sacred Heart of Jesus, aflame with an unquenchable fire, stands today against lingering traces of Jansenism as a powerful symbol of Christ's unquenchable love for the whole human race.

QUOTE: "Whoever does not love does not know God. Why? Because God is Love. What more can be said, my Brothers? If one did not find one word in praise of love through this epistle, nor the least word throughout all the other pages of Scripture, and we heard only this one word from the voice of the Spirit of God: Because 'God is Love,' we should seek for nothing more" (St. Augustine, *Homily on the First Epistle of St. John*).

SATURDAY AFTER CORPUS CHRISTI   OPTIONAL

Immaculate Heart of Mary

In the 17th century St. John Eudes promoted devotion to the hearts of Jesus and Mary. He even composed an Office and Mass in honor of the Heart of Mary. It became a feast of the universal Church only in the 20th century and is celebrated on the day after the feast of the Sacred Heart of Jesus.

The New Testament mentions Mary's heart only twice. Luke 2:19 says: "Mary treasured all these things and reflected on them in her heart." Luke 2:51 has a similar text, though the *New American Bible* translates "heart" as "memory."

Both in Scripture and in later reflections on Mary's heart, it is obvious that the usage is symbolic. The physical heart stands for the inner reaches of the human personality. It includes or connotes the mind, the soul, the will, the spirit, the core of one's being. It is the place where a person thinks, remembers, feels, desires, makes decisions.

Medieval saints such as Mechtild, Gertrude and Bridget promoted devotion to the heart of Mary. Franciscan and Jesuit theologians made their contributions. St. Francis de Sales dedicated his *Treatise on the Love of God* to Mary's heart. But it was St. John Eudes who wrote extensively about this theme. He says that the divine Word printed on Mary's heart a perfect likeness of the divine attributes and a share in the properties of each person of the Trinity.

Perhaps this devotion is coming into its own in the 20th century. It is a special theme of Fatima. In 1942 Pius XII consecrated the world to the Immaculate Heart of Mary and established the feast for the universal Church.

COMMENT: To honor Mary's heart is to honor her total dedication to God. As she pondered in her heart the mysteries of Jesus' infancy and childhood (Luke 2:19, 51), she must have done the same for all the mysteries of his life, death and resurrection. This feast suggests that Mary is the greatest of the mystics—totally wrapped up in God and committed to God's will. Her spirituality is a model for all the members of the Church.

QUOTE: "We can say that the mystery of the redemption took shape beneath the heart of the Virgin of Nazareth when she pronounced her 'fiat.' From then on, under the special influence of the Holy Spirit, this heart, the heart of both a virgin and a mother, has always followed the work of her Son and has gone out to all those whom Christ has embraced and continues to embrace with inexhaustible love. For that reason her heart must have the inexhaustibility of a mother" (John Paul II, *Redeemer of Man*, 22).

Justin

Martyr (d. 165)

Justin never ended his quest for religious truth even when he converted to Christianity after years of studying various pagan philosophies.

As a young man, he was principally attracted to the school of Plato. However, he found that the Christian religion answered the great questions about life and existence better than the philosophers.

Upon his conversion he continued to wear the philosopher's mantle, and became the first Christian philosopher. He combined the Christian religion with the best elements in Greek philosophy. In his view, philosophy was a pedagogue of Christ, an educator that was to lead one to Christ.

Justin is known as an apologist, one who defends in writing the Christian religion against the attacks and misunderstandings of the pagans. Two of his apologies have come down to us; they are addressed to the Roman emperor and to the Senate.

For his staunch adherence to the Christian religion, Justin was beheaded in Rome in 165.

COMMENT: As patron of philosophers, Justin may inspire us to use our natural powers (especially our power to know and understand) in the service of Christ and to build up the Christian life within us. Since we are prone to error, especially in reference to the deep questions concerning life and existence, we should also be willing to correct and check our natural thinking in light of religious truth. Thus we will be able to say with the learned saints of the Church: I believe in order to understand, and I understand in order to believe.

"Philosophy is the knowledge of that which exists, and a clear understanding of the truth; and happiness is the reward of such knowledge and understanding" (Justin, *Dialogue with Trypho*, 3).

OPTIONAL

Marcellinus and Peter

Martyrs (d. 304)

Marcellinus and Peter were prominent enough in the memory of the Church to be included among the saints of the Roman canon. Mention of their names is optional in our present Eucharistic Prayer I.

Marcellinus was a priest and Peter was an exorcist (strange that this order, one of the four "minor" orders, was dropped just at the time when Hollywood discovered the devil). They were beheaded during the persecution of Diocletian.

Pope Damasus wrote an epitaph apparently founded on the report of their executioner, and Constantine erected a basilica over the crypt in which they were buried in Rome. Numerous legends sprang from an early account of their death.

COMMENT: Why are these men included in our Eucharistic prayer, and given their own feast day, in spite of the fact that almost nothing is known about them? Probably because the Church respects its collective memory. They once sent an impulse of encouragement through the whole Church. They made the ultimate step of faith.

QUOTE: "The Church has always believed that the apostles, and Christ's martyrs who had given the supreme witness of faith and charity by the shedding of their blood, are quite closely joined with us in Christ" (*Constitution of the Church*, 50).

Charles Lwanga and Companions

Martyrs (d. 1886)

One of 22 Ugandan martyrs, Charles Lwanga is the patron of youth and Catholic action in most of tropical Africa. He protected his fellow pages, ages 13-30, from the homosexual demands of the Bagandan ruler, Mwanga, and encouraged and instructed them in the Catholic faith during their imprisonment for refusing the demands.

For his own unwillingness to submit to the immoral acts and his efforts to safeguard the faith of his friends, Charles was burned to death at Namugongo on June 3, 1886, by Mwanga's order.

Charles first learned of Christ's teachings from two retainers in the court of Chief Mawulugungu. While a catechumen, he entered the royal household as assistant to Joseph Mukaso, head of the court pages.

On the night of Mukaso's martyrdom for encouraging the African youths to resist Mwanga, Charles requested and received Baptism. Imprisoned with his friends, Charles's courage and belief in God inspired them to remain chaste and faithful.

The 22 martyrs were canonized by Pope Paul VI, on October 18, 1964.

COMMENT: Like Charles Lwanga, we are all teachers and witnesses to Christian living by the examples of our own lives. We are all called upon to spread the word of God, whether by word or deed. By remaining courageous and unshakable in our faith during times of great moral and physical temptation, we live as Christ lived.

QUOTE: On his African tour in 1969, Pope Paul VI told 22 young Ugandan converts that "being a Christian was a fine thing but not always an easy one."

Boniface
Bishop and Martyr (672?-754)

Boniface, known as the apostle of the Germans, was an English Benedictine monk who gave up the honors of an abbatial election to devote his life to the conversion of the Germanic tribes. Two characteristics stand out: his Christian orthodoxy and his fidelity to the pope of Rome.

How absolutely necessary this orthodoxy and fidelity were is borne out by the conditions he found on his first missionary journey in 719 at the request of Pope Gregory II. Paganism was a way of life. What Christianity he did find had either lapsed into paganism or was mixed with error. The clergy were mainly responsible for these latter conditions since they were in many instances uneducated, lax and questionably obedient to their bishops. In particular instances their very ordination was questionable.

These are the conditions that Boniface was to report in 722 on his first return visit to Rome. The Holy Father instructed him to reform the German Church. The pope sent letters of recommendation to religious and civil leaders. Boniface later admitted that his work would have been unsuccessful, from a human viewpoint, without a letter of safe conduct from Charles Martel, the powerful Frankish ruler, grandfather of Charlemagne. Boniface was finally made a regional bishop and authorized to organize the whole German Church. He was eminently successful.

In the Frankish kingdom, he met great problems because of lay interference in bishops' elections, the worldliness of the clergy and lack of papal control.

During a final mission to the Frisians, he and 53 companions were massacred while he was preparing converts for Confirmation.

In order to restore the Germanic Church to its fidelity to Rome and to convert the pagans, he had been guided by two principles. The first was to restore the obedience of the clergy to their bishops in union with the pope of Rome. The second was the establishment of many houses of prayer which took the form of Benedictine monasteries. A great number of Anglo-Saxon monks and nuns followed him to the continent. He introduced Benedictine nuns to the active apostolate of education.

COMMENT: Boniface bears out the Christian rule: to follow Christ is to follow the way of the cross. For Boniface, it was not only physical suffering or death, but the painful, thankless, bewildering task of Church reform. Missionary glory is often thought of in terms of bringing new persons to Christ. It seems—but is not—less glorious to heal the household of the faith.

STORY: Boniface literally struck a blow for Christianity in his attempt to destroy pagan superstitions. On a day previously announced, in the presence of a tense crowd, he attacked with an axe Donar's sacred oak on Mount Gudenburg. The huge tree crashed, splitting into four parts. The people waited for the gods to strike Boniface dead—then realized their gods were powerless, nonexistent. He used planks from the tree to build a chapel.

Norbert
Bishop (1080?-1134)

Friends sometimes jokingly mangle the name of the Premonstratensians into "Monstrous Pretensions," just as the Franciscan O.F.M. is said to mean "Out For Money." The name actually derives from Premontre, the region of France where Norbert established the order in the 12th century.

Recalling the nickname, Norbert's founding of the order was in truth a monstrous task: combating rampant heresies particularly regarding the Blessed Sacrament, revitalizing many of the faithful who had grown indifferent and dissolute and effecting peace and reconciliation among enemies.

Norbert entertained no pretensions about his own ability to accomplish this multiple task. Even with the aid of a goodly number of men who joined his order, he realized that nothing could be effectively done without God's power. Finding this help especially in devotion to the Blessed Sacrament, he and his Norbertines praised God for success in converting heretics, reconciling numerous enemies and rebuilding faith in indifferent believers.

Reluctantly, Norbert became Archbishop of Magdeburg in southern Germany, a territory half pagan and half Christian. In this position he zealously and courageously continued his work for the Church until his death on June 6, 1134.

COMMENT: A different world cannot be built by indifferent people. The same is true in regard to the Church. Sad to say, the so-called updating of the Church has not engendered the different Church which was so devoutly and hopefully envisioned by Vatican Council II. A principal reason for this failure was—and is—the indifference of vast numbers of nominal faithful, their indifference to ecclesiastical authority and essential doctrines of the faith. Unswerving loyalty to the Church and fervent devotion to the Eucharist, as practiced by Norbert, will continue immeasurably towards maintaining the people of God in accord with the heart of Christ.

QUOTE: On the occasion of his ordination to the priesthood, Norbert said, "O Priest! You are not yourself because you are God. You are not of yourself because you are the servant and minister of Christ. You are not your own because you are the spouse of the Church. You are not yourself because you are the mediator between God and man. You are not from yourself because you are nothing. What then are you? Nothing and everything. O Priest! Take care lest what was said to Christ on the cross be said to you: 'He saved others, himself he cannot save!' "

JUNE 9   OPTIONAL

Ephrem

Deacon and Doctor (306?-373)

Poet, teacher, orator and defender of the faith, Ephrem is the only Syrian ever to be acclaimed a doctor of the Church. He took upon himself the special task of opposing the many false doctrines rampant at his time, always remaining a true and forceful defender of the Catholic Church.

Born in Nisibis, Mesopotamia, he was baptized as a young man and became famous as a teacher in his native city. When the

Christian emperor had to cede Nisibis to the Persians, Ephrem, along with many Christians, fled as a refugee to Edessa. He is credited with attracting great glory to the biblical school there. He was ordained a deacon but declined becoming a priest (and was said to have avoided episcopal consecration by feigning madness!).

He had a prolific pen and his writings best illumine his holiness. Although he was not a man of great scholarship, his works reflect deep insight and knowledge of the Scriptures. In writing about the mysteries of humanity's redemption, Ephrem reveals a realistic and humanly sympathetic spirit and a great devotion to the humanity of Jesus and Mary. It is said that his poetic account of the Last Judgment inspired Dante.

It is surprising to read that he wrote hymns against the heretics of his day. He would take the popular songs of the heretical groups and, using their melodies, compose beautiful hymns embodying orthodox doctrine. Ephrem became one of the first to introduce song into the Church's public worship as a means of instruction for the faithful. His many hymns have earned him the title "Harp of the Holy Spirit."

He preferred a simple, austere life, living in a small cave overlooking the city of Edessa. It was here he died around 373.

COMMENT: Many Catholics still find singing in church a problem, probably because of the rather individualistic piety that they inherited. Yet singing has been a tradition of both the Old and the New Testament. It is an excellent way of expressing and creating a community spirit of unity as well as joy. Ephrem's hymns, an ancient historian testifies, "lent luster to the Christian assemblies." We need some modern Ephrems—and cooperating singers—to do the same for our Christian assemblies today.

QUOTE: "Lay me not with sweet spices,
        For this honor avails me not,
        Nor yet use incense and perfumes,

For the honor befits me not.
Burn yet the incense in the holy place;
As for me, escort me only with your prayers,
Give ye your incense to God,
And over me send up hymns.
Instead of perfumes and spices,
Be mindful of me in your intercessions."

(From The Testament of St. Ephrem)

Barnabas

Apostle

Barnabas, a Jew of Cyprus, comes as close as anyone outside the Twelve to being a full-fledged apostle. He was closely associated with St. Paul (he introduced Paul to Peter and the other apostles) and served as a kind of mediator between the former persecutor and the still suspicious Jewish Christians.

When a Christian community developed at Antioch, Barnabas was sent as the official representative of the Church of Jerusalem to incorporate them into the fold. He and Paul instructed in Antioch for a year, after which they took relief contributions to Jerusalem.

Later, Paul and Barnabas, now clearly seen as charismatic leaders, were sent by Antioch officials to preach to the Gentiles. Enormous success crowned their efforts. After a miracle at Lystra, the people wanted to offer sacrifice to them as gods—Barnabas being Zeus, and Paul, Hermes—but the two said, "We are of the same nature as you, human beings. We proclaim to you good news that you should turn from these idols to the living God" (see Acts 14:8-18).

But all was not peaceful. They were expelled from one town, they had to go to Jerusalem to clear up the ever-recurring controversy about circumcision and even the best of friends can have differences. When Paul wanted to revisit the places they had evangelized, Barnabas wanted to take along John Mark, his cousin, author of the Gospel, but Paul insisted that, since Mark had deserted them once, he was not fit to take along now. The disagreement that followed was so sharp that Barnabas and Paul separated, Barnabas taking Mark to Cyprus, Paul taking Silas to Syria. Later, they were reconciled—Paul, Barnabas and Mark.

When Paul stood up to Peter for not eating with Gentiles for fear of his Jewish friends, we learn that "even Barnabas was carried away by their hypocrisy" (see Galatians 2:1-13).

COMMENT: Barnabas is spoken of simply as one who dedicated his life to the Lord. He was a man "filled with the Holy Spirit and faith. *Thereby* large numbers were added to the Lord." Even when he and Paul were expelled from Antioch in Pisidia, they were "filled with joy and the Holy Spirit."

STORY: Barnabas is mentioned by name as one of the generous members of the idyllic and extremely poor Church in Jerusalem: "The community of believers was of one heart and mind, and no one claimed that any of his possessions was his own, but they had everything in common....There was no needy person among them, for those who owned property or houses would sell them, bring the proceeds of the sale, and put them at the feet of the apostles, and they were distributed to each according to need.

"Thus Joseph, also named by the apostles Barnabas (which is translated 'son of encouragement'), a Levite, a Cypriot by birth, sold a piece of property that he owned, then brought the money and put it at the feet of the apostles" (Acts 4:32, 34-37).

Anthony of Padua

Priest and Doctor (1195-1231)

The Gospel call to leave everything and follow Christ was the rule of Anthony's life. Over and over again God called him to something new in his plan. Every time Anthony responded with renewed zeal and self-sacrificing to serve his Lord Jesus more completely.

His journey as the servant of God began as a very young man when he decided to join the Augustinians, giving up a future of wealth and power to be a servant of God. Later, when the bodies of the first Franciscan martyrs went through the town where he was stationed, he was again filled with an intense longing to be one of those closest to Jesus himself: those who die for the Good News.

So Anthony entered the Franciscan Order and set out to preach to the Moors. But an illness prevented him from achieving his goal. He returned to Italy and was stationed in a small hermitage where he spent most of his time praying, reading the Scriptures and doing menial tasks.

The call of God came again at an ordination where no one was prepared to speak. The humble and obedient Anthony hesitantly accepted the task. The years of searching for Jesus in prayer, of reading sacred Scripture and of serving him in poverty, chastity and obedience had prepared Anthony to allow the Spirit to use his talents. Anthony's sermon was astounding to those who expected an unprepared speech and knew not the Spirit's power to give people words.

Recognized as a great man of prayer and a great Scripture and theology scholar, Anthony became the first friar to teach theology to the other friars. Again he was called from that post to preach to the heretics, to use his profound knowledge of Scripture

132

and theology to convert and reassure those who had been misled.

COMMENT: Anthony should be the patron of those who find their lives completely uprooted and set in a new and unexpected direction. Like all saints, he is a perfect example of turning one's life completely over to Christ. God did with Anthony as God pleased—and what God pleased was a life of spiritual power and brilliance that still attracts admiration today. He whom popular devotion has nominated as finder of lost objects found himself by losing himself totally to the providence of God.

QUOTE: In his *Sermons*, Anthony says: "The saints are like the stars. In his providence Christ conceals them in a hidden place that they may not shine before others when they might wish to do so. Yet they are always ready to exchange the quiet of contemplation for the works of mercy as soon as they perceive in their heart the invitation of Christ."

Romuald

Abbot (950?-1027)

After a wasted youth, Romuald saw his father kill a relative in a duel over property. In horror he fled to a monastery near Ravenna in Italy. After three years he was found to be uncomfortably holy by some of the monks, and was eased out.

He spent the next 30 years going about Italy founding monasteries and hermitages. He longed to give his life to Christ in martyrdom, and got the pope's permission to preach the gospel in Hungary. But he was struck with illness as soon as he arrived, and the illness recurred as often as he tried to proceed.

During another period of his life, he suffered great spiritual dryness. One day as he was praying Psalm 31 ("I will give you understanding and I will instruct you"), he was given an extraordinary light and spirit which never left him.

At the next monastery where he stayed, he was accused of a scandalous crime by a young nobleman he had rebuked for a dissolute life. Amazingly, his fellow monks believed the accusation. He was given a severe penance, forbidden to offer Mass and excommunicated, an unjust sentence he endured in silence for six months.

The most famous of the monasteries he founded was that of the Camaldoli (Campus Maldoli, name of the owner) in Tuscany. Here he founded the order of the Camaldolese Benedictines, uniting a monastic and hermit life.

His father later became a monk, wavered and was kept faithful by the encouragement of his son.

COMMENT: Christ is a gentle leader, but he calls us to total holiness. Now and then men and women are raised up to challenge us by the absoluteness of their dedication, the vigor of their spirit, the depth of their conversion. The fact that we cannot duplicate their lives does not change the call to us to be totally open to God in our own particular circumstances.

STORY: A Polish duke had a son in the monastery where Romuald was living. The son, on behalf of his father, presented Romuald with a fine horse. Romuald exchanged it for a donkey, saying that he felt closer to Jesus Christ on such a mount.

Aloysius Gonzaga
Religious (1568-1591)

The Lord can make saints anywhere, even amid the brutality and license of Renaissance life. Florence was the "mother of piety" for Aloysius Gonzaga despite his exposure to a "society of fraud, dagger, poison and lust." As a son of a princely family, he grew up in royal courts and army camps. His father wanted Aloysius to be a military hero.

At age seven he experienced a profound spiritual quickening. His prayers included the Office of Mary, the psalms and other devotions. At age nine he came from his hometown of Castiglione to Florence to be educated; by age 11 he was teaching catechism to poor children, fasting three days a week and practicing great austerities. When he was 13 years old he traveled with his parents and the Empress of Austria to Spain and acted as a page in the court of Philip II. The more Aloysius saw of court life, the more he was turned off, seeking relief in learning about the lives of saints.

A book about the experience of Jesuit missionaries in India suggested to him the idea of entering the Society of Jesus, and in Spain his decision became final. Now began a four-year contest with his father. Eminent churchmen and laypeople were pressed into service to persuade him to remain in his "normal" vocation. Finally he prevailed, was allowed to renounce his right to succession and was received into the Jesuit novitiate.

Like other seminarians, Aloysius was faced with a new kind of penance—that of accepting different ideas about the exact nature of penance. He was obliged to eat more, to take recreation with the other students. He was forbidden to pray except at stated times. He spent four years in the study of philosophy and had St. Robert Bellarmine as his spiritual adviser.

In 1591, a plague struck Rome. The Jesuits opened a hospital of their own. The general himself and many other Jesuits rendered personal service. Because he nursed patients, washing them and making their beds, Aloysius caught the disease himself. A fever persisted after his recovery and he was so weak he could scarcely rise from bed. Yet, he maintained his great discipline of prayer, knowing that he would die within the octave of Corpus Christi, three months later. He was 23.

COMMENT: As a saint who fasted, scourged himself, sought solitude and prayer and did not look on the faces of women, Aloysius seems an unlikely patron of youth in a society where asceticism is confined to training camps of football teams and boxers, and sexual permissiveness has little left to permit. Can an overweight and air-conditioned society deprive itself of *anything*? It will when it discovers a reason, as Aloysius did. The motivation for letting God purify us is the experience of God loving us, in prayer.

QUOTE: "When we stand praying, beloved brethren, we ought to be watchful and earnest with our whole heart, intent on our prayers. Let all carnal and worldly thoughts pass away, nor let the soul at that time think on anything except the object of its prayer" (St. Cyprian, *On the Lord's Prayer*, 31).

Paulinus of Nola

Bishop (354?-431)

Anyone who is praised in the letters of six or seven saints undoubtedly must be of extraordinary character. Such a person was Paulinus of Nola, correspondent and friend of Augustine,

Jerome, Melania, Martin, Gregory and Ambrose.

Born near Bordeaux, he was the son of the Roman prefect of Gaul, who had extensive property in both Gaul and Italy. Paulinus became a distinguished lawyer, holding several public offices in the Empire. With his Spanish wife Therasia, he retired at an early age to a life of cultured leisure.

The two were baptized by the saintly bishop of Bordeaux and moved to Therasia's estate in Spain. After many childless years, they had a son who died a week after birth. This occasioned their beginning a life of great austerity and charity, giving away most of their Spanish property. Possibly as a result of this great example, Paulinus was rather unexpectedly ordained priest at Christmas by the bishop of Barcelona.

He and his wife then moved to Nola, near Naples. He had a great love for St. Felix of Nola, and spent much effort in promoting devotion to the saint. He gave away most of his remaining property (to the consternation of his relatives) and continued his work for the poor. Supporting a host of debtors, tramps and other needy people, he lived a monastic life in another part of his home. By popular demand he was made bishop of Nola and guided that diocese for 21 years.

His last years were saddened by the invasion of the Huns. Among his few writings is the earliest extant Christian wedding song.

COMMENT: Many of us are tempted to "retire" early in life, after an initial burst of energy. Devotion to Christ and to his work is waiting to be done all around us. Paulinus's life had scarcely begun when he thought it was over, as he took his ease on that estate in Spain. "Man proposes, but God disposes."

STORY: An eyewitness described Paulinus's last days: A priest came to him three days before his death, saying that 40 pieces of silver were needed for the poor. He smiled and said that someone would pay the debt of the poor. Almost immediately a messenger came with a gift of 50 silver pieces. On his last day, when the lamps were being lighted for Vespers, after having said nothing for a long time, he stretched out his hands and said, "I have prepared a lamp for my Christ."

John Fisher

Bishop and Martyr (1469-1535)

John Fisher is usually associated with Erasmus, Thomas More and other Renaissance humanists. His life, therefore, did not have the external simplicity found in the lives of some saints. Rather, he was a man of learning, associated with the intellectuals and political men of his day. He was interested in the contemporary culture and eventually became chancellor at Cambridge. He had been made a bishop at 35, and one of his specific interests was in raising the standard of preaching in England. Fisher himself was an accomplished preacher and writer. His sermons on the penitential psalms were reprinted seven times before his death. With the coming of Lutheranism, he was drawn into controversy. His eight books against heresy gave him a leading position among European theologians.

In 1527 he was asked to study the problem of Henry VIII's marriage. He incurred Henry's anger by defending the validity of his marriage with Catherine and later by rejecting Henry's claim to be the supreme head of the Church of England.

In an attempt to be rid of him, Henry first had him accused of not reporting all the "revelations" of the nun of Kent, Elizabeth Barton. He was summoned, in feeble health, to take the oath to the new Act of Succession. He and Thomas More refused because the Act presumed the legality of Henry's divorce and his claim to be head of the English Church. They were sent to the Tower, where Fisher remained 14 months without trial. They were finally sentenced to life imprisonment and loss of goods.

When the two were called to further interrogations, they remained silent. Fisher was tricked, on the supposition he was speaking privately as a priest, and declared again that the king was not supreme head. The king, further angered that the pope had made John Fisher a cardinal, had him brought to trial on the charge of high treason. He was condemned and executed, his body left to lie all day on the scaffold and his head hung on London Bridge. More was executed two weeks later.

COMMENT: Today many questions are raised about Christians' and priests' active involvement in social issues. John Fisher remained faithful to his calling as a bishop. He strongly upheld the teachings of the Church; the very cause of his martyrdom was his loyalty to Rome. He was involved in the cultural enrichment circles as well as in the political struggles of his time. This involvement caused him to question the moral conduct of the leadership of his country. "The Church has the right, indeed the duty, to proclaim justice on the social, national and international level, and to denounce instances of injustice, when the fundamental rights of man and his very salvation demand it" (*Justice in the World*, 1971 Synod of Bishops).

QUOTE: Erasmus said of John Fisher: "He is the one man at this time who is incomparable for uprightness of life, for learning and for greatness of soul."

Thomas More

Martyr (1478-1535)

His belief that no lay ruler has jurisdiction over the Church of Christ cost Thomas More his life.

Beheaded on Tower Hill, London, June 6, 1535, he steadfastly refused to approve Henry VIII's divorce and remarriage and establishment of the Church of England.

Described as "a man for all seasons," More was a literary scholar, eminent lawyer, gentleman, father of four children and chancellor of England. An intensely spiritual man, he would not support the king's divorce from Catherine of Aragon in order to marry Anne Boleyn. Nor would he acknowledge Henry as supreme head of the Church in England, breaking with Rome and denying the pope as head.

He was committed to the Tower of London to await trial for treason: not swearing to the Act of Succession and the Oath of Supremacy. Upon conviction, More declared he had all the councils of Christendom and not just the council of one realm to support him in the decision of his conscience.

COMMENT: Four hundred years later, in 1935, Thomas More was canonized a saint of God. Few saints are more relevant to the 20th century. The supreme diplomat and counselor, he did not compromise his own moral values in order to please the king, knowing that true allegiance to authority is not blind acceptance of everything that authority wants. Henry himself realized this and tried desperately to win his chancellor to his side because he knew More was a man whose approval counted, a man whose personal integrity no one questioned. But when Thomas resigned as chancellor, unable to approve the two matters that meant most to Henry, Henry had to get rid of Thomas.

STORY: When the executioner offered to blindfold him, More said that he would do this himself. But after he had stretched his head over the low block—it was merely a log of wood—he made a signal to the man to wait a moment. Then he made his last joke: His beard was lying on the block and he would like to remove it. At least *that* had committed no treason. The heavy axe went slowly up, hung a moment in the air and fell.

Birth of John the Baptist

Jesus called John the greatest of all those who had preceded him: "I tell you, among those born of women, no one is greater than John...." But John would have agreed completely with what Jesus added: "[Y]et the least in the kingdom of God is greater than he" (Luke 7:28).

John spent his time in the desert, an ascetic. He began to announce the coming of the Kingdom, and to call everyone to a fundamental reformation of life.

His purpose was to prepare the way for Jesus. His baptism, he said, was for repentance. But One would come who would baptize with the Holy Spirit and fire. John is not worthy even to carry his sandals. His attitude toward Jesus was: "He must increase; I must decrease" (John 3:30).

John was humbled to find among the crowd of sinners who came to be baptized the one whom he already knew to be the Messiah. "I need to be baptized by you" (Matthew 3:14b). But Jesus insisted, "Allow it now, for thus it is fitting for us to fulfill all righteousness" (Matthew 3:15b). Jesus, true and humble human as well as eternal God, was eager to do what was required of any good Jew. John thus publicly entered the community of those awaiting the Messiah. But making himself part of that community, he made it truly messianic.

The greatness of John, his pivotal place in the history of salvation, is seen in the great emphasis Luke gives to the annunciation of his birth and the event itself—both made prominently parallel to the same occurrences in the life of Jesus. John attracted countless people ("all Judea") to the banks of the Jordan, and it occurred to some people that he might be the Messiah. But he constantly deferred to Jesus, even to sending away some of his followers to become the first disciples of Jesus.

Perhaps John's idea of the coming of the Kingdom was not being perfectly fulfilled in the public ministry of Jesus. For whatever reason, he sent his disciples (when he was in prison) to ask Jesus if he was the Messiah. Jesus' answer showed that the Messiah was to be a figure like that of the Suffering Servant in Isaiah. John himself would share in the pattern of messianic suffering, losing his life to the revenge of Herodias.

COMMENT: John challenges us Christians to the fundamental attitude of Christianity—total dependence on the Father, in Christ. Except for the Mother of God, no one had a higher function in the unfolding of salvation. Yet the least in the Kingdom, Jesus said, is greater than he, for the pure gift that the Father gives. The attractiveness as well as the austerity of John, his fierce courage in denouncing evil—all stem from his fundamental and total placing of his life within the will of God.

QUOTE: "And this is not something which was only true once, long ago in the past. It is always true, because the repentance which he preached always remains the way into the kingdom which he announced. He is not a figure that we can forget now that Jesus, the true light, has appeared. John is always relevant because he calls for a preparation which all men need to make. Hence every year there are four weeks in the life of the Church in

which it listens to the voice of the Baptist. These are the weeks of
Advent" (*A New Catechism*).

Cyril of Alexandria

Bishop and Doctor (376?-444)

Saints are not born with halos around their heads. Cyril,
recognized as a great teacher of the Church, began his career as
archbishop of Alexandria (Egypt) with impulsive, often violent,
actions. He pillaged and closed the churches of the Novatian
heretics, participated in the deposing of St. John Chrysostom and
confiscated Jewish property, expelling the Jews from Alexandria
in retaliation for their attacks on Christians.

Cyril's importance for theology and Church history lies in
his championing the cause of orthodoxy against the heresy of
Nestorius.

The controversy centered around the two natures in Christ.
Nestorius would not agree to the word "God-bearer" for Mary. He
preferred "Christ-bearer," saying there are two distinct persons in
Christ (divine and human) joined only by a moral union. He said
Mary was not the mother of God but only of the man Christ,
whose humanity was only a temple of God. Nestorianism implied
that the humanity of Christ was a mere disguise.

Cyril, presiding as the pope's representative at the Council
of Ephesus (431), condemned Nestorianism and proclaimed Mary
truly the "God-bearer" (the mother of the one Person who is truly
God and truly human). In the confusion that followed, Cyril was
deposed and imprisoned for three months, after which he was
welcomed back to Alexandria as a second Athanasius (the
champion against Arianism).

Besides needing to soften some of his opposition to those who had sided with Nestorius, Cyril had difficulties with some of his own allies, who thought he had gone too far, sacrificing not only language but orthodoxy. Until his death, his policy of moderation kept his extreme partisans under control. On his deathbed, despite pressure, he refused to condemn the teacher of Nestorius.

COMMENT: Lives of the saints are valuable not only for the virtue they reveal but also for the less admirable qualities that also appear. Holiness is a gift of God to us as human beings. Life is a process. We respond to God's gift, but sometimes with a lot of zigzagging. If Cyril had been more patient and diplomatic, the Nestorian Church might not have risen and maintained power so long. But even saints must grow out of immaturity, narrowness and selfishness. It is because they—and we—do grow, that we are truly saints, persons who live the life of God.

QUOTE: Cyril's theme: "Only if it is one and the same Christ who is consubstantial with the Father and with men can he save us, for the meeting ground between God and man is the flesh of Christ. Only if this is God's own flesh can man come into contact with Christ's divinity through his humanity. Because of our kinship with the Word made flesh we are sons of God. The Eucharist consummates our kinship with the word, our communion with the Father, our sharing in the divine nature—there is very real contact between our body and that of the Word" (*New Catholic Encyclopedia*).

Irenaeus

Bishop and Martyr (130?-220)

The Church is fortunate that Irenaeus was involved in much of its controversy in the second century. He was a student, well trained, no doubt, with great patience in investigating, tremendously protective of apostolic teaching, but prompted more by a desire to win over his opponents than to prove them in error.

As bishop of Lyons he was especially concerned with the Gnostics, whose teaching was attracting and confusing many of the Gallic Christians. After thoroughly investigating the various Gnostic sects and their "secret," he set about showing to what logical conclusions their tenets led. These he contrasted with the teaching of the apostles and the text of Holy Scripture, giving us, in five books, a system of theology of great importance to subsequent times. Moreover, his work, widely used and translated into Latin and Armenian, gradually ended the influence of the Gnostics.

The circumstances and manner of his death, like those of his birth and early life in Asia Minor, are not at all clear.

COMMENT: A deep and genuine concern for other people will remind us that the discovery of truth is not to be a victory for some and a defeat for others. Unless all can claim a share in that victory, truth itself will continue to be rejected by the losers, because it will be regarded as inseparable from the yoke of defeat. And so, confrontation, controversy and the like might yield to a genuine united search for God's truth and how it can best be served.

STORY: A group of Christians in Asia Minor had been put under the ban of excommunication by Pope Victor III because of their refusal to accept the date of the Western Church for the celebration of Easter. Irenaeus, the "lover of peace" as his name indicates, interceded with the pope to lift the ban, indicating that this was not an essential matter and that these people were merely following an old tradition, one that men such as St. Polycarp and Pope Anicetus had not seen as divisive. The pope responded favorably and the rift was healed. Some one hundred years later, the Western practice was voluntarily adopted.

Peter and Paul

Apostles

Peter (d. 64?). St. Mark ends the first half of his Gospel with a triumphant climax. He has recorded doubt, misunderstanding and the opposition of many to Jesus. Now Peter makes his great confession of faith: "You are the Messiah" (Mark 8:29b).

It was one of the many glorious moments in Peter's life, beginning with the day he was called from his nets along the Sea of Galilee to become a fisher of men for Jesus.

The New Testament clearly shows Peter as the leader of the apostles, chosen by Jesus to have a special relationship with him. With James and John he was privileged to witness the Transfiguration, the raising of a dead child to life and the agony in Gethsemani. His mother-in-law was cured by Jesus. He was sent with John to prepare for the last Passover before Jesus' death. His name is first on every list of apostles.

And to Peter only did Jesus say, "Blessed are you, Simon son of Jonah. For flesh and blood has not revealed this to you, but my heavenly Father. And so I say to you, you are Peter, and upon this rock I will build my church, and the gates of the netherworld shall not prevail against it. I will give you the keys to the kingdom of heaven. Whatever you bind on earth shall be bound in heaven; and whatever you loose on earth shall be loosed in heaven" (Matthew 16:17b-19).

But the Gospels prove their own veracity by the unflattering details they include about Peter. He clearly had no PR man. It is a great comfort for ordinary mortals to know that Peter also has his human weakness, even in the presence of Jesus.

He generously gave up all things, yet he can ask in childish self-regard, "What are we going to get for all this?" (see Matthew 19:27). He receives the full force of Christ's anger when he objects to the idea of a suffering Messiah: "Get behind me, Satan! You are an obstacle to me. You are thinking not as God does, but as human beings do" (Matthew 16:23b).

Peter is willing to accept Jesus' doctrine of forgiveness, but suggests a limit of seven times. He walks on the water in faith, but sinks in doubt. He refuses to let Jesus wash his feet, then wants his whole body cleansed. He swears at the Last Supper that he will never deny Jesus, and then swears to a servant maid that he has never known the man. He loyally resists the first attempt to arrest Jesus by cutting off Malchus's ear, but in the end he runs away with the others. In the depth of his sorrow, Jesus looks on him and forgives him, and he goes out and sheds bitter tears.

COMMENT: We would probably go to confession to Peter sooner than to any of the other apostles. He is perhaps a more striking example of the simple fact of holiness. Jesus says to us as he said, in effect, to Peter: "It is not you who have chosen me, but I who have chosen you. Peter, it is not human wisdom that makes it possible for you to believe, but my Father's revelation. I, not you, build my Church."

QUOTE: "So humble yourselves under the mighty hand of God, that he may exalt you in due time. Cast all your worries upon him because he cares for you.

"Be sober and vigilant. Your opponent the devil is prowling around like a roaring lion looking for [someone] to devour. Resist him, steadfast in faith, knowing that your fellow believers thoughout the world undergo the same sufferings. The God of all grace who called you to his eternal glory through Christ [Jesus] will himself restore, confirm, strengthen, and establish you after you have suffered a little" (1 Peter 5:6-10).

Paul (d. 64?). If Billy Graham suddenly began preaching that the United States should adopt Marxism and not rely on the Constitution, the angry reaction would help us understand Paul's life when he started preaching that Christ alone can save us. He had been the most Pharisaic of Pharisees, the most legalistic of Mosaic lawyers. Now he suddenly appears to other Jews as a heretical welcomer of Gentiles, a traitor and apostate.

Paul's central conviction was simple and absolute: Only God can save humanity. No human effort—even the most scrupulous observance of law—can create a human good which we can bring to God as reparation for sin and payment for grace. To be saved from itself, from sin, from the devil and from death, humanity must open itself completely to the saving power of Jesus.

Paul never lost his love for his Jewish family, though he carried on a lifelong debate with them about the uselessness of the Law without Christ. He reminded the Gentiles that they were grafted on the parent stock of the Jews, who were still God's chosen people, the children of the promise.

COMMENT: Paul's experience of the risen Jesus on the road to Damascus was the driving force that made him one of the most zealous, dynamic and courageous ambassadors of Christ the Church has ever had. But persecution, humiliation and weakness became his day-by-day carrying of the cross, material for further transformation. The dying Christ was in him; the living Christ was his life.

QUOTE: Paul talks about his sufferings: "Five times at the hands of the Jews I received forty lashes minus one. Three times I was beaten with rods, once I was stoned, three times I was shipwrecked, I passed a night and a day on the deep; on frequent journeys, in dangers from rivers, dangers from robbers, dangers from my own race, dangers from Gentiles, dangers in the city, dangers in the wilderness, dangers at sea, dangers among false brothers; in toil and hardship, through many sleepless nights, through hunger and thirst, through frequent fastings, through cold and exposure....I am content with weaknesses, insults, hardships, persecutions, and constraints, for the sake of Christ; for when I am weak, then I am strong" (2 Corinthians 11:24-27; 12:10).

First Martyrs of the Church of Rome

(A.D. 64)

There were Christians in Rome within a dozen or so years after the death of Jesus, though they were not the converts of the "apostle of the Gentiles" (Romans 15:20). Paul had not yet visited them at the time he wrote his great letter in A.D. 57-58.

There was a large Jewish population in Rome. Probably as a result of controversy between Jews and Jewish Christians, the Emperor Claudius expelled all Jews from Rome in A.D. 49-50. Suetonius the historian says that the expulsion was due to disturbances in the city "caused by the certain *Chrestus*" [Christ]. Perhaps many came back after Claudius's death in A.D. 54. Paul's letter seems addressed to a largely Gentile Church.

In July of A.D. 64 more than half of Rome was destroyed by fire. Rumor blamed the tragedy on Nero, who wanted to enlarge his palace. He shifted the blame by accusing the Christians. According to the historian Tacitus a "great multitude" of Christians were put to death because of their "hatred of the human race." Peter and Paul were probably among the victims.

Threatened by an army revolt and condemned to death by the senate, Nero committed suicide in A.D. 68 at the age of 31.

COMMENT: Wherever the Good News of Jesus was preached, it met the same opposition as Jesus did, and many of those who began to follow him shared his suffering and death. But no human force could stop the power of the Spirit unleashed upon the world. The blood of martyrs has always been, and will always be, the seed of Christians.

QUOTE: From Pope Clement I, successor of St. Peter: "It was through envy and jealousy that the greatest and most upright pillars of the Church were persecuted and struggled unto death....First of all, Peter, who because of unreasonable jealousy suffered not merely once or twice but many times, and, having thus given his witness, went to the place of glory that he deserved. It was through jealousy and conflict that Paul showed the way to the prize for perseverance. He was put in chains seven times, sent into exile, and stoned; a herald both in the east and the west, he achieved a noble fame by his faith....

"Around these men with their holy lives there are gathered a great throng of the elect, who, though victims of jealousy, gave us the finest example of endurance in the midst of many indignities and tortures. Through jealousy women were tormented, like Dirce or the daughters of Danaus, suffering terrible and unholy acts of violence. But they courageously finished the course of faith and despite their bodily weakness won a noble prize."

Junipero Serra
Priest (1713-1784)

In 1776, when the American revolution was beginning in the east, another part of the future United States was being born in California. That year a gray-robed Franciscan founded Mission San Juan Capistrano, now famous for its annually returning swallows. It was the seventh of nine missions established under the direction of the indomitable Spaniard.

Born in Spain's island of Majorca, Serra entered the Franciscan Order at 17 and was given the name of St. Francis' childlike companion, Brother Juniper. His years until 35 were spent in the classroom as student and doctor of theology. He became famous as a preacher. Suddenly he gave it all up and followed the yearning he had conceived when hearing of the South American missionary work of St. Francis Solanus. Junipero's desire was to convert the American Indians.

Arriving by ship at Vera Cruz, Mexico, he and a companion walked the 250 miles to Mexico City. On the way his left leg became infected by an insect bite and would remain a cross—even life-threatening—the rest of his life. For 18 years his work was in Mexico's Lower California, the Baja Peninsula. He became president of the missions there.

Enter politics: the threat of a Russian invasion south from Alaska. Charles III of Spain ordered an expedition to beat Russia to the territory. So the last two *conquistadors*—one military, one spiritual—began their quest. Jose de Galvez persuaded Junipero to set out with him for present-day Monterey. The first mission founded after the 900-mile journey north was San Diego (1769). In the same year a shortage of food almost canceled the expedition. Junipero and another friar vowed to stay with the Indians. They began a novena in preparation for St. Joseph's day,

March 19, the scheduled day of departure. On that day, the relief ship was sighted.

Other missions followed: Monterey/Carmel (1770); San Antonio and San Gabriel (1771); San Luis Obispo (1772); San Francisco and San Juan Capistrano (1776); Santa Clara (1777); San Buenaventura (1782). Twelve more were founded after Serra's death.

Junipero had to make the long trip back to Mexico City to settle great differences with the military commander. He arrived at the point of death. The outcome was substantially Junipero's: the famous "Regulation" protecting the Indians and the missions. It was the basis for the first significant legislation in California, a "Bill of Rights" for Native Americans.

Because the Native Americans were living an almost nonhuman life, the friars were made their legal guardians. They were kept at the mission after Baptism lest they be corrupted in their former haunts—a move that has brought cries of "injustice" from some moderns.

Junipero's missionary life was a long battle with cold and hunger, with unsympathetic military commanders and even with danger of death from his beloved Indians. Through it all his unquenchable zeal was fed by prayer each night, often from midnight till dawn. He baptized over 6,000 and confirmed 5,000. His travels would have circumnavigated the globe. He brought the Native Americans not only the gift of faith but also a decent standard of living. He won their love, as witnessed especially at his death. He is buried at Carmel, Monterey.

COMMENT: The word that best describes Junipero is *zeal*. It was a spirit that came from his deep prayer and dauntless will. "Always forward, never back" was his motto. His work bore fruit for 50 years after his death as the rest of the missions were founded in a kind of Christian communal living by the Indians. Then both Mexican and American greed caused the secularization of the missions. The Indians went back to what they had been, God again writing straight with crooked lines.

QUOTE: Spoken at the unveiling of his statue in the Capitol's Statuary Hall: "This man, whose memory is indissolubly one with the epic of California, was great in his humility. He triumphed by his courage, when everything would have appeared to discourage him and beat him down. He is one who is worthy of first place among the immortal heroes who created our nation. So his memory will never die, and his name will be blessed from generation to generation."

JULY 3   FEAST

Thomas

Apostle

Poor Thomas! He made one remark and has been branded as "Doubting Thomas" for 20 centuries. But if he doubted, he also believed. He made what is certainly the most explicit statement of faith in the New Testament: "My Lord and My God!" (see John 20:24-28) and, in so expressing his faith, gave Christians a prayer that will be said till the end of time. He also occasioned a compliment from Jesus to us 20th-century Christians: "Have you come to believe because you have seen me? Blessed are those who have not seen and have believed" (John 20:29).

Thomas should be equally well known for his courage. Perhaps what he said was impetuous—since he ran, like the rest, at the showdown—but he can scarcely have been insincere when he expressed his willingness to die with Jesus. The occasion was when Jesus proposed to go to Bethany after Lazarus had died. Since Bethany was near Jerusalem, this meant walking into the very midst of his enemies and to almost certain death. Realizing this, Thomas said to the other apostles, "Let us also go to die with him" (John 11:16b).

COMMENT: Thomas shares the lot of Peter the impetuous, James and John, the "sons of thunder," Philip and his foolish request to see the Father—indeed all the apostles in their weakness and lack of understanding. We must not exaggerate these facts, however, for Christ did not pick worthless men. But their human weakness again points up the fact that holiness is a gift of God, not a human creation; it is given to ordinary men and women with weaknesses; it is God who gradually transforms the weaknesses into the image of Christ, the courageous, trusting and loving one.

QUOTE: "...[P]rompted by the Holy Spirit, the Church must walk the same road which Christ walked: a road of poverty and obedience, of service and self-sacrifice to the death....For thus did all the apostles walk in hope. On behalf of Christ's Body, which is the Church, they supplied what was wanting in the sufferings of Christ by their own trials and sufferings (cf. Colossians 1:24)" (*Decree on the Church's Missionary Activity*, 5).

Elizabeth of Portugal
(1271-1336)

Elizabeth is usually depicted in royal garb with a dove or an olive branch. At her birth in 1271, her father, Pedro III, future king of Aragon, was reconciled with his father James, the reigning monarch. This proved to be a portent of things to come. Under the healthful influences with which her early years were surrounded, she quickly learned self-discipline and acquired a taste for spirituality. Thus fortunately prepared, she was able to meet the challenge when, at the age of 12, she was given in marriage to Denis, king of Portugal. She was able to establish for herself a pattern of life conducive to growth in God's love, not merely through her exercises of piety, including daily Mass, but also through her exercise of charity, by which she was able to befriend and help pilgrims, strangers, the sick, the poor—in a word, all those whose need came to her notice. At the same time she remained devoted to her husband, whose infidelity to her was a scandal to the kingdom.

He too was the object of many of her peace endeavors. She long sought peace for him with God, and was finally rewarded when he gave up his life of sin. She repeatedly sought and effected peace between the king and their rebellious son, Alfonso, who thought that he was passed over to favor the king's illegitimate children. She acted as peacemaker in the struggle between Ferdinand, king of Aragon, and his cousin James, who claimed the crown. And finally from Coimbra, where she had retired as a Franciscan tertiary to the monastery of the Poor Clares after the death of her husband, she set out and was able to bring about a lasting peace between her son Alfonso, now king of Portugal, and his son-in-law, the king of Castile.

COMMENT: The work of promoting peace is anything but a calm and quiet endeavor. It takes a clear mind, a steady spirit and a brave soul to intervene between people whose emotions are so aroused that they are ready to destroy one another. This is all the more true of a woman in the early 14th century. But Elizabeth had a deep and sincere love and sympathy for humankind, almost a total lack of concern for herself and an abiding confidence in God. These were the tools of her success.

STORY: Elizabeth was not well enough to undertake her final peacemaking journey, made all the more difficult by the oppressive heat of the season. She would not, however, permit

155

herself to be dissuaded from it. She answered that there was no better way to give of her life and her health than by averting the miseries and destruction of war. By the time she had successfully brought about peace, she was so sick that death was imminent. After her death in 1336, her body was returned to the monastery at Coimbra for burial.

Anthony Zaccaria
Priest (1502-1539)

At the same time that Martin Luther was attacking abuses in the Church, a reformation within the Church was already being attempted. Among the early movers of the Counter-Reformation was Anthony Zaccaria.

His mother became a widow at 18 and devoted herself to the spiritual education of her son. He received a medical doctorate at 22 and, while working among the poor of his native Cremona, was attracted to the religious apostolate. He renounced his rights to any future inheritance, worked as a catechist, and was ordained priest at the age of 26.

Called to Milan in a few years, he laid the foundations of two religious congregations, one for men and one for women. Their aim was the reform of the decadent society of their day, beginning with the clergy and religious.

Greatly inspired by St. Paul (his congregation is named the Barnabites, after the companion of that saint), he preached with great vigor in church and street, conducted popular missions and was not ashamed of doing public penance.

He encouraged such innovations as the collaboration of the laity in the apostolate, frequent Communion, the Forty Hours devotion and the ringing of church bells at 3:00 p.m. on Fridays.

His holiness moved many to reform their lives but, as with all saints, it also moved many to oppose him. Twice his community had to undergo official religious investigation, and twice was exonerated.

While on a mission of peace, he became seriously ill and was brought home for a visit to his mother. He died at Cremona at the age of 36.

COMMENT: The austerity of Anthony's spirituality and the Pauline ardor of his preaching would probably "turn off" many people today, as the atrocious phrase puts it. When even some psychiatrists complain at the lack of a sense of sin, it may be time to tell ourselves that not *all* evil is explained by emotional disorder, subconscious and unconscious drives, parental influence and so on. The old-time "hell and damnation" mission sermons have given way to positive, encouraging, biblical homilies. We do indeed need assurance of forgiveness, relief from existential anxiety and future shock. But we still need prophets to stand up and tell us, "He who says he is without sin is a liar."

QUOTE: "I charge you in the presence of God and of Christ Jesus, who will judge the living and the dead, and by his appearing and his kingly power: proclaim the word; be persistent whether it is convenient or inconvenient; convince, reprimand, encourage through all patience and teaching. For the time will come when people will not tolerate sound doctrine but, following their own desires and insatiable curiosity, will accumulate teachers and will stop listening to the truth and will be diverted to myths" (2 Timothy 4:1-4).

Maria Goretti

Virgin and Martyr (1890-1902)

The largest crowd ever assembled for a canonization—250,000—symbolized the reaction of millions touched by the simple story of Maria Goretti.

She was the daughter of a poor Italian tenant-farmer, had no chance to go to school, never learned to read or write. When she made her First Communion not long before her death at age 12, she was one of the larger and somewhat backward members of the class.

On a hot afternoon in July, Maria was sitting at the top of the stairs of her cottage, mending a shirt. She was not quite 12 years old, but physically mature. A cart stopped outside, and a neighbor, Alessandro, 18 years old, ran up the stairs. He seized her and pulled her into a bedroom. She struggled and tried to call for help, gasping that she would be killed rather than submit. "No, God does not wish it. It is a sin. You would go to hell for it." Alessandro began striking at her blindly with a long dagger.

She was taken to a hospital. Her last hours were marked by the usual simple compassion of the good—concern about where her mother would sleep, forgiveness of her murderer (she had been in fear of him, but did not say anything lest she cause trouble to his family) and her devout welcoming of Viaticum. She died about 24 hours after the attack.

Her murderer was sentenced to 30 years in prison. For a long time he was unrepentant and surly. One night he had a dream or vision of Maria, gathering flowers and offering them to him. His life changed. When he was released after 27 years, his first act was to go to beg the forgiveness of Maria's mother.

Devotion to the young martyr grew, miracles were worked, and in less than a half-century she was canonized. At her beatification in 1947, her mother (then 82), two sisters and a brother appeared with Pope Pius XII on the balcony of St. Peter's. Three years later, at her canonization, a 66-year-old Alessandro Serenelli knelt among the quarter-million people and cried tears of joy.

COMMENT: Maria may have had trouble with catechism, but she had no trouble with faith. God's will was holiness, decency, respect for one's body, absolute obedience, total trust. In a complex world, her faith was simple: It is a privilege to be loved by God, and to love him—at any cost. As the virtue of chastity dies the death of a thousand qualifications, she is a breath of sweet fresh air.

QUOTE: "Even if she had not been a martyr, she would still have been a saint, so holy was her everyday life" (Cardinal Salotti).

Benedict

Abbot (480?-543)

It is unfortunate that no contemporary biography was written of a man who has exercised measureless influence on monasticism in the West. Benedict is well recognized in the later *Dialogues* of St. Gregory, but these are sketches to illustrate miraculous elements of his career.

He was born of a distinguished family in central Italy, studied at Rome and early in life was drawn to the monastic life. At first he became a hermit, leaving a depressing world—pagan armies on the march, the Church torn by schism, people suffering from war, morality at a low ebb.

He soon realized that he could not live a hidden life in a small town any better than in a large city, so he withdrew to a cave high in the mountains for three years. Some monks chose him as their leader for a while, but found his strictness not to their taste. Still, the shift from hermit to community life had begun for him. He had an idea of gathering various families of monks into one "Grand Monastery" to give them the benefit of unity, fraternity, permanent worship in one house. Finally he began to build what was to become one of the most famous monasteries in the world—Monte Cassino, commanding three narrow valleys running toward the mountain.

The rule that gradually developed prescribed a life of liturgical prayer, study, manual labor and living together in community under a common father (abbot). Benedictine asceticism is known for its moderation, and Benedictine charity has always shown concern for the people in the surrounding countryside. In the course of the Middle Ages, all monasticism in the West was gradually brought under the rule of St. Benedict.

Today the Benedictine family is represented by two branches: the Benedictine Federation and the Cistercians.

The feast of Benedict's sister, Scholastica, is celebrated February 10.

COMMENT: The Church has been blessed through Benedictine devotion to the liturgy, not only in its actual celebration with rich and proper ceremony in the great abbeys, but also through the scholarly studies of many of its members. Liturgy is sometimes confused with guitars or choirs, Latin or Bach. We should be grateful to those who both preserve and adapt the genuine tradition of worship in the Church.

QUOTE: "Rightly, then, the liturgy is considered as an exercise of the priestly office of Jesus Christ. In the liturgy the sanctification of man is manifested by signs perceptible to the senses...; in the liturgy full public worship is performed by the Mystical Body of

Jesus Christ, that is, by the Head and his members.

"From this it follows that every liturgical celebration, because it is an action of Christ the priest and of his Body the Church, is a sacred action, surpassing all others" (*Constitution on the Liturgy*, 7).

Henry
(972-1024)

As German king and Roman Emperor, Henry was a practical man of affairs. He was energetic in consolidating his rule. He crushed rebellions and feuds. On all sides he had to deal with drawn-out disputes so as to protect his frontiers. This involved him in a number of battles, especially in the south in Italy; he also helped Pope Benedict VIII quell disturbances in Rome. Always his ultimate purpose was to establish a stable peace in Europe.

According to 11th-century custom, Henry took advantage of his position and filled bishoprics with men loyal to him. In his case, however, he avoided the pitfalls of this practice and actually fostered the reform of ecclesiastical and monastic life.

COMMENT: All in all, this saint was a man of his times. From our standpoint, he may have been too quick to do battle and too ready to use power to accomplish reforms. But, granted such limitations, he shows that holiness is possible in a busy secular life. It is in doing our job that we become saints.

QUOTE: "We deem it opportune to remind our children of their duty to take an active part in public life and to contribute toward the attainment of the common good of the entire human family as well as to that of their own political community. They should endeavor, therefore, in the light of their Christian faith and led by love, to insure that the various institutions—whether economic, social, cultural or political in purpose—should be such as not to create obstacles, but rather to facilitate or render less arduous man's perfecting of himself in both the natural order and the supernatural....Every believer in this world of ours must be a spark of light, a center of love, a vivifying leaven amidst his fellow men. And he will be this all the more perfectly, the more closely he lives in communion with God in the intimacy of his own soul" (*Pacem in Terris*, 146, 164).

Kateri Tekakwitha

Virgin (1656-1680)

The blood of martyrs is the seed of saints. Nine years after the Jesuits Isaac Jogues and John de Brébeuf were tortured to death by Huron and Iroquois Indians, a baby girl was born near the place of their martyrdom, Auriesville, New York. She was to be the first North American native to be canonized. Her mother was a Christian Algonquin, taken captive by the Iroquois and given as wife to the chief of the Mohawk clan, the boldest and fiercest of the Five Nations. When she was only four, she lost her parents and little brother in a smallpox epidemic that left her disfigured and half blind. She was adopted by an uncle, who succeeded her father as chief. He hated the coming of the Blackrobes, but could do nothing to them because a peace treaty with the French required their presence in villages with Christian captives. She was moved by the words of three Blackrobes who lodged with her uncle, but fear of him kept her from seeking instruction. She refused to marry a Mohawk brave and at 19 finally got the courage to take the step of converting. She was baptized with the name Kateri (Catherine) on Easter Sunday.

Now she would be treated as a slave. Because she would not work on Sunday, she received no food that day. Her life in grace grew rapidly. She told a missionary that she often meditated on the great dignity of being baptized. She was powerfully moved by God's love for human beings and saw the dignity of each of her people. She was always in danger, for her conversion and holy life created great opposition. On the advice of a priest, she stole away one night and began a 200-mile walking journey to a Christian Indian village at Sault St. Louis, near Montreal.

For three years she grew in holiness under the direction of a priest and an older Iroquois woman, giving herself totally to God in long hours of prayer, in charity and in strenuous penance. At 23 she took a vow of virginity, an unprecedented act for an Indian woman, whose maintenance depended on being married. She found a place in the woods where she could pray an hour a day—and was accused of meeting a man there! Her dedication to virginity was instinctive: She did not know about religious life for women until she visited Montreal. Inspired by this, she and two friends wanted to start a community, but the local priest dissuaded her. She humbly accepted an "ordinary" life. She practiced extremely severe fasting as penance for the conversion of her nation. She died the afternoon before Holy Thursday. Witnesses said that her emaciated face changed color and became like that of a healthy child. The lines of suffering, even the pockmarks, disappeared and the touch of a smile came upon her lips.

COMMENT: We like to think that our proposed holiness is thwarted by our situation. If only we could have more solitude, less opposition, better health. Kateri repeats the example of the saints: Holiness thrives on the cross, anywhere. Yet she did have what Christians—all people—need: the support of a community.

She had a good mother, helpful priests, Christian friends. These were present in what we call primitive conditions, and blossomed in the age-old Christian triad of prayer, fasting and alms: union with God in Jesus and the Spirit, self-discipline and often suffering, and charity for her brothers and sisters.

QUOTE: "I am not my own; I have given myself to Jesus. He must be my only love. The state of helpless poverty that may befall me if I do not marry does not frighten me. All I need is a little food and a few pieces of clothing. With the work of my hands I shall always earn what is necessary and what is left over I'll give to my relatives and to the poor. If I should become sick and unable to work, then I shall be like the Lord on the cross. He will have mercy on me and help me, I am sure."

JULY 15   MEMORIAL

Bonaventure

Bishop and Doctor (1221-1274)

Bonaventure, Franciscan, theologian, doctor of the Church, was both learned and holy. Because of the spirit that filled him and his writings, he was at first called the Devout Doctor; but in more recent centuries he has been known as the Seraphic Doctor after the "Seraphic Father" Francis because of the truly Franciscan spirit he possessed.

Born in Bagnoregio, a town in central Italy, he was cured of a serious illness as a boy through the prayers of Francis of Assisi. Later, he studied the arts at Paris. Inspired by Francis and the example of the friars, especially of his master in theology, Alexander of Hales, he entered the Franciscan order, and became in turn a teacher of theology in the University. Chosen as general of the order in 1257, he was God's instrument in bringing the order back to a deeper love of the way of St. Francis, both through the life of Francis which he wrote at the behest of the brothers and through other works which defended the order or explained its ideals and way of life.

COMMENT: Bonaventure so united holiness and theological knowledge that he rose to the heights of mysticism while yet remaining a very active preacher and teacher, one beloved by all who met him. To know him was to love him; to read him is still for us today to meet a true Franciscan and a gentleman.

STORY: The morning of the 15th of July, 1274, in the midst of the Second Council of Lyons, Pope Gregory X and the Fathers of the Council were shocked to learn that toward dawn Brother Bonaventure, bishop of Albano, had sickened and died. An unknown chronicler provides his impression of the Franciscan cardinal: "A man of eminent learning and eloquence, and of outstanding holiness, he was known for his kindness, approachableness, gentleness and compassion. Full of virtue, he was beloved of God and man. At his funeral Mass that same day, many were in tears, for the Lord had granted him this grace, that whoever came to know him was forthwith drawn to a deep love of him."

Our Lady of Mount Carmel

Hermits lived on Mount Carmel near the Fountain of Elijah in the 12th century. They had a chapel dedicated to Our Lady. By the 13th century they became known as "Brothers of Our Lady of

Mount Carmel." They soon celebrated a special Mass and Office in honor of Mary. In 1726 it became a celebration of the universal Church under the title of Our Lady of Mount Carmel. For centuries the Carmelites have seen themselves as specially related to Mary. Their great saints and theologians have promoted devotion to her and often championed the mystery of her Immaculate Conception.

St. Teresa of Avila called Carmel "the order of the Virgin." St. John of the Cross credited Mary with saving him from drowning as a child, leading him to Carmel and helping him escape from prison. St. Theresa of the Child Jesus believed that Mary cured her from illness. On her First Communion she dedicated her life to Mary. During the last days of her life she frequently spoke of Mary.

There is a tradition (which may not be historical) that Mary appeared to St. Simon Stock, a Carmelite General, and gave him a scapular, telling him to promote devotion to it. The scapular is a modified version of Mary's own garment. It symbolizes her special protection and calls the wearers to consecrate themselves to her in a special way. Obviously, no magic way of salvation is intended. Rather, the scapular is a reminder of the gospel call to prayer and penance—a call that Mary models in a most splendid way.

COMMENT: The Carmelites were known from early on as "Brothers of Our Lady of Mount Carmel." The title suggests that they saw Mary not only as "mother," but also as "sister." The word sister is a reminder that Mary is very close to us. She is the daughter of God and therefore can help us be authentic daughters and sons of God. She also can help us grow in appreciation of being sisters and brothers to one another. She leads us to a new realization that all human beings belong to the family of God. When such a conviction grows, there is hope that the human race can find its way to peace.

QUOTE: "The various forms of piety toward the Mother of God, which the Church has approved within the limits of sound and orthodox doctrine, according to the dispositions and understanding of the faithful, ensure that while the mother is honored, the Son through whom all things have their being (cf. Colossians 1:15-16) and in whom it has pleased the Father that all fullness should dwell (cf. Colossians 1:19) is rightly known, loved and glorified and his commandments are observed" (*Constitution on the Church*, 66).

Lawrence of Brindisi
Priest and Doctor (1559-1619)

At first glance perhaps the most remarkable quality of Lawrence of Brindisi is his outstanding gift of languages. In addition to a thorough knowledge of his native Italian, he had complete reading and speaking ability in Latin, Hebrew, Greek, German, Bohemian, Spanish and French.

He was born on July 22, 1559, and died exactly 60 years later on his birthday in 1619. His parents William and Elizabeth Russo gave him the name of Julius Caesar, *Caesare* in Italian. After the early death of his parents he was educated by his uncle at the College of St. Mark in Venice.

When he was just 16 he entered the Capuchin Franciscan order in Venice and received the new name of Lawrence. He completed his studies of philosophy and theology at the University of Padua and was ordained a priest at 23.

With his facility for languages he was able to study the Bible in its original texts. At the request of Pope Clement VIII he spent much time preaching to the Jews in Italy. So excellent was his knowledge of Hebrew, the rabbis felt sure he was a Jew who had become a Christian.

The Capuchin order completed a compilation of 15 volumes of his writings in 1956. Eleven of these 15 contain his sermons, each of which relies chiefly on scriptural quotations to illustrate his teaching.

Lawrence's sensitivity to the needs of people—a character trait perhaps unexpected in such a talented scholar—began to surface. He was elected major superior of the Capuchin Franciscan Province of Tuscany at the age of 31. He had the combination of brilliance, human compassion and administrative skill needed to carry out his duties. In rapid succession he was promoted by his fellow Capuchins and was elected minister-general of the entire order in 1602. In this position he was responsible for great growth and geographical expansion of the order.

Lawrence was appointed papal emissary and peacemaker, a job which took him to a number of foreign countries. An effort to achieve peace in his native kingdom of Naples took him on a journey to Lisbon to visit the king of Spain. Serious illness in Lisbon took his life in 1619.

COMMENT: His constant devotion to Scripture, coupled with great sensitivity to the needs of people, present a life-style which appeals to 20th-century Christians. Lawrence had a balance in his life that blended self-discipline with a keen appreciation for the needs of those whom he was called to serve.

QUOTE: "God is love, and all his operations proceed from love. Once he wills to manifest that goodness by sharing his love outside himself, then the Incarnation becomes the supreme manifestation of his goodness and love and glory. So, Christ was intended before all other creatures and for his own sake. For him all things were created and to him all things must be subject, and God loves all creatures in and because of Christ. Christ is the first-born of every creature, and the whole of humanity as well as the created world finds its foundation and meaning in him. Moreover, this would have been the case even if Adam had not sinned" (*St. Lawrence of Brindisi, Doctor of the Universal Church,* Capuchin Educational Conference, Washington, D.C.).

Mary Magdalene

Except for the mother of Jesus, few women are more honored in the Bible than Mary Magdalene. Yet she could well be the patron of the slandered, since there has been a persistent legend in the Church that she is the unnamed sinful woman who anointed the feet of Jesus in Luke 7:36-50.

Most Scripture scholars today point out that there is no scriptural basis for confusing the two. Mary Magdalene, that is, "of Magdala" was the one from whom Christ cast out "seven demons" (Luke 8:2)—an indication, at the worst, of extreme demonic possession or, possibly, severe illness.

Father W.J. Harrington, O.P., writing in the *New Catholic Commentary*, says that "seven demons" "does not mean that Mary had lived an immoral life—a conclusion reached only by means of a mistaken identification with the anonymous woman of Luke 7:36." Father Edward Mally, S.J., writing in the *Jerome Biblical Commentary*, agrees that she "is not...the same as the sinner of Luke 7:37, despite the later Western romantic tradition about her."

Mary Magdalene was one of the many "who were assisting them (Jesus and the Twelve) out of their means." She was one of those who stood by the cross of Jesus with his mother. And, of all the "official" witnesses that might have been chosen for the first awareness of the Resurrection, she was the one to whom that privilege was given.

COMMENT: Mary Magdalene has been smiling at her "mistaken identity" for 19 centuries. Yet she would no doubt insist that it makes no difference. We are all sinners in need of the saving power of God, whether our sins have been lurid or not. More importantly, we are all, with her, "unofficial" witnesses of the Resurrection.

STORY: Today's Gospel (John 20:1-2, 11-18) shows Mary at first not recognizing the risen Jesus in the garden, then knowing him as he spoke her name. Her great love bursts forth, echoing the first reading, "I took hold of him and would not let him go" (Songs 3:4b). Jesus says, "Stop holding on to me, for I have not yet ascended to the Father" (John 20:17a). The meaning probably is that there is an entirely new relationship now—a much deeper one, resting in faith rather than the former relationship that was possible because of his visible body. St. John may also be stressing the fact that Jesus' exaltation at the right hand of the Father is the completion of the Resurrection.

At first, the apostles did not believe Mary. Christ's followers, even today, meet disbelief in their witness to the Resurrection.

Bridget

Religious (1303?-1373)

From age seven on, Bridget had visions of Christ crucified. Her visions formed the basis for her activity—always with the value on charity rather than spiritual favors.

She lived her married life in the court of the Swedish king Magnus II. Mother of eight children (the second eldest was St. Catherine of Sweden), she lived the strict life of a penitent after her husband's death.

Bridget constantly strove to exert her good influence over Magnus; while never fully reforming, he did give her land and buildings to found a monastery for men and women. This group eventually expanded into an order known as the Bridgetines (still in existence).

In 1350, a year of jubilee, Bridget braved a plague-stricken Europe to make a pilgrimage to Rome. She never returned to Sweden and her years in Rome were far from happy, being hounded by debts and by opposition to her work against Church abuses.

A final pilgrimage to the Holy Land, marred by shipwreck and the death of her son, Charles, eventually led to her death in 1373.

COMMENT: Bridget's visions, rather than isolating her from the affairs of the world, involved her in many contemporary issues, whether they be royal policy or the Avignon papacy. She saw no contradiction between mystical experience and secular activity, and her life is a testimony to the possibility of a holy life in the market place.

QUOTE: Despite the hardships of life and wayward children (not all became saints), Margery Kempe of Lynn says Bridget was "kind and meek to every creature" and "she had a laughing face."

James

Apostle

This James is the brother of John the Evangelist. The two were called by Jesus as they worked with their father in a fishing boat on the Sea of Galilee. Jesus had already called another pair of brothers from a similar occupation: Peter and Andrew. "He walked along a little farther and saw James, the son of Zebedee, and his brother John. They too were in a boat mending their nets. Then he called them. So they left their father Zebedee in the boat along with the hired men and followed him" (Mark 1:19-20).

James was one of the favored three who had the privilege of witnessing the Transfiguration, the raising to life of the daughter of Jairus and the agony in Gethsemane.

Two incidents in the Gospels describe the temperament of this man and his brother. St. Matthew tells that their mother came (Mark says it was the brothers themselves) to ask that they have the seats of honor (one on the right, one on the left of Jesus) in the kingdom. "Jesus said in reply, 'You do not know what you are asking. Can you drink the cup that I am going to drink?' They said to him, 'We can'" (Matthew 20:22). Jesus then told them they would indeed drink the cup and share his baptism of pain and death, but that sitting at his right hand or left was not his to give—it "is for those for whom it has been prepared by my Father" (Matthew 20:23b). It remained to be seen how long it would take to realize the implications of their confident "We can!"

The other disciples became indignant at the ambition of James and John. Then Jesus taught them all the lesson of humble service: The purpose of authority is to serve. They are not to impose their will on others, or lord it over them. This is the position of Jesus himself. He was the servant of all; the service imposed on him was the supreme sacrifice of his own life.

On another occasion, James and John gave evidence that the nickname Jesus gave them—"sons of thunder"—was an apt one. The Samaritans would not welcome Jesus because he was on his way to hated Jerusalem. "When the disciples James and John saw this they asked, 'Lord, do you want us to call down fire from heaven to consume them?' Jesus turned and rebuked them..." (Luke 9:54-55).

James was apparently the first of the apostles to be martyred. "About that time King Herod laid hands upon some members of the church to harm them. He had James, the brother of John, killed by the sword, and when he saw that this was pleasing to the Jews he proceeded to arrest Peter also" (Acts 12:1-3a).

This James is not to be confused with the author of the Letter of James, or with the leader of the Jerusalem community.

COMMENT: The way the Gospels treat the apostles is a good reminder of what holiness is all about. There is very little about their virtues as static possessions whereby they would have some title to heavenly reward. Rather, the great emphasis is on the Kingdom, on God's giving them the power to proclaim the Good News. As far as their personal lives are concerned, there is much about Jesus' purifying them of narrowness, pettiness, fickleness.

QUOTE: "...Christ the Lord, in whom the full revelation of the supreme God is brought to completion (cf. 2 Corinthians 1:20; 3:16; 4:6), commissioned the apostles to preach to all men that gospel which is the source of all saving truth and moral teaching, and thus to impart to them divine gifts....This commission was faithfully fulfilled by the apostles, who, by their oral preaching, by example, and by ordinances, handed on what they had received from the lips of Christ, from living with him, and from what he did, or what they had learned through the promptings of the Holy Spirit" (*Constitution on Divine Revelation*, 7).

Joachim and Ann

Parents of Mary

In the Scriptures, Matthew and Luke furnish a legal family history of Jesus, tracing ancestry to show that Jesus is the culmination of great promises. Not only is his mother's family neglected, we also know nothing factual about them except that they existed. Even the names *Joachim* and *Ann* come from a legendary source written more than a century after Jesus died.

The heroism and holiness of these people, however, is inferred from the whole family atmosphere around Mary in the Scriptures. Whether we rely on the legends about Mary's childhood or make guesses from the information in the Bible, we see in her a fulfillment of many generations of prayerful persons, herself steeped in the religious traditions of her people.

The strong character of Mary in making decisions, her continuous practice of prayer, her devotion to the laws of her faith, her steadiness at moments of crisis, and her devotion to her relatives—all indicate a close-knit, loving family that looked forward to the next generation even while retaining the best of the past.

Joachim and Ann—whether these are their real names or not—represent that entire quiet series of generations who faithfully perform their duties, practice their faith and establish an atmosphere for the coming of the Messiah, but remain obscure.

COMMENT: This is the "feast of grandparents." It reminds grandparents of their responsibility to establish a tone for generations to come: They must make the traditions live and offer them as a promise to little children. But the feast has a message for the younger generation as well. It reminds the young that older people's greater perspective, depth of experience and appreciation of life's profound rhythms are all part of a wisdom not to be taken lightly or ignored.

QUOTE: "...[T]he family is the foundation of society. In it the various generations come together and help one another to grow wise and to harmonize personal rights with the other requirements of social life" (*The Church in the Modern World*, 52).

Martha

Martha, Mary and their brother Lazarus were evidently close friends of Jesus. He came to their home simply as a welcomed guest, rather than as one celebrating the conversion of a sinner like Zacchaeus or one unceremoniously received by a suspicious Pharisee. The sisters feel free to call on Jesus at their brother's death, even though a return to Judea at that time seems almost certain death.

No doubt Martha was an active sort of person. On one occasion (see Luke 10:38-42) she prepares the meal for Jesus and possibly his fellow guests and forthrightly states the obvious: All hands should pitch in to help with the dinner.

Yet, as Father John McKenzie points out, she need not be rated as an "unrecollected activist." The evangelist is emphasizing what our Lord said on several occasions about the primacy of the spiritual: "...[D]o not worry about your life, what you will eat [or drink], or about your body, what you will wear....But seek first the kingdom [of God] and his righteousness" (Matthew 6:25b, 33a); "One does not live by bread alone" (Luke 4:4b); "Blessed are they who hunger and thirst for righteousness..." (Matthew 5:6a).

Martha's great glory is her simple and strong statement of

faith in Jesus at the time of her brother's death. "Jesus told her, 'I am the resurrection and the life; whoever believes in me, even if he dies, will live, and everyone who lives and believes in me will never die. Do you believe this?' She said to him, 'Yes, Lord. I have come to believe that you are the Messiah, the Son of God, the one who is coming into the world' " (John 11:25-27).

COMMENT: Scripture commentators point out that in writing his account of the raising of Lazarus, St. John intends that we should see Martha's words to Mary before the resurrection of Lazarus as a summons that every Christian must obey. In her saying "The teacher is here and is asking for you," Jesus is calling every one of us to resurrection—now in baptismal faith, forever in sharing his victory over death. And all of us, as well these three friends, are in our own unique way called to special friendship with him.

QUOTE: "Even in this life the Spirit transforms us....When Moses turned towards the Lord, his face shone in the reflection of God: when the believer turns towards the Lord Jesus and contemplates his glorious face, he is transformed into an ever brighter image of that same glory. And this irradiating power which transforms us into beings of light only comes from Christ because he himself is wholly penetrated by that Spirit" (Durrwell, *The Resurrection*).

Peter Chrysologus

Bishop and Doctor (406-450?)

A man who vigorously pursues a goal may produce results far beyond his expectations and his intentions. Thus it was with Peter of the Golden Words, as he was called, who as a young man became Bishop of Ravenna, the capital of the empire in the West. At the time there were abuses and vestiges of paganism evident in his diocese, and these he was determined to battle and overcome. His principal weapon was the short sermon, and many of them have come down to us. They do not contain great originality of thought. They are, however, full of moral applications, sound in doctrine and historically significant in that they reveal Christian life in fifth-century Ravenna. So authentic were the contents of his sermons that, some 13 centuries later, he was declared a doctor of the Church by Pope Benedict XIII. He who had earnestly sought to teach and motivate his own flock was recognized as a teacher of the universal Church.

In addition to his zeal in the exercise of his office, Peter Chrysologus was distinguished by a fierce loyalty to the Church, not only in its teaching, but in its authority as well. He looked upon learning not as a mere opportunity but as an obligation for all, both as a development of God-given faculties and as a solid support for the worship of God.

Some time before his death, St. Peter returned to Imola, his birthplace, where he died c. A.D. 450.

COMMENT: Quite likely, it was St. Peter Chrysologus's attitude toward learning that gave substance to his exhortations. Next to virtue, learning, in his view, was the greatest improver of the human mind and the support of true religion. Ignorance is not a virtue, nor is anti-intellectualism. Knowledge is neither more nor less a source of pride than physical, administrative or financial prowess. To be fully human is to expand our knowledge—whether sacred or secular—according to our talent and opportunity.

STORY: Eutyches, the leader of the heresy denying the humanity of Christ, sought support from Church leaders, Peter Chrysologus among them, after his condemnation in A.D. 448. Peter frankly told him: "In the interest of peace and the faith, we cannot judge in matters of faith without the consent of the Roman bishop." He further exhorted Eutyches to accept the mystery of the Incarnation in simple faith. Peter reminded him that if the peace of the Church causes joy in heaven, then divisions must give birth to grief.

JULY 31   MEMORIAL

Ignatius of Loyola
Priest (1491-1556)

The founder of the Jesuits was on his way to military fame and fortune when a cannon ball shattered his leg. Because there were no books of romance on hand during his convalescence, he whiled away the time reading a life of Christ and lives of the saints. His conscience was deeply touched, and a long, painful turning to Christ began. Having seen the Mother of God in a vision, he made a pilgrimage to her shrine at Monserrat. He remained for almost a year at nearby Manresa, sometimes with the Dominicans, sometimes in a pauper's hospice, often in a cave in the hills praying. After a period of great peace of mind, he went through a harrowing trial of scruples. There was no comfort in anything—prayer, fasting, sacraments, penance. At length, his peace of mind returned.

It was during this year of conversion that he began to write down material that later became his greatest work, the *Spiritual Exercises*.

He finally achieved his purpose of going to the Holy Land, but could not remain, as he planned, because of the hostility of the Turks. He spent the next 11 years in various European universities, studying with great difficulty, beginning almost as a child. Like many others, he fell victim twice to the suspicions of the time, and was twice jailed for brief periods.

In 1534, at the age of 33, he and six others (one of whom was Francis Xavier) vowed to live in poverty and chastity and to go to the Holy Land. If this became impossible, they vowed to offer themselves to the apostolic service of the pope. The latter became the only choice. Four years later Ignatius made the association permanent. The new Society of Jesus was approved by Paul III, and Ignatius was elected to serve as the first general.

When companions were sent on various missions by the pope, Ignatius remained in Rome, consolidating the new venture, but still finding time to found homes for orphans, catechumens and penitents. He founded the Roman College, intended to be the model of all other colleges of the Society.

Ignatius was a true mystic. He centered his spiritual life on the essential foundations of Christianity—the Trinity, Christ, the Eucharist. His spirituality is expressed in the Jesuit motto, *ad majorem Dei gloriam*—"for the greater glory of God." In his concept, obedience was to be the prominent virtue, to assure the effectiveness and mobility of his men. All activity was to be guided by a true love of the Church and unconditional obedience to the Holy Father, for which reason all professed members took a fourth vow to go wherever the pope should send them for the salvation of souls.

COMMENT: Luther nailed his theses to the church door at Wittenberg in 1517. Seventeen years later, Ignatius founded the

Society that was to play so prominent a part in the Counter-Reformation. He was an implacable foe of Protestantism. Yet the seeds of ecumenism may be found in his words: "Great care must be taken to show forth orthodox truth in such a way that if any heretics happen to be present they may have an example of charity and Christian moderation. No hard words should be used nor any sort of contempt for their errors be shown." One of the greatest figures in the modern ecumenical movement was Cardinal Bea, a Jesuit.

QUOTE: Ignatius recommended this prayer to penitents: "Receive, Lord, all my liberty, my memory, my understanding and my whole will. You have given me all that I have, all that I am, and I surrender all to your divine will, that you dispose of me. Give me only your love and your grace. With this I am rich enough, and I have no more to ask."

Alphonsus Liguori

Bishop and Doctor (1696-1787)

Moral theology, Vatican II said, should be more thoroughly
nourished by Scripture, and show the nobility of the Christian
vocation of the faithful and their obligation to bring forth fruit in
charity for the life of the world. Alphonsus, declared patron of
moral theologians by Pius XII in 1950, would rejoice in that
statement. In his day, he fought for the liberation of moral
theology from the rigidity of Jansenism. His moral theology,
which went through 60 editions in the century following him,
concentrated on the practical and concrete problems of pastors
and confessors. If a certain legalism and minimalism crept into
moral theology, it should not be attributed to this model of
moderation and gentleness.

At the University of Naples he received, at the age of 16, a
doctorate in both canon and civil law by acclamation, but soon
gave up the practice of law for apostolic activity. He was ordained
priest and concentrated his pastoral efforts on popular (parish)
missions, hearing confessions, forming Christian groups.

He founded the Redemptorist congregation in 1732. It was
an association of priests and brothers living a common life,
dedicated to the imitation of Christ, and working mainly in
popular missions for peasants in rural areas. Almost as an omen of
what was to come later, he found himself deserted, after a while,
by all his original companions except one lay brother. But the
congregation managed to survive and was formally approved 17
years later, though its troubles were not over.

Alphonsus' great pastoral reforms were in the pulpit and
confessional—replacing the pompous oratory of the time with
simplicity, and the rigorism of Jansenism with kindness. His great
fame as a writer has somewhat eclipsed the fact that for 26 years

he traveled up and down the kingdom of Naples preaching popular missions.

He was made bishop (after trying to reject the honor) at 66 and at once instituted a thorough reform of the diocese.

His greatest sorrow came at the end of his life. The Redemptorists, precariously continuing after the suppression of the Jesuits, had difficulty in getting their rule approved by the Kingdom of Naples. Alphonsus acceded to the condition that they possess no property in common, but a royal official, with the connivance of a high Redemptorist official, changed the rule substantially. Alphonsus, old, crippled and with very bad sight, signed the document, unaware that he had been betrayed. The Redemptorists in the Papal States then put themselves under the pope, who withdrew those in Naples from the jurisdiction of Alphonsus. It was only after his death that the branches were united.

At 71 he was afflicted with rheumatic pains which left incurable bending of his neck; until it was straightened a little, the pressure of his chin caused a raw wound on his chest. He suffered a final 18 months of "dark night" scruples, fears, temptations against every article of faith and every virtue, interspersed with intervals of light and relief, when ecstasies were frequent.

Alphonsus is best known for his moral theology, but he also wrote well in the field of spiritual and dogmatic theology. His *Glories of Mary* is one of the great works on that subject, and his book *Visits to the Blessed Sacrament* went through 40 editions in his lifetime, greatly influencing the practice of this devotion in the Church.

COMMENT: St. Alphonsus was known above all as a practical man who dealt in the concrete rather than the abstract. His life is indeed a "practical" model for the everyday Christian who has difficulty recognizing the dignity of Christian life amid the swirl of problems, pain, misunderstanding and failure. Alphonsus suffered all these things. He is a saint because he was able to maintain an intimate sense of the presence of the suffering Christ through it all.

QUOTE: Someone once remarked, after a sermon by Alphonsus, "It is a pleasure to listen to your sermons; you forget yourself and preach Jesus Christ."

AUGUST 2   OPTIONAL

Eusebius of Vercelli
Bishop (283?-371)

Someone has said that if there had been no Arian heresy it would be very difficult to write the lives of many early saints. Eusebius is another of the defenders of the Church during one of its most trying periods.

Born on the isle of Sardinia, he became a member of the Roman clergy and is the first recorded bishop of Vercelli in Piedmont. He is also the first to join the monastic life with that of the clergy, establishing a community of his diocesan clergy on the principle that the best way to sanctify his people was to have them see a clergy formed in solid virtue and living in community.

He was sent by Pope Liberius to persuade the emperor to call a council to settle Catholic-Arian troubles. When it was called at Milan, Eusebius went reluctantly, sensing that the Arian block would have its way, although the Catholics were more numerous. He refused to go along with the condemnation of Athanasius; instead, he laid the Nicene Creed on the table and insisted that all sign it before taking up any other matter. The emperor put pressure on him, but Eusebius insisted on Athanasius' innocence and reminded the emperor that secular force should not be used to influence Church decisions. At first the emperor threatened to kill him, but later sent him into exile in Palestine. There the Arians dragged him through the streets and shut him up in a little room, releasing him only after his four-day hunger strike, but continuing their harassment shortly after.

His exile continued in Asia Minor and Egypt, until the new emperor permitted him to be welcomed back to his see in Vercelli. He attended the Council of Alexandria with Athanasius and approved the leniency shown to bishops who had wavered. He also worked with St. Hilary of Poitiers against the Arians.

He died peacefully in his own diocese at an advanced age.

COMMENT: Catholics in the U.S. have sometimes felt penalized by an unwarranted interpretation of the principle of separation of Church and state, especially in the matter of Catholic schools. Be that as it may, the Church is happily free today from the tremendous pressure put on it after its becoming an "established" Church under Constantine. We are happily rid of such things as a pope asking an emperor to call a Church council, Pope John I being sent by the emperor to negotiate in the East, the pressure of kings on papal elections. The Church cannot be a prophet if it's in anybody's pocket.

QUOTE: "To render the care of souls more efficacious, community life for priests is strongly recommended, especially for those attached to the same parish. While this way of living encourages apostolic action, it also affords an example of charity and unity to the faithful" (*Decree on the Bishops' Pastoral Office*, 30).

John Vianney
Priest (1786-1859)

A man with vision overcomes obstacles and performs deeds that seem impossible. John Vianney was a man with vision: He wanted to become a priest. But he had to overcome his meager formal schooling which did not equip him adequately for seminary studies.

His failure to comprehend Latin lectures forced him to discontinue. But his vision of being a priest urged him to seek private tutoring. After a lengthy battle with the books, John was ordained.

Situations calling for "impossible" deeds followed him everywhere. As pastor of the parish at Ars, John encountered people who were indifferent and quite comfortable with their style of living. His vision lead him through severe fasts and short nights of sleep. (Some devils can only be cast out by prayer and fasting.)

With Catherine Lassagne and Benedicta Lardet, he established La Providence, a home for girls. Only a man of vision could have such trust that God would provide for the spiritual and material needs of all those who came to make La Providence their home.

His work as a confessor is John Vianney's most remarkable accomplishment. In the winter months he was to spend 11 to 12 hours daily reconciling people with God. In the summer months this time was increased to 16 hours. Unless a man was dedicated to his vision of a priestly vocation, he could not have endured this giving of self day after day.

Many people look forward to retirement and taking it easy, doing the things they always wanted to do but never had the time for. But John Vianney had no thoughts of retirement. As his fame spread, more hours were consumed in serving God's people. Even the few hours he would allow himself for sleep were disturbed frequently by the devil.

Who, but a man with vision, could keep going with ever-increasing strength?

COMMENT: Indifference toward religion, coupled with a love for material comfort, seem to be common signs of our times. A person from another planet observing us would not likely judge us to be pilgrim people, on our way to somewhere else. John Vianney, on the other hand, was a man on a journey with his goal before him at all times.

QUOTE: Recommending liturgical prayer, John Vianney would say, "Private prayer is like straw scattered here and there: If you set it on fire it makes a lot of little flames. But gather these straws into a bundle and light them, and you get a mighty fire, rising like a column into the sky; public prayer is like that."

AUGUST 5   OPTIONAL

Dedication of St. Mary Major

First raised at the order of Pope Liberius in the mid-fourth century, the Liberian Basilica was rebuilt by Pope Sixtus III shortly after the Council of Ephesus affirmed Mary's title as Mother of God in 431. Rededicated at that time to the Mother of God, St. Mary Major is the largest church in the world honoring God through Mary. Standing atop one of Rome's seven hills, the Esquiline, it has survived many restorations without losing its character as an early Roman basilica. Its interior retains three naves divided by colonnades in the style of Constantine's era.

Fifth-century mosaics on its walls testify to its antiquity.

St. Mary Major is one of the four Roman basilicas known as patriarchal cathedrals in memory of the first centers of the Church. St. John Lateran (see November 9) represents Peter's see, Rome; St. Paul Outside the Walls, the See of Alexandria, allegedly the see presided over by Mark; St. Peter's, the See of Constantinople; and St. Mary's, the See of Antioch, where Mary is supposed to have spent most of her life.

A now discredited legend, unreported before the year 1000, gives another name to this feast: Our Lady of the Snows. According to that story, a wealthy Roman couple pledged their fortune to the Mother of God. In affirmation, she produced a miraculous midsummer snowfall and told them to build a church on the site. The legend was long celebrated by releasing a shower of white rose petals from the dome every August 5.

COMMENT: Theological debate over Christ's nature as God and man reached fever pitch in Constantinople in the early fifth century. Athanasius, chaplain to Bishop Nestorius, began preaching against the title *Theotokos*, "Mother of God," insisting that the Virgin was mother only of the human Jesus. Nestorius agreed, decreeing that Mary would henceforth be named "Mother of Christ" in his see. The people of Constantinople virtually revolted against their bishop's refutation of a cherished belief. When the Council of Ephesus refuted Nestorius, believers took to the streets, enthusiastically chanting, "*Theotokos! Theotokos!*"

QUOTE: "From the earliest times the Blessed Virgin is honored under the title of Mother of God, in whose protection the faithful take refuge together in prayer in all their perils and needs. Accordingly, following the Council of Ephesus, there was a remarkable growth in the cult of the People of God towards Mary, in veneration and love, in invocation and imitation..." (*Constitution on the Church*, 66).

Transfiguration of the Lord

All three Synoptics tell the story of the Transfiguration
(Matthew 17:1-8; Mark 9:2-9; Luke 9:28-36). With remarkable
agreement, all three place the event shortly after Peter's
confession of faith that Jesus is the Messiah and Jesus' first
prediction of his passion and death. Peter's eagerness to erect
tents or booths on the spot suggests it occurred during the Jewish
week-long fall Feast of Booths.

In spite of the texts' agreement, it is difficult to reconstruct
the disciples' experience, according to Scripture scholars, for the
Gospels draw heavily on Old Testament descriptions of the Sinai
encounter with God and prophetic visions of the Son of Man.
Certainly Peter, James and John had a glimpse of Jesus' divinity
strong enough to strike fear into their hearts. Such an experience
defies description, so they drew on familiar religious language to
describe it. And certainly Jesus warned them that his glory and his
suffering were to be inextricably connected—a theme John plays
throughout his Gospel.

Tradition names Mt. Tabor as the site of the revelation. A
church first raised there in the fourth century was dedicated on
August 6. A feast in honor of the Transfiguration was celebrated
in the Eastern Church from about that time. Western observance
began in some localities about the eighth century.

On July 22, 1456, Crusaders defeated the Turks at Belgrade.
News of the victory reached Rome on August 6, and Pope
Callistus III placed the feast on the Roman calendar the following
year.

COMMENT: One of the Transfiguration accounts is read on the
second Sunday of Lent each year, proclaiming Christ's divinity to
catechumens and baptized alike. The Gospel for the first Sunday

of Lent, by contrast, is the story of the temptation in the desert—affirmation of Jesus' humanity. The two distinct but inseparable natures of the Lord were a subject of much theological argument at the beginning of the Church's history; it remains hard for believers to grasp.

QUOTE: At his Transfiguration Christ showed his disciples the splendor of his beauty, to which he will shape and color those who are his: "He will reform our lowness configured to the body of his glory" (Philippians 3:21) (St. Thomas Aquinas, *Summa Theoligica*).

Sixtus II and Companions

Pope and Martyr; Martyrs (d. 258)

Freedom to assemble has always been one of the first liberties that dictators deny to subjects (and one highly prized by our American forebears). The emperor Valerian published his first decree against Christians in 257, and forbade them to hold assemblies. Pope Sixtus had been pope for just one year when he was murdered while presiding at the Eucharist in one of the underground caverns used as cemeteries (catacombs). He and four deacons were seized and beheaded. Two other deacons were probably martyred the same day, and St. Lawrence (August 10) four days later.

During his year in office Sixtus had to deal with the controversy about the validity of Baptism by heretics. He supported the positive view, but was tolerant toward the practice of the Eastern Church, which rebaptized those who had received the sacrament from heretics. The negative view was shared by St.

Cyprian (September 16), to whom Sixtus sent messengers for discussion. Sixtus was asked to be patient with those in error, and contented himself with a strong recommendation of the truth. Other popes did the same, until the error was finally condemned.

COMMENT: What are we willing to suffer to practice our faith? In times of persecution Christians have always dared to come together to celebrate the Eucharist—huddled in a corner of the prison, risking life and possessions—in Ireland, for example, by providing "priest's holes." Those of us who live in Christian lands can scarcely comprehend the possibility: Does the Eucharist mean so much to us that, under government persecution, we would gather at night in one of our homes to celebrate the mystery of the Body and Blood of Jesus, risking that fatal knock on the door?

QUOTE: "...[B]aptism, of itself, is only a beginning, a point of departure, for it is wholly directed toward the acquiring of fullness of life in Christ. Baptism is thus oriented toward a complete profession of faith, a complete incorporation into the system of salvation such as Christ himself willed it to be, and finally, toward a complete participation in Eucharistic communion" (*Decree on Ecumenism*, 22).

Cajetan
Priest (1480-1557)

Like most of us, Cajetan seemed headed for an "ordinary" life—first as a lawyer, then as a priest engaged in the work of the Roman Curia.

His life took a characteristic turn when he joined the Oratory of Divine Love in Rome, a group devoted to piety and charity, shortly after his ordination at 36. When he was 42 he founded a hospital for incurables at Venice. At Vicenza, he entered a "disreputable" religious community that consisted only of men of the lowest stations of life—and was roundly censured by his friends, who thought his action was a reflection on his family. He sought out the sick and poor of the town and served them.

The greatest need of the time was the reformation of a Church that was "sick in head and members." Cajetan and three friends decided that the best road to reformation lay in reviving the spirit and zeal of the clergy. (One of them later became Paul IV.) Together they founded a congregation known as the Theatines (from Teate [*Chieti*] where their first superior-bishop had his see). They managed to escape to Venice after their house in Rome was wrecked when Charles V sacked Rome in 1527. The Theatines were outstanding among the Catholic reform movements that took shape before the Protestant Reformation.

He founded a *monte de pieta* ("mountain [or fund] of piety") in Naples—one of many charitable, nonprofit credit organizations that lent money on the security of pawned objects. The purpose was to help the poor and protect them against usurers. Cajetan's little organization ultimately became the Bank of Naples, with great changes in policy.

STORY: When Cajetan was sent to establish a house of his congregation in Naples, a count tried to prevail upon him to accept an estate in lands. He refused. The count pointed out that he would need the money, for the people of Naples were not as generous as the people of Venice. "That may be true," replied Cajetan, "but God is the same in both cities."

COMMENT: If Vatican II had been summarily stopped after its first session in 1962, many Catholics would have felt that a great blow had been dealt to the growth of the Church. Cajetan had the same feeling about the Council of Trent. But, as he said, God is the same in Naples as in Venice, with or without Trent or Vatican II (or III). We open ourselves to God's power in whatever circumstances we find ourselves, and God's will is done. God has standards of success that are different from ours.

Dominic

Priest (1170-1221)

If he hadn't taken a trip with his bishop, Dominic would probably have remained within the structure of contemplative life; after the trip, he spent the rest of his life being a contemplative in active apostolic work.

Born in old Castile, Spain, he was trained for the priesthood by a priest-uncle, studied the arts and theology, and became a canon of the cathedral at Osma, where there was an attempt to revive the apostolic common life of the Acts of the Apostles.

On a journey to northern Europe with his bishop, he came face to face with the then virulent Albigensian heresy at Languedoc. The Albigensians (Cathari, "the pure") held to two principles—one good, one evil—in the world. All matter is evil—hence they denied the Incarnation and sacraments. On the same principle they abstained from procreation and took a minimum of food and drink. The inner circle led what must be called a heroic life of purity and asceticism not shared by ordinary followers.

Dominic sensed the need for the Church to combat the heresy, and was commissioned to be part of the preaching crusade against it. He saw immediately why the preaching was not succeeding: the ordinary people admired and followed the ascetical heroes of the Albigenses. Understandably, they were not impressed by the Catholic spokesmen who traveled with horse and retinues, stayed at the best inns and had servants. Dominic therefore, with three Cistercians, began itinerant preaching according to the gospel ideal. He continued this work for 10 years, being successful with the ordinary people but not with the leaders.

His fellow preachers gradually became a community, and in 1215 he founded a religious house at Toulouse which was to be the beginning of the Dominican Order.

His ideal, and that of his order, was to link organically a life with God, study and prayer in all forms, with a ministry of salvation to people by the word of God. His ideal: *contemplata tradere*: "to pass on the fruits of contemplation" or "to speak only of God or with God."

COMMENT: The Dominican ideal, like that of all religious communities, is for the imitation, not merely the admiration, of the rest of the Church. The effective combining of contemplation and activity is the vocation of truck driver Smith as well as theologian Aquinas. Acquired contemplation is the tranquil abiding in the presence of God, and is an integral part of any full human life. It must be the wellspring of all Christian activity.

STORY: Legend has it that Dominic saw the sinful world threatened by God's anger but saved by the intercession of our Lady, who pointed out to her Son two figures: One was Dominic himself, the other a stranger. In church the next day he saw a ragged beggar enter—the man in the vision. He went up to him, embraced him and said, "You are my companion and must walk with me. If we hold together, no earthly power can withstand us." The beggar was Francis of Assisi. The meeting of the two founders is commemorated twice a year, when on their respective feast days Dominicans and Franciscans celebrate Mass in each other's churches, and afterwards sit at the same table "to eat the bread which for seven centuries has never been wanting" (*Butler's Lives of the Saints*).

FEAST

Lawrence

Deacon and Martyr (d. 258?)

The esteem in which the Church holds Lawrence is seen in the fact that today's celebration ranks as a feast. We know very little about his life. He is one of those whose martyrdom made a deep and lasting impression on the early Church. Celebration of his feast day spread rapidly.

He was a Roman deacon under Pope St. Sixtus II (August 5). Four days after this pope was put to death, Lawrence and four clerics suffered martyrdom, probably during the persecution of the Emperor Valerian.

Legendary details of his death were known to Damasus, Prudentius, Ambrose and Augustine. The church built over his tomb became one of the seven principal churches in Rome and a favorite place for Roman pilgrimages.

COMMENT: Once again we have a saint about whom almost nothing is known, yet one who has received extraordinary honor in the Church since the fourth century. Almost nothing—yet the greatest fact of his life is certain: He died for Christ. We who are hungry for details about the lives of the saints are again reminded that their holiness was, after all, total response to Christ, expressed perfectly by a death like this.

STORY: A well-known legend has persisted from earliest times. As deacon in Rome, Lawrence was charged with the responsibility for the material goods of the Church, and the distribution of alms to the poor. When Lawrence knew he would be arrested like the pope, he sought out the poor, widows and orphans of Rome and gave them all the money he had on hand, selling even the sacred vessels to increase the sum. When the prefect of Rome heard of this, he imagined that the Christians must have considerable treasure. He sent for Lawrence and said, "You Christians say we are cruel to you, but that is not what I have in mind. I am told that your priests offer in gold, that the sacred blood is received in silver cups, that you have golden candlesticks at your evening services. Now, your doctrine says you must render to Caesar what is his. Bring these treasures—the emperor needs them to maintain his forces. God does not cause money to be counted: He brought none of it into the world with him—only words. Give me the money, therefore, and be rich in words."

Lawrence replied that the Church was indeed rich. "I will show you a valuable part. But give me time to set everything in order and make an inventory." After three days he gathered a great number of blind, lame, maimed, leprous, orphaned and widowed persons and put them in rows. When the prefect arrived, Lawrence simply said, "These are the treasure of the Church."

The prefect was so angry he told Lawrence that he would indeed have his wish to die—but it would be by inches. He had a great gridiron prepared, with coals beneath it, and had Lawrence's body placed on it. After the martyr had suffered the pain for a long time, the legend concludes, he made his famous cheerful remark, "It is well done. Turn it over and eat it!"

Clare

Virgin (1194-1253)

One of the more sugary movies made about Francis of Assisi pictures Clare as a golden-haired beauty floating through sun-drenched fields, a sort of one-girl counterpart to the new Franciscan Order.

The beginning of her religious life was indeed movie material. Having refused to marry at 15, she was moved by the dynamic preaching of Francis. He became her lifelong friend and spiritual guide.

At 18, she escaped one night from her father's home, was met on the road by friars carrying torches, and in the poor little chapel called the *Portiuncula* received a rough woolen habit, exchanged her jeweled belt for a common rope with knots in it, and sacrificed the long tresses to Francis' scissors. He placed her in a Benedictine convent which her father and uncles immediately stormed in rage. She clung to the altar of the church, threw aside her veil to show her cropped hair and remained adamant.

End of movie material. Sixteen days later her sister Agnes joined her. Others came. They lived a simple life of great poverty, austerity and complete seclusion from the world, according to a rule Francis gave them as a Second Order (Poor Clares). At 21, Francis obliged her under obedience to accept the office of abbess in which she continued until her death.

The nuns went barefoot, slept on the ground, ate no meat and observed almost complete silence. (Later Clare, like Francis, persuaded her sisters to moderate this rigor: "Our bodies are not made of brass.") The greatest emphasis, of course, was on gospel poverty. They possessed no property, even in common, subsisting on daily contributions. When even the pope tried to persuade her to mitigate this practice, she showed her characteristic firmness: "I need to be absolved from my sins, but I do not wish to be absolved from the obligation of following Jesus Christ."

Contemporary accounts glow with admiration of her life in the convent of San Damiano in Assisi. She served the sick, waited on table, washed the feet of the begging nuns. She came from prayer, it was said, with her face so shining it dazzled those about her. She suffered serious illness for the last 27 years of her life. Her influence was such that popes, cardinals and bishops often came to consult her—she herself never left the walls of San Damiano.

Francis always remained her great friend and inspiration. She was always obedient to his will and to the great ideal of gospel life which he was making real.

A well-known story concerns her prayer and trust. She had the Blessed Sacrament placed on the walls of the convent when it faced attack by invading Saracens. "Does it please you, O God, to deliver into the hands of these beasts the defenseless children I have nourished with your love? I beseech you, dear Lord, protect these whom I am now unable to protect." To her sisters she said, "Don't be afraid. Trust in Jesus." The Saracens fled.

COMMENT: The 41 years of Clare's religious life are poor movie material, but they are a scenario of sanctity: an indomitable resolve to lead the simple, literal gospel life as Francis taught her; courageous resistance to the ever-present pressure to dilute the ideal; a passion for poverty and humility; an ardent life of prayer; and a generous concern for her sisters.

STORY: On her deathbed, Clare was heard to say to herself: "Go forth in peace, for you have followed the good road. Go forth without fear, for he who created you has made you holy, has always protected you, and loves you as a mother. Blessed be you, my God, for having created me."

Pontian and Hippolytus

Pope and Martyr; Priest and Martyr (d. 235)

Two men died for the faith after harsh treatment and exhaustion
in the mines of Sardinia. One had been pope for five years, the
other an antipope for 18. They died reconciled.

Pontian. Pontian was a Roman who served as pope from 230 to
235. During his reign he held a synod which confirmed the
excommunication of the great theologian Origen in Alexandria.
He was banished to exile by the Roman emperor in 235, and
resigned so that a successor could be elected in Rome. He was sent
to the "unhealthy" island of Sardinia, where he died of harsh
treatment in 235. With him was Hippolytus (see below) with
whom he was reconciled. The bodies of both martyrs were
brought back to Rome and buried with solemn rites as martyrs.

Hippolytus. As a presbyter in Rome, Hippolytus (the name
means "a horse turned loose") was at first "holier than the
Church." He censured the pope for not coming down hard
enough on a certain heresy—calling him a tool in the hands of
one Callistus, a deacon—and coming close to advocating the
opposite heresy himself. When Callistus was elected pope,
Hippolytus accused him of being too lenient with penitents, and
had himself elected antipope by a group of followers. He felt that
the Church must be composed of pure souls uncompromisingly
separated from the world, and evidently thought that his group
fitted the description. He remained in schism through the reigns
of three popes. In 235 he was also banished to the island of
Sardinia. Shortly before or after this event, he was reconciled to
the Church, and died with Pope Pontian in exile.

Hippolytus was a rigorist, a vehement and intransigent man

for whom even orthodox doctrine and practice were not purified enough. He is, nevertheless, the most important theologian and prolific religious writer before the age of Constantine. His writings are the fullest source of our knowledge of the Roman liturgy and the structure of the Church in the second and third centuries. His works include many Scripture commentaries, polemics against heresies and a history of the world. A marble statue, dating from the third century, representing the saint sitting in a chair, was found in 1551. On one side is inscribed his table for computing the date of Easter, on the other a list of how the system works out until the year 224. Pope John XXIII installed the statue in the Vatican library.

COMMENT: Hippolytus was a strong defender of orthodoxy, and admitted his excesses by his humble reconciliation. He was not a formal heretic, but an overzealous disciplinarian. What he could not learn in his prime as a reformer and purist, he learned in the pain and desolation of imprisonment. It was a fitting symbolic event that Pope Pontian shared his martyrdom.

QUOTE: "Christ, like a skillful physician, understands the weakness of men. He loves to teach the ignorant and the erring he turns again to his own true way. He is easily found by those who live by faith; and to those of pure eye and holy heart, who desire to knock at the door, he opens immediately. He does not disdain the barbarian, nor does he set the eunuch aside as no man. He does not hate the female on account of the woman's act of disobedience in the beginning, nor does he reject the male on account of the man's transgression. But he seeks all, and desires to save all, wishing to make all the children of God, and calling all the saints unto one perfect man" (Hippolytus, *Treatise on Christ and Antichrist*).

Maximilian Mary Kolbe

Priest and Martyr (1894-1941)

"I don't know what's going to become of you!" How many parents have said that? Maximilian Mary Kolbe's reaction was, "I prayed very hard to our Lady to tell me what *would* happen to me. She appeared, holding in her hands two crowns, one white, one red. She asked if I would like to have them—one was for purity, the other for martyrdom. I said, 'I choose both.' She smiled and disappeared." After that he was not the same.

He entered the minor seminary of the Conventual Franciscans in Lwow, Poland, near his birthplace, and at 16 became a novice. Though he later achieved doctorates in philosophy and theology, he was deeply interested in science, even drawing plans for rocket ships.

Ordained at 24, he saw religious indifference as the deadliest poison of the day. His mission was to combat it. He had already founded the Militia of the Immaculata, whose aim was to fight evil with the witness of the good life, prayer, work and suffering. He dreamed of and then founded *Knight of the Immaculata*, a religious magazine under Mary's protection to teach the Gospel to all nations. For the work of publication he established a "City of the Immaculata"—Niepolalanow—which housed 700 of his Franciscan brothers. He later founded one in Nagasaki, Japan. Both the Militia and the magazine ultimately reached the one-million mark in members and subscribers. His love of God was daily filtered through devotion to Mary.

In 1939 the Nazi panzers overran Poland with deadly speed. Niepolalanow was severely bombed. Kolbe and his friars were arrested, then released in less than three months, on the feast of the Immaculate Conception.

In 1941 he was arrested again. The Nazis' purpose was to

liquidate the select ones, the leaders. The end came quickly, in Auschwitz three months later, after terrible beatings and humiliations.

A prisoner had escaped. The commandant announced that ten men would die. He relished walking along the ranks. "This one. That one." As they were being marched away to the starvation bunkers, Number 16670 dared to step from the line. "I would like to take that man's place. He has a wife and children." "Who are you?" "A priest." No name, no mention of fame. Silence. The commandant, dumbfounded, perhaps with a fleeting thought of history, kicked Sergeant Francis Gajowniczek out of line and ordered Father Kolbe to go with the nine. In the "block of death" they were ordered to strip naked and the slow starvation began in darkness. But there was no screaming—the prisoners sang. By the eve of the Assumption four were left alive. The jailer came to finish Kolbe off as he sat in a corner praying. He lifted his fleshless arm to receive the bite of the hypodermic needle. It was filled with carbolic acid. They burned his body with all the others.

COMMENT: Father Kolbe's death was not a sudden, last-minute act of heroism. His whole life had been a preparation. His holiness was a limitless, passionate desire to convert the whole world to God. And his beloved Immaculata was his inspiration.

QUOTE: "Courage, my sons. Don't you see that we are leaving *on a mission?* They pay our fare in the bargain. What a piece of good luck! The thing to do now is to pray well in order to win as many souls as possible. Let us, then, tell the Blessed Virgin that we are content, and that she can do with us anything she wishes" (Maximilian Mary Kolbe, when first arrested).

Assumption

On November 1, 1950, Pius XII defined the Assumption of Mary to be a dogma of faith: "We pronounce, declare and define it to be a divinely revealed dogma that the immaculate Mother of God, the ever Virgin Mary, having completed the course of her earthly life, was assumed body and soul to heavenly glory." The pope proclaimed this dogma only after a broad consultation of bishops, theologians and laity. There were few dissenting voices. What the pope solemnly declared was already a common belief in the Catholic Church.

We find homilies on the Assumption going back to the sixth century. In following centuries the Eastern Churches held steadily to the doctrine, but some authors in the West were hesitant. However, by the 13th century there was universal agreement. The feast was celebrated under various names (Commemoration, Dormition, Passing, Assumption) from at least the fifth or sixth century.

Scripture does not give an account of Mary's Assumption into heaven. Nevertheless, Revelation 12 speaks of a woman who is caught up in the battle between good and evil. Many see this woman as God's people. Since Mary best embodies the people of both Old and New Testament, her Assumption can be seen as an exemplification of the woman's victory. Furthermore, in 1 Corinthians 15:20 Paul speaks of Christ's resurrection as the firstfruits of those who have fallen asleep. Since Mary is closely associated with all the mysteries of Jesus' life, it is not surprising that the Holy Spirit has led the Church to belief in Mary's share in his glorification. So close was she to Jesus on earth, she must be with him body and soul in heaven.

COMMENT: In the light of the Assumption of Mary, it is easy to pray her Magnificat with new meaning. In her glory she proclaims the greatness of the Lord and finds joy in God her savior. God has done marvels to her and she leads others to recognize God's holiness. She is the lowly handmaid who deeply reverenced her God and has been raised to the heights. From her position of strength she will help the lowly and the poor find justice on earth and she will challenge the rich and powerful to distrust wealth and power as a source of happiness.

QUOTE: "In the bodily and spiritual glory which she possesses in heaven, the Mother of Jesus continues in this present world as the image and first flowering of the Church as she is to be perfected in the world to come. Likewise, Mary shines forth on earth, until the day of the Lord shall come (cf. 2 Peter 3:10), as a sign of certain hope and comfort for the pilgrim People of God" (*Constitution on the Church*, 68).

Stephen of Hungary
(975-1038)

The Church is universal, but its expression is always affected—for good or ill—by local culture. There are no "generic" Christians; there are Mexican Christians, Polish Christians, Filipino Christians. This fact is evident in the life of Stephen, national hero and spiritual patron of Hungary.

Born a pagan, he was baptized at about the age of ten, together with his father, chief of the Magyars, a fierce group of marauders who came to the Danube in the ninth century. At 20 he married Gisela, sister to the future emperor St. Henry (July 13). When he succeeded his father, Stephen adopted a policy of

Christianization of the country for both political and religious reasons. He suppressed a series of revolts by pagan nobles and welded the Magyars into a strong national group. He sent to Rome to get ecclesiastical organization—and also to ask the pope to confer the title of king upon him. He was crowned on Christmas day in 1001.

Stephen established a system of tithes to support churches and pastors and to relieve the poor. Out of every 10 towns one had to build a church and support a priest. He abolished pagan customs with a certain amount of violence, and commanded all to marry, except clergy and religious. He was easily accessible to all, especially the poor.

In 1031 his son Emeric died, and the rest of his days were embittered by controversy over his successor. His nephews attempted to kill him. He died in 1038 and was canonized, along with his son, in 1083.

COMMENT: God's gift of holiness is a Christlike love of God and humanity. Love must sometimes bear a stern countenance for the sake of ultimate good. Christ attacked the hypocrisy of the Pharisees, but died forgiving them. Paul excommunicated the incestuous man at Corinth "that his spirit may be saved." Some Christians fought the Crusades with noble zeal, in spite of the unworthy motives of others. Today, after senseless wars, and with a deeper understanding of the complex nature of human motives, we shrink from any use of violence, physical or "silent." This wholesome development continues as people debate whether it is possible for a Christian to be an absolute pacifist or whether evil must sometimes be repelled by force.

QUOTE: "Although the Church has contributed much to the development of culture, experience shows that, because of circumstances, it is sometimes difficult to harmonize culture with Christian teaching.

"These difficulties do not necessarily harm the life of faith.

Indeed they can stimulate the mind to a more accurate and penetrating grasp of the faith. For recent studies and findings of science, history and philosophy raise new questions which influence life and demand new theological investigations" (*Constitution on the Church in the Modern World*, 62).

Jane Frances de Chantal
Religious (1562-1641)

Jane Frances was wife, mother, nun and founder of a religious community. Her mother died when she was 18 months old, and her father, head of parliament at Dijon, France, became the main influence on her education. She developed into a woman of beauty and refinement, lively and cheerful in temperament. At 21 she married Baron de Chantal, by whom she had six children, three of whom died in infancy. At her castle she restored the custom of daily Mass, and was seriously engaged in various charitable works. Her husband was killed after seven years of marriage, and she sank into deep dejection for four months at her family home. Her father-in-law threatened to disinherit her children if she did not return to his home. He was then 75, vain, fierce and extravagant. Jane Frances managed to remain cheerful in spite of him and his insolent housekeeper.

When she was 32 she met St. Francis de Sales, who became her spiritual director, softening some of the severities imposed by her former director. She wanted to become a nun but he persuaded her to defer this decision. She took a vow to remain unmarried and to obey her director.

After three years Francis told her of his plan to found an institute of women which would be a haven for those whose health, age or other considerations barred them from entering the already established orders. There would be no cloister, and they would be free to undertake spiritual and corporal works of mercy. They were primarily intended to exemplify the virtues of Mary at the Visitation (hence their name, the Visitation nuns): humility and meekness.

The usual opposition to women in active ministry arose and Francis de Sales was obliged to make it a cloistered community, with the rule of St. Augustine. Francis wrote his famous *Treatise on the Love of God* for them. The congregation (three women) began when Jane Frances was 45. She underwent great sufferings: Francis de Sales died; her son was killed; a plague ravaged France; her daughter-in-law and son-in-law died. She whipped up the local authorities to great efforts for the victims of the plague and put all the resources of her convent at the disposal of the sick.

During a part of her religious life she had to undergo great trials of the spirit—interior anguish, darkness and spiritual dryness. She died while on a visitation of convents of the community.

COMMENT: It may strike some as unusual that a saint should be subject to spiritual dryness, darkness, interior anguish. We tend to think that such things are the usual condition of "ordinary" sinful people. Some of our lack of spiritual liveliness may indeed be our fault. But the life of faith is still one that is lived in trust, and sometimes the darkness is so great that trust is pressed to its limit.

QUOTE: St. Vincent de Paul said of Jane Frances: "She was full of faith, yet all her life had been tormented by thoughts against it. While apparently enjoying the peace and easiness of mind of souls who have reached a high state of virtue, she suffered such interior trials that she often told me her mind was so filled with all sorts of temptations and abominations that she had to strive not to look within herself...But for all that suffering her face never lost its serenity, nor did she once relax in the fidelity God asked of her. And so I regard her as one of the holiest souls I have ever met on this earth" (*Butler's Lives of the Saints*).

John Eudes
Priest (1601-1680)

How little we know where God's grace will lead. Born on a farm in northern France, John died at 79 in the next "county" or department. In that time he was a religious, a parish missionary, founder of two religious communities and a great promoter of the devotion to the Sacred Heart and the Heart of Mary.

He joined the religious community of the Oratorians and was ordained priest at 24. During severe plagues in 1627 and 1631 he volunteered to care for the stricken in his own diocese. Lest he infect his fellow religious, he lived in a huge cask in the middle of a field during the plague.

At age 32, John became a parish missionary. His gifts as preacher and confessor won him great popularity. He preached over 100 parish missions, some lasting from several weeks to several months.

In his concern with the spiritual improvement of the clergy, he realized that the greatest need was for seminaries. He had permission from his general superior, the bishop and even Cardinal Richelieu to begin this work, but the succeeding general superior disapproved. After prayer and counsel, John decided it was best to leave the religious community. The same year he founded a new one, ultimately called the Eudist (Congregation of Jesus and Mary), devoted to the formation of the clergy by conducting diocesan seminaries. The new venture, while approved by individual bishops, met with immediate opposition, especially from Jansenists and some of his former associates. John founded several seminaries in Normandy, but was unable to get approval from Rome (partly, it was said, because he did not use the most tactful approach).

In his parish mission work John was disturbed by the sad condition of prostitutes who sought to escape their miserable life. Temporary shelters were found but arrangements were not satisfactory. A certain Madeleine Lamy, who had cared for several of the women, one day said to him, "Where are you off to now? To some church, I suppose, where you'll gaze at the images and think yourself pious. And all the time what is really wanted of you is a decent house for these poor creatures." The words, and the laughter of those present, struck deeply within him. The result was another new religious community, called the Sisters of Charity of the Refuge.

He is probably best known for the central theme of his writings: Jesus as the source of holiness, Mary as the model of the Christian life. His devotion to the Sacred Heart and to the Heart of Mary led Pius XI to declare him the father of the liturgical cult of the Hearts of Jesus and Mary.

COMMENT: Holiness is the wholehearted openness to the love of God. It is visibly expressed in many ways, but the variety of expression has one common quality: concern for the needs of others. In John's case, those who were in need were plague-stricken people, ordinary parishioners, those preparing for the priesthood, prostitutes and all Christians called to imitate the love of Jesus and his mother.

QUOTE: "Our wish, our object, our chief preoccupation must be to form Jesus in ourselves, to make his spirit, his devotion, his affections, his desires and his disposition live and reign there. All our religious exercises should be directed to this end. It is the work which God has given us to do unceasingly" (St. John Eudes, *The Life and Reign of Jesus in Christian Souls*).

Bernard

Abbot and Doctor (1091-1153)

Man of the century! Woman of the century! You see such terms
applied to so many today—"golfer of the century," "composer of
the century," "right tackle of the century"—that the line no
longer has any punch. But the "man of the 12th century," without
doubt or controversy, has to be Bernard of Clairvaux. Adviser of
popes, preacher of the Second Crusade, defender of the faith,
healer of a schism, reformer of a monastic order, Scripture
scholar, theologian and eloquent preacher: any one of these titles
would distinguish an ordinary man. Yet Bernard was all of
these—and he still retained a burning desire to return to the
hidden monastic life of his younger days.

In the year 1111, at the age of 16, Bernard left his home to
join the monastic community of Citeaux. His five brothers, two
uncles and some 30 young friends followed him into the
monastery. Within four years a dying community had recovered
enough vitality to establish a new house in the nearby valley of
Wormwoods, with Bernard as abbot. The zealous young man was
quite demanding, though more on himself than others. A slight
breakdown of health taught him to be more patient and
understanding. The valley was soon renamed Clairvaux, the
valley of light.

His ability as arbitrator and counselor became widely
known. More and more he was lured away from the monastery to
settle long-standing disputes. On several of these occasions he
apparently stepped on some sensitive toes in Rome. Bernard was
completely dedicated to the primacy of the Roman See. But to a
letter of warning from Rome he replied that the good fathers in
Rome had enough to do to keep the Church in one piece. If any
matters arose that warranted their interest, he would be the first

to let them know.

Shortly thereafter it was Bernard who intervened in a full-blown schism and settled it in favor of the Roman pontiff against the antipope.

The Holy See prevailed on Bernard to preach the Second Crusade throughout Europe. His eloquence was so overwhelming that a great army was assembled and the success of the crusade seemed assured. The ideals of the men and their leaders, however, were not those of Abbot Bernard, and the project ended as a complete military and moral disaster.

Bernard felt responsible in some way for the degenerative effects of the crusade. This heavy burden possibly hastened his death, which came August 20, 1153.

COMMENT: Bernard's life in the Church was more active than we can imagine possible today. His efforts produced far-reaching results. But he knew that they would have availed little without the many hours of prayer and contemplation that brought him strength and heavenly direction. His life was characterized by a deep devotion to the Blessed Mother. His sermons and books about Mary are still the standard of Marian theology.

QUOTE: "In dangers, in doubts, in difficulties, think of Mary, call upon Mary. Let not her name depart from your lips, never suffer it to leave your heart. And that you may more surely obtain the assistance of her prayer, neglect not to walk in her footsteps. With her for guide, you shall never go astray; while invoking her, you shall never lose heart; so long as she is in your mind, you are safe from deception; while she holds your hand, you cannot fall; under her protection you have nothing to fear; if she walks before you, you shall not grow weary; if she shows you favor, you shall reach the goal" (St. Bernard).

Pius X

Pope (1835-1914)

Pope Pius X is perhaps best remembered for his encouragement of the frequent reception of Holy Communion, especially by children.

The second of 10 children in a poor Italian family, Joseph Sarto became Pius X at 68, one of the 20th century's greatest popes.

Ever mindful of his humble origin, he stated, "I was born poor, I lived poor, I will die poor." He was embarrassed by some of the pomp of the papal court. "Look how they have dressed me up," he said in tears to an old friend. To another, "It is a penance to be forced to accept all these practices. They lead me around surrounded by soldiers like Jesus when he was seized in Gethsemane."

Interested in politics, he encouraged Italian Catholics to become more politically involved. One of his first papal acts was to end the supposed right of governments to interfere by veto in papal elections—a practice that threatened the freedom of the conclave in which he was elected.

In 1905, when France renounced its agreement with the Holy See and threatened confiscation of Church property if governmental control of Church affairs were not granted, Pius X courageously rejected the demand.

While he did not author a famous social encyclical as his predecessor had done, he denounced the ill treatment of the Indians on the plantations of Peru, sent a relief commission to Messina after an earthquake and sheltered refugees at his own expense.

On the 11th anniversary of his election as pope, Europe was plunged into World War I. Pius had foreseen it, but it killed him.

"This is the last affliction the Lord will visit on me. I would gladly give my life to save my poor children from this ghastly scourge." He died a few weeks after the war began.

COMMENT: His humble background was no obstacle in relating to a personal God and to people whom he loved genuinely. He gained his strength, his gentleness and warmth for people from the source of all gifts, the Spirit of Jesus. In contrast, we often feel embarrassed by our backgrounds. Shame makes us prefer to remain aloof from people whom we perceive as superior. If we are in a superior position, on the other hand, we often ignore simpler people. Yet we, too, have to help "restore all things in Christ," especially the wounded people of God.

QUOTE: Describing Pius X, a historian wrote that he was "a man of God who knew the unhappiness of the world and the hardships of life, and in the greatness of his heart wanted to comfort everyone."

Queenship of Mary

Pius XII established this feast in 1954. But Mary's queenship has roots in Scripture. At the Annunciation Gabriel announced that Mary's Son would receive the throne of David and rule forever. At the Visitation Elizabeth calls Mary "mother of my Lord." As in all the mysteries of Mary's life, Mary is closely associated with Jesus: Her queenship is a share in Jesus' kingship. We can also recall that in the Old Testament the mother of the king has great influence in court.

In the fourth century St. Ephrem called Mary Lady and

Queen and Fathers and Doctors continued to use the title. Hymns of the 11th to 13th centuries address Mary as queen: "Hail, Holy Queen," "Hail, Queen of Heaven," "Queen of Heaven." The Dominican rosary and the Franciscan crown as well as numerous invocations in Mary's litany celebrate her queenship.

The feast is a logical follow-up to the Assumption and is now celebrated on the octave day of that feast. In his encyclical *To the Queen of Heaven* Pius XII points out that Mary deserves the title because she is Mother of God, because she is closely associated as the New Eve with Jesus' redemptive work, because of her preeminent perfection and because of her intercessory power.

COMMENT: As St. Paul suggests in Roman 8:28-30, God has predestined human beings from all eternity to share the image of his Son. All the more was Mary predestined to be the mother of Jesus. As Jesus was to be king of all creation, Mary, in dependence on Jesus, was to be queen. All other titles to queenship derive from this eternal intention of God. As Jesus exercised his kingship on earth by serving his Father and his fellow human beings, so did Mary exercise her queenship. As the glorified Jesus remains with us as our king till the end of time (Matthew 28:20), so does Mary, who was assumed into heaven and crowned queen of heaven and earth.

QUOTE: "Let the entire body of the faithful pour forth persevering prayer to the Mother of God and Mother of men. Let them implore that she who aided the beginnings of the Church by her prayers may now, exalted as she is in heaven above all the saints and angels, intercede with her Son in the fellowship of all the saints. May she do so until all the peoples of the human family, whether they are honored with the name of Christian or whether they still do not know their Savior, are happily gathered together in peace and harmony into the one People of God, for the glory of the Most Holy and Undivided Trinity" (*Constitution on the Church*, 69).

Rose of Lima

Virgin (1586-1617)

The first canonized saint of the New World has one characteristic of all saints—the suffering of opposition—and another characteristic which is more for admiration than for imitation—excessive practice of mortification.

She was born to parents of Spanish descent in Lima, Peru, at a time when South America was in its first century of evangelization. She seems to have taken Catherine of Siena as a model, in spite of the objections and ridicule of parents and friends.

The saints have so great a love of God that what seems bizarre to us, and is indeed sometimes imprudent, is simply a logical carrying out of a conviction that *anything* that might endanger a loving relationship with God must be rooted out. So, because her beauty was so often admired, Rose used to rub her face with pepper to produce disfiguring blotches. Later, she wore a thick circlet of silver on her head, studded on the inside, like a crown of thorns.

When her parents fell into financial trouble, she worked in the garden all day and sewed at night. Ten years of struggle against her parents began when they tried to make Rose marry. They refused to let her enter a convent, and out of obedience she continued her life of penance and solitude at home as a member of the Third Order of St. Dominic. So deep was her desire to live the life of Christ that she spent most of her time at home in solitude.

During the last few years of her life, Rose set up a room in the house where she cared for homeless children, the elderly and the sick. This was a beginning of social services in Peru. Though secluded in life and activity, she was brought to the attention of

Inquisition interrogators, who could only say that she was influenced by grace.

What might have been a merely eccentric life was transfigured from the inside. If we remember some unusual penances, we should also remember the greatest thing about Rose: a love of God so ardent that it withstood ridicule from without, violent temptation and lengthy periods of sickness. When she died at 31, the city turned out for her funeral. Prominent men took turns carrying her coffin.

COMMENT: It is easy to dismiss "excessive" penances of the saints as the expression of a certain culture or temperament. But a woman wearing a crown of thorns may at least prod our consciences. We enjoy the most comfort-oriented life in human history. We eat too much, drink too much, use a million gadgets, fill our eyes and ears with everything imaginable. Commerce thrives on creating useless needs to spend our money on. It seems that when we have become most like slaves, there is the greatest talk of "freedom." Are we willing to discipline ourselves in such an atmosphere?

QUOTE: "If your hand or your foot causes you to sin, cut it off and throw it away. It is better for you to enter into life maimed or crippled than with two hands or two feet to be thrown into eternal fire. And if your eye causes you to sin, tear it out and throw it away. It is better for you to enter into life with one eye than with two eyes to be thrown into fiery Gehenna" (Matthew 18:8-9).

Bartholomew

Apostle

In the New Testament, Bartholomew is mentioned only in the lists of the apostles. Some scholars identify him with Nathanael, a man of Cana in Galilee who was summoned to Jesus by Philip. Jesus paid him a great compliment: "Here is a true Israelite. There is no duplicity in him" (John 1:47b). When Nathanael asked how Jesus knew him, Jesus said, "I saw you under the fig tree" (John 1:48b). Whatever amazing revelation this involved, it brought Nathanael to exclaim, "Rabbi, you are the Son of God; you are the King of Israel" (John 1:49b). But Jesus countered with, "Do you believe because I told you that I saw you under the fig tree? You will see greater things than this" (John 1:50b).

Nathanael did see greater things. He was one of those to whom Jesus appeared on the shore of the Sea of Tiberias after his resurrection (see John 21:1-14). They had been fishing all night without success. In the morning, they saw someone standing on the shore though no one knew it was Jesus. He told them to cast their net again, and they made so great a catch that they could not haul the net in. Then John cried out to Peter, "It is the Lord."

When they brought the boat to shore, they found a fire burning, with some fish laid on it and some bread. Jesus asked them to bring some of the fish they had caught, and invited them to come and eat their meal. John relates that although they knew it was Jesus, none of the apostles presumed to inquire who he was. This, John notes, was the third time Jesus appeared to the apostles.

COMMENT: Bartholomew or Nathanael? We are confronted again with the fact that we know almost nothing about most of the apostles. Yet the unknown ones were also foundation stones, the

12 pillars of the new Israel whose 12 tribes now encompass the whole earth. Their personalities were secondary (without thereby being demeaned) to their great office of bearing tradition from their firsthand experience, speaking in the name of Jesus, putting the Word made flesh into human words for the enlightenment of the world. Their holiness was not an introverted contemplation of their status before God. It was a gift that they had to share with others. The Good News was that all are called to the holiness of being Christ's members, by the gracious gift of God.

The simple fact is that humanity is totally meaningless unless God is its total concern. Then humanity, made holy with God's own holiness, becomes the most precious creation of God.

QUOTE: "Like Christ himself, the apostles were unceasingly bent upon bearing witness to the truth of God. They showed special courage in speaking 'the word of God with boldness' (Acts 4:31) before the people and their rulers. With a firm faith they held that the gospel is indeed the power of God unto salvation for all who believe....They followed the example of the gentleness and respectfulness of Christ" (*Declaration on Religious Freedom*, 11).

OPTIONAL

Louis

(1226-1270)

At his coronation as king of France, Louis bound himself by oath to behave as God's anointed, as the father of his people and feudal lord of the King of Peace. Other kings had done the same, of course. Louis was different in that he actually interpreted his kingly duties in the light of faith. After the violence of two previous reigns, he brought peace and justice.

He was crowned king at 12, at his father's death. His mother, Blanche of Castile, ruled during his minority. When he was 19, (and his bride 12) he was married to Marguerite of Province. It was a loving marriage, despite her arrogant and restless nature. They had 10 children.

Louis "took the cross" for a Crusade when he was 30. His army took Damietta on the Nile but not long after, weakened by dysentery and without support, they were surrounded and captured. Louis obtained the release of the army by giving up the city of Damietta in addition to paying a ransom. He stayed in Syria four years.

He is admired as a crusader, but perhaps greater credit is due him for his concern for justice in civil administration. He drew up regulations for his officials which became the first of a series of reform laws. He replaced trial by battle with a form of examination of witnesses and encouraged the beginning of using written records in court.

Louis was always respectful of the papacy, but defended royal interests against the popes and refused to acknowledge Innocent IV's sentence against the emperor Frederick II.

He was devoted to his people, founding hospitals, visiting the sick and, like his patron St. Francis, caring even for people with leprosy. (He is one of the patrons of the Third Order of St. Francis.) Louis united France—lords and townsfolk, peasants and priests and knights—by the force of his personality and holiness. For many years the nation was at peace.

Disturbed by new Moslem advances in Syria, he led another Crusade in 1267, at the age of 41. His Crusade was diverted to Tunis for his brother's sake. The army was decimated by disease within a month, and Louis himself died on foreign soil at the age of 44. He was canonized 27 years later.

COMMENT: Louis was strong-willed, strong-minded. His word was trusted utterly, and his courage in action was remarkable. What is most remarkable was his sense of respect for anyone with whom he dealt, especially the "humble folk of the Lord." To care for his people he built cathedrals, churches, libraries, hospitals and orphanages. He dealt with princes honestly and equitably. He hoped to be treated the same way by the King of Kings, to whom he gave his life, his family and his country.

STORY: Every day Louis had 13 special guests from among the poor to eat with him, and a large number of poor were served meals near his palace. During Advent and Lent all who presented themselves were given a meal, and Louis often served them in person. He kept lists of needy people, whom he regularly relieved, in every province of his dominion.

Joseph Calasanz
Priest (1556-1648)

From Aragon, where he was born in 1556, to Rome, where he died 92 years later, fortune alternately smiled and frowned on the work of Joseph Calasanz. A priest with university training in canon law and theology, respected for his wisdom and administrative expertise, he put aside his career because he was deeply concerned with the need for education of poor children. When he was unable to get other institutes to undertake this apostolate at Rome, he and several companions personally provided a free school for deprived children. So overwhelming was the response that there was a constant need for larger facilities to house their effort. Soon Pope Clement VIII gave support to the school, and this aid continued under Pope Paul V. Other schools were opened; other men were attracted to the work and in 1621 the community (for so the teachers lived) was recognized as a religious community, the Clerks Regular of Religious Schools (Piarists or Scolopi). Not long after, Joseph was appointed superior for life.

A combination of various prejudices and political ambition and maneuvering was to cause the institute much turmoil. Some did not favor educating the poor, for education would leave the poor dissatisfied with their lowly tasks for society! Others were shocked that some of the Piarists were sent for instruction to Galileo (a friend of Joseph) as superior, thus dividing the members into opposite camps. Repeatedly investigated by papal commissions, Joseph was demoted; when the struggle within the institute persisted, the Piarists were suppressed. Only after Joseph's death were they restored to status as a religious community.

COMMENT: No one knew better than Joseph the need for the work he was doing; no one knew better than he how baseless were the charges brought against him. Yet if he were to work within the Church, he realized that he must submit to its authority, that he must accept a setback if he was unable to convince authorized investigators. While the prejudice, the scheming, and the ignorance of men often keep the truth from emerging for a long period of time, Joseph was convinced, even under suppression, that his institute would again be recognized and authorized. With this trust he joined exceptional patience and a genuine spirit of forgiveness.

QUOTE: Even in the days after his own demotion, Joseph protected his persecutors against his enraged partisans; and when the community was suppressed, he stated with Job, to whom he was often compared: "The LORD gave and the LORD has taken away;/blessed be the name of the LORD!" (Job 1:21b).

Monica

(322?-387)

The circumstances of St. Monica's life could have made her a nagging wife, a bitter daughter-in-law and a despairing parent, yet she did not give way to any of these temptations. Although she was a Christian, her parents gave her in marriage to a pagan, Patricius, who lived in her hometown of Tagaste in North Africa. Patricius had some redeeming features, but he had a violent temper and was licentious. Monica also had to bear with a cantankerous mother-in-law who lived in her home. Patricius criticized his wife because of her charity and piety, but always respected her. Monica's prayers and example finally won her husband and mother-in-law to Christianity. Her husband died in 371, one year after his baptism.

Monica had at least three children who survived infancy. The oldest, Augustine, is the most famous. At the time of his father's death, Augustine was 17 and a rhetoric student in Carthage. Monica was distressed to learn that her son had accepted the Manichean heresy and was living an immoral life. For a while, she refused to let him eat or sleep in her house. Then one night she had a vision that assured her Augustine would return to the faith. From that time on she stayed close to her son, praying and fasting for him. In fact, she often stayed much closer that Augustine wanted.

When he was 29, Augustine decided to go to Rome to teach rhetoric. Monica was determined to go along. One night he told his mother that he was going to the dock to say good-bye to a friend. Instead, he set sail for Rome. Monica was heartbroken when she learned of Augustine's trick, but she still followed him. She arrived in Rome only to find that he had left for Milan. Although travel was difficult, Monica pursued him to Milan.

In Milan Augustine came under the influence of the bishop, St. Ambrose, who also became Monica's spiritual director. She accepted his advice in everything and had the humility to give up some practices that had become second nature to her (see Quote, below). Monica became a leader of the devout women in Milan as she had been in Tagaste.

She continued her prayers for Augustine during his years of instruction. At Easter, 387, St. Ambrose baptized Augustine and several of his friends. Soon after, his party left for Africa. Although no one else was aware of it, Monica knew her life was near the end. She told Augustine, "Son, nothing in this world now affords me delight. I do not know what there is now left for me to do or why I am still here, all my hopes in this world being now fulfilled." She became ill shortly after and suffered severely for nine days before her death.

Almost all we know about St. Monica is in the writings of St. Augustine, especially his *Confessions*.

COMMENT: Today, with our instant cereal, instant cures and instant credit, we have little patience for things that take time. Likewise, we want instant answers to our prayers. Monica is a model of patience. Her long years of prayer, coupled with a strong, well-disciplined character, finally led to the conversion of her hot-tempered husband, her cantankerous mother-in-law and her brilliant but wayward son, Augustine.

QUOTE: When Monica moved from North Africa to Milan, she found religious practices new to her and also that some of her former customs, such as a Saturday fast, were not common there. She asked St. Ambrose which customs she should follow. His classic reply was: "When I am here, I do not fast on Saturday, but I fast when I am in Rome; do the same and always follow the custom and discipline of the Church as it is observed in the particular locality in which you find yourself."

Augustine
Bishop and Doctor (354-430)

A Christian at 33, a priest at 36, a bishop at 41: everyone is familiar with the biographical sketch of Augustine of Hippo, sinner turned saint. But really to get to know the man is a rewarding experience.

There quickly surfaces the intensity with which he lived his life, whether his path led away from or toward God. The tears of his mother, the instructions of Ambrose and, most of all, God himself speaking to him in the Scriptures redirected Augustine's love of life to a life of love.

Having been so deeply immersed in creature-pride of life in his early days and having drunk deeply of its bitter dregs, it is not surprising that Augustine should have turned, with a holy fierceness, against the many demon-thrusts rampant in his day. His times were truly decadent—politically, socially, morally. He was both feared and loved, like the Master. The perennial criticism leveled against him: a fundamental rigorism.

In his day, he providentially fulfilled the office of prophet. Like Jeremiah and other greats, he was hard-pressed but could not keep quiet. "I say to myself, I will not mention him,/I will speak in his name no more./But then it becomes like fire burning in my heart,/imprisoned in my bones;/I grow weary holding it in,/I cannot endure it" (Jeremiah 20:9).

COMMENT: Augustine is still acclaimed and condemned in our day. (cf. *Whatever Became of Sin?* by Karl Menninger). He is a prophet for today, trumpeting the need to scrap escapisms and stand face-to-face with personal responsibility and dignity.

QUOTE: "Too late have I loved you, O Beauty of ancient days, yet ever new! Too late I loved you! And behold, you were within, and I abroad, and there I searched for you; I was deformed, plunging amid those fair forms, which you had made. You were with me, but I was not with you. Things held me far from you—things which, if they were not in you, were not at all. You called, and shouted, and burst my deafness. You flashed and shone, and scattered my blindness. You breathed odors and I drew in breath—and I pant for you. I tasted, and I hunger and thirst. You touched me, and I burned for your peace" (St. Augustine, *Confessions*).

Beheading of John the Baptist
Martyr

The drunken oath of a king with a shallow sense of honor, a seductive dance and the hateful heart of a queen joined together to bring about the martyrdom of John the Baptist. The greatest of prophets suffered the fate of so many Old Testament prophets before him: rejection and martyrdom. The "voice crying in the desert" did not hesitate to accuse the guilty, did not hesitate to speak the truth. But why? What possesses a man that he would give us his very life?

This great religious reformer was sent by God to prepare the people for the Messiah. His vocation was one of selfless giving. The only power that he claimed was the Spirit of Yahweh. "I am baptizing you with water, for repentance, but the one who is coming after me is mightier than I. I am not worthy to carry his sandals. He who will baptize you with the Holy Spirit and fire" (Matthew 3:11). Scripture tells us that many people followed John looking to him for hope, perhaps in anticipation of some great Messianic power. John never allowed himself the false honor of receiving these people for his own glory. He knew his calling was one of preparation. When the time came, he led his disciples to Jesus: "The next day John was there again with two of his disciples, and as he watched Jesus walk by, he said, 'Behold, the Lamb of God.' The two disciples heard what he said and followed Jesus" (John 1:35-37).

It is John the Baptist who has pointed the way to Christ. John's life and death were a giving over of self for God and man. His simple style of life was one of complete detachment from earthly possessions. His heart was centered on God and the call that he heard from the Spirit of God speaking to his heart. Confident of God's grace, he had the courage to speak words of condemnation or repentance, of salvation.

COMMENT: Each person has a calling to which he must listen. No one will ever repeat the mission of John, and yet all of us are called to that very mission. It is the role of the Christian to witness to Jesus. Whatever our position in this world, we are called to be disciples of Christ. By our words and deeds others should realize that we live in the joy of knowing that Jesus is Lord. We do not have to depend upon our own limited resources, but can draw strength from the vastness of Christ's saving grace.

QUOTE: "So they came to John and said to him, 'Rabbi, the one who was with you across the Jordan, to whom you testified, here he is baptizing and everyone is coming to him.' John answered and said, 'No one can receive anything except what has been given him from heaven. You yourselves can testify that I said [that] I am not the Messiah, but that I was sent before him. The one who has the bride is the bridegroom; the best man, who stands and listens for him, rejoices greatly at the bridegroom's voice. So this joy of mine has been made complete. He must increase; I must decrease' " (John 3:26-30).

225

Gregory the Great

Pope and Doctor (540?-604)

Coming events cast their shadows before: Gregory was the prefect of Rome before he was 30. After five years in office, he resigned, founded six monasteries on his Sicilian estate, and became a Benedictine monk in his own home at Rome.

Ordained a priest, he became one of the pope's seven deacons, and also served six years in the East as papal nuncio in Constantinople. He was recalled to become abbot, and at the age of 50 was elected pope by the clergy and people of Rome.

He was direct and firm. He removed unworthy priests from office, forbade taking money for many services, emptied the papal treasury to ransom prisoners of the Lombards and to care for persecuted Jews and the victims of plague and famine. He was very concerned about the conversion of England, sending 40 monks from his own monastery. He is known for his reform of the liturgy, for strengthening respect for doctrine. Whether he was largely responsible for the revision of "Gregorian" chant is disputed.

Gregory lived in a time of perpetual strife with invading Lombards and difficult relations with the East. When Rome itself was under attack, it was he who went to interview the Lombard king.

An Anglican historian has written: "It is impossible to conceive what would have been the confusion, the lawlessness, the chaotic state of the middle ages without the medieval papacy; and of the medieval papacy, the real father is Gregory the Great."

His book, *Pastoral Care*, on the duties and qualities of a bishop, was read for centuries after his death. He described bishops mainly as physicians whose main duties were preaching and the enforcement of discipline. In his own down-to-earth preaching, Gregory was skilled at applying the daily Gospel to the needs of his listeners.

Called "the Great," Gregory has been given a place with Augustine, Ambrose and Jerome as one of the four key doctors of the Western Church.

COMMENT: Gregory was content to be a monk, but he willingly served the Church in other ways when asked. He sacrificed his own preferences in many ways, especially when he was called to be bishop of Rome. Once he was called to public service, Gregory gave his considerable energies completely to this work.

QUOTE: "Perhaps it is not after all so difficult for a man to part with his possessions, but it is certainly most difficult for him to part with himself. To renounce what one has is a minor thing; but to renounce what one is, that is asking a lot" (St. Gregory, *Homilies on the Gospels*).

Birth of Mary

The Church has celebrated Mary's birth since at least the sixth century. A September birth was chosen because the Eastern Church begins its Church year with September. The September 8 date helped determine the date for the feast of the Immaculate Conception on December 8 (nine months earlier).

Scripture does not give an account of Mary's birth. However, the apocryphal *Protoevangelium of James* fills in the gap. This work has no historical value, but it does reflect the development of Christian piety. According to this account, Anna and Joachim are infertile but pray for a child. They receive the promise of a child that will advance God's plan of salvation for the world. Such a story (like many biblical counterparts) stresses the special presence of God in Mary's life from the beginning.

St. Augustine connects Mary's birth with Jesus' saving work. He tells the earth to rejoice and shine forth in the light of her birth. "She is the flower of the field from whom bloomed the precious lily of the valley. Through her birth the nature inherited from our first parents is changed." The opening prayer at Mass speaks of the birth of Mary's Son as the dawn of our salvation and asks for an increase of peace.

COMMENT: We can see every human birth as a call for new hope in the world. The love of two human beings has joined with God in his creative work. The loving parents have shown hope in a world filled with travail. The new child has the potential to be a channel of God's love and peace to the world.

This is all true in a magnificent way in Mary. If Jesus is the perfect expression of God's love, Mary is the foreshadowing of that love. If Jesus has brought the fullness of salvation, Mary is its dawning.

Birthday celebrations bring happiness to the celebrant as well as to family and friends. Next to the birth of Jesus, Mary's birth offers the greatest possible happiness to the world. Each time we celebrate her birth we can confidently hope for an increase of peace in our hearts and in the world at large.

QUOTE: "Today the barren Anna claps her hands for joy, the earth radiates with light, kings sing their happiness, priests enjoy every blessing, the entire universe rejoices, for she who is queen and the Father's immaculate bride buds forth from the stem of Jesse" (adapted from *Byzantine Daily Worship*).

Peter Claver

Priest (1581-1654)

A native of Spain, young Jesuit Peter Claver left his homeland forever in 1610 to be a missionary in the colonies of the New World. He sailed into Cartagena (now in Columbia), a rich port city washed by the Caribbean. He was ordained there in 1615.

By this time the slave trade had been established in the Americas for nearly 100 years, and Cartegena was a chief center for it. Ten thousand slaves poured into the port each year after crossing the Atlantic from West Africa under conditions so foul and inhuman that an estimated one-third of the passengers died in transit. Although the practice of slave-trading was condemned by Pope Paul III and later labeled "supreme villainy" by Pius IX, it continued to flourish.

Peter Claver's predecessor, Jesuit Father Alfonso de Sandoval, had devoted himself to the service of the slaves for 40 years before Claver arrived to continue his work, declaring himself "the slave of the Negroes forever."

As soon as a slave ship entered the port, Peter Claver moved into its infested hold to minister to the ill-treated and miserable passengers. After the slaves were herded out of the ship like chained animals and shut up in nearby yards to be gazed at by the crowds, Claver plunged in among them with medicines, food, bread, brandy, lemons and tobacco. With the help of interpreters, he gave basic instructions and assured his brothers and sisters of their human dignity and God's saving love. During the 40 years of his ministry, Claver instructed and baptized an estimated 300,000 slaves.

His apostolate extended beyond his care for slaves. He became a moral force, indeed, the apostle of Cartagena. He preached in the city square, gave missions to sailors and traders as well as country missions, during which he avoided, when possible, the hospitality of the planters and owners and lodged in the slave quarters instead.

After four years of sickness which forced the saint to remain inactive and largely neglected, he died on September 8, 1654. The city magistrates, who had previously frowned at his solicitude for the black outcasts, ordered that he should be buried at public expense and with great pomp.

He was canonized in 1888, and Pope Leo XIII declared him the worldwide patron of missionary work among black slaves.

COMMENT: The Holy Spirit's might and power is manifested in the striking decisions and bold actions of Peter Claver. A decision to leave one's homeland never to return reveals a gigantic act of will difficult for the contemporary mind to imagine. Peter's determination to serve forever the most abused, rejected and lowly of all people is stunningly heroic. When we measure our lives against such a man's, we became aware of our own barely used potential and of our need to open ourselves more to the jolting power of Jesus' Spirit.

QUOTE: Peter Claver understood that concrete service like the distributing of medicine, food or brandy to his black brothers and sisters could be as effective a communication of the word of God as mere *verbal* preaching. As Peter Claver often said, "We must speak to them with our hands before we try to speak to them with our lips."

John Chrysostom
Bishop and Doctor (d. 407)

The ambiguity and intrigue surrounding John, the great preacher
(his name means "golden-mouthed") from Antioch, are
characteristic of the life of any great man in a capital city.
Brought to Constantinople after a dozen years of priestly service
in Syria, John found himself the reluctant victim of an imperial
ruse to make him bishop in the greatest city of the empire.
Ascetic, unimposing but dignified, and troubled by stomach
ailments from his desert days as a monk, John began his
episcopate under the cloud of imperial politics.

If his body was weak, his tongue was powerful. The content
of his sermons, his exegesis of Scripture, were never without a
point. Sometimes the point stung the high and mighty. Some
sermons lasted up to two hours.

His life-style at the imperial court was not appreciated by
some courtiers. He offered a modest table to episcopal sycophants
hanging around for imperial and ecclesiastical favors. John
deplored the court protocol that accorded him precedence before
the highest state officials. He would not be a kept man.

His zeal led him to decisive action. Bishops who bribed their
way into their office were deposed. Many of his sermons called for
concrete steps to share wealth with the poor. The rich did not
appreciate hearing from John that private property existed
because of Adam's fall from grace any more than married men
liked to hear that they were bound to marital fidelity just as much
as their wives. When it came to justice and charity, John
acknowledged no double standards.

Aloof, energetic, outspoken, especially when he became
excited in the pulpit, John was a sure target for criticism and
personal trouble. He was accused of gorging himself secretly on

rich wines and fine foods. His faithfulness as spiritual director to the rich widow, Olympia, provoked much gossip attempting to prove him a hypocrite where wealth and chastity were concerned. His action taken against unworthy bishops in Asia Minor was viewed by other ecclesiastics as a greedy, uncanonical extension of his authority.

Two prominent personages who personally undertook to discredit John were Theophilus, archbishop of Alexandria, and the empress Eudoxia. Theophilus feared the growth in importance of the bishop of Constantinople and took occasion to charge John with fostering heresy. Theophilus and other angered bishops were supported by Eudoxia. The empress resented his sermons contrasting gospel values with the excesses of imperial court life. Whether intended or not, sermons mentioning the lurid Jezebel and impious Herodias were associated with the empress, who finally did manage to have John exiled. He died in exile in 407.

COMMENT: John Chrysostom's preaching, by word and example, exemplifies the role of the prophet to comfort the disturbed and to disturb the comfortable. For his honesty and courage he paid the price of a turbulent ministry as bishop, personal vilification and exile.

QUOTE: Bishops "should set forth the ways by which are to be solved very grave questions concerning the ownership, increase, and just distribution of material goods, peace and war, and brotherly relations among all people" (*Decree on the Bishops' Pastoral Office*, 12).

Triumph of the Cross

Early in the fourth century St. Helena, mother of the Roman
Emperor Constantine, went to Jerusalem in search of the holy
places of Christ's life. She razed the Temple of Aphrodite, which
tradition held was built over the Savior's tomb, and her son built
the Basilica of the Holy Sepulcher over the tomb. During the
excavation, workers found three crosses. Legend has it that the
one on which Jesus died was identified when its touch healed a
dying woman.

The cross immediately became an object of veneration. At
a Good Friday celebration in Jerusalem toward the end of the
fourth century, according to an eyewitness, the wood was taken
out of its silver container and placed on a table together with the
inscription Pilate ordered placed above Jesus' head. Then "all the
people pass through one by one; all of them bow down, touching
the cross and the inscription, first with their foreheads, then with
their eyes; and, after kissing the cross, they move on."

To this day the Eastern Churches, Catholic and Orthodox
alike, celebrate the Exaltation of the Holy Cross on the
September anniversary of the basilica's dedication. The feast
entered the Western calendar in the seventh century after
Emperor Heraclius recovered it from the Persians, who had
carried it off in 614, 15 years earlier. According to the story, the
emperor intended to carry the cross back into Jerusalem himself,
but was unable to move forward until he put off his imperial garb
and became a barefoot pilgrim.

COMMENT: The cross is today the universal image of Christian
belief. Countless generations of artists have turned it into a thing
of beauty to be carried in procession or worn as jewelry. To the
eyes of the first Christians, it had no beauty. It stood outside too

233

many city walls, decorated only with decaying corpses, as a threat to anyone who defied Rome's authority—including the heretic sect which refused sacrifice to Roman gods. Although believers spoke of the cross as the instrument of salvation, it seldom appeared in Christian art unless disguised as an anchor or the Chi-Rho until after Constantine's edict of toleration.

QUOTE: "How splendid the cross of Christ! It brings life, not death; light, not darkness; Paradise, not its loss. It is the wood on which the Lord, like a great warrior, was wounded in hands and feet and side, but healed thereby our wounds. A tree has destroyed us, a tree now brought us life" (Theodore of Studios).

SEPTEMBER 15   MEMORIAL

Our Lady of Sorrows

For a while there were two feasts in honor of the Sorrowful Mother: one going back to the 15th century, the other to the 17th century. For a while both were celebrated by the universal Church: one on the Friday before Palm Sunday, the other in September.

The principal biblical references to Mary's sorrows are in Luke 2:35 and John 19:26-27. The Lucan passage is Simeon's prediction about a sword piercing Mary's soul; the Johannine passage relates Jesus' words to Mary and to the beloved disciple.

Many early Church writers interpret the sword as Mary's sorrows, especially as she saw Jesus die on the cross. Thus, the two passages are brought together as prediction and fulfillment.

St. Ambrose in particular sees Mary as a sorrowful yet powerful figure at the cross. Mary stood fearlessly at the cross while others fled. Mary looked on her Son's wounds with pity, but saw in them the salvation of the world. As Jesus hung on the cross, Mary did not fear to be killed but offered herself to her persecutors.

COMMENT: John's account of Jesus' death is highly symbolic. When Jesus gives the beloved disciple to Mary, we are invited to appreciate Mary's role in the Church: She symbolizes the Church; the beloved disciple represents all believers. As Mary mothered Jesus, she is now mother to all his followers. Furthermore, as Jesus died, he handed over his Spirit. Mary and the Spirit cooperate in begetting new children of God—almost an echo of Luke's account of Jesus' conception. Christians can trust that they will continue to experience the caring presence of Mary and Jesus' Spirit throughout their lives and throughout history.

QUOTE: "At the cross her station keeping,
Stood the mournful mother weeping,
Close to Jesus to the last.
Through her heart, his sorrow sharing,
All his bitter anguish bearing,
Now at length the sword has passed."

(*Stabat Mater*)

Cornelius and Cyprian

Pope and Martyr; Bishop and Martyr

Cornelius (d. 253). There was no pope for 14 months after the martyrdom of St. Fabian because of the intensity of the persecution of the Church. During the interval, the Church was governed by a college of priests. St. Cyprian, a friend of Cornelius, writes that he was elected pope "by the judgment of God and of Christ, by the testimony of most of the clergy, by the vote of the people, with the consent of aged priests and of good men."

The greatest problem of Cornelius's two-year term as pope had to do with the Sacrament of Penance and centered on the readmission of Christians who had apostatized during the time of persecution. Two extremes were finally both condemned. Cyprian, primate of Africa, appealed to the pope to confirm his stand that the relapsed could be reconciled only by the decision of the bishop (against the very indulgent practice of Novatus).

In Rome, however, Cornelius met with the opposite view. After his election, a priest named Novatian (one of those who had governed the Church) had himself consecrated a rival bishop of Rome—the first antipope. He denied that the Church had any power to reconcile not only the apostates, but also those guilty of murder, adultery, fornication or second marriage! Cornelius had the support of most of the Church (especially of Cyprian of Africa) in condemning Novatianism, though the sect persisted for several centuries. Cornelius held a synod at Rome in 251 and ordered the "relapsed" to be restored to the Church with the usual "medicines of repentance."

The friendship of Cornelius and Cyprian was strained for a time when one of Cyprian's rivals made accusations about him. But the problem was cleared up.

A document from Cornelius shows the extent of organization in the Church of Rome in the mid-third century: 46 priests, seven deacons, seven subdeacons. It is estimated that the number of Christians totaled about 50,000.

Cornelius died as a result of the hardships of his exile in what is now Civita Vecchia.

COMMENT: It seems fairly true to say that almost every possible false doctrine has been proposed at some time or other in the history of the Church. The third century saw the resolution of a problem we scarcely consider—the penance to be done before reconciliation with the Church after mortal sin. Men like Cornelius and Cyprian were God's instruments in helping the Church find a prudent path between extremes of rigorism and laxity. They are part of the Church's ever-living stream of tradition, ensuring the continuance of what was begun by Christ, and evaluating new experiences through the wisdom and experience of those who have gone before (Roliner).

QUOTE: "There is one God and one Christ and but one episcopal chair, originally founded on Peter, by the Lord's authority. There cannot, therefore, be set up another altar or another priesthood. Whatever any man in his rage or rashness shall appoint, in defiance of the divine institution, must be a spurious, profane and sacrilegious ordinance" (St. Cyprian, *The Unity of the Catholic Church*).

Cyprian (d. 258). Cyprian is important in the development of Christian thought and practice in the third century, especially in northern Africa.

Highly educated, a famous orator, he was converted to Christianity as an adult. He distributed his goods to the poor, and amazed his fellow citizens by making a vow of chastity before his baptism. Within two years he had been ordained priest and was chosen, against his will, as bishop of Carthage (near modern Tunis).

Cyprian complained that the peace the Church had enjoyed had weakened the spirit of many Christians and had opened the door to converts who did not have the true spirit of faith. When the Decian persecution began, many Christians easily abandoned the Church. It was their reinstatement that caused the great controversies of the third century, and helped the Church progress in its understanding of the Sacrament of Penance. Novatus, a priest who had opposed Cyprian's election, set himself up in Cyprian's absence (he had fled to a hiding place from which to direct the Church—bringing criticism on himself) and received back all apostates without imposing any canonical penance. Ultimately he was condemned. Cyprian held a middle course, holding that those who had actually sacrificed to idols could receive Communion only at death, whereas those who had only bought certificates saying they had sacrificed could be admitted after a more or less lengthy period of penance. Even this was relaxed during a new persecution.

During a plague in Carthage, he urged Christians to help everyone, including their enemies and persecutors.

A friend of Pope Cornelius, he opposed the following pope, Stephen. He and the other African bishops would not recognize the validity of Baptism conferred by heretics and schismatics. This was not the universal view of the Church, but Cyprian was not intimidated even by Stephen's threat of excommunication.

He was exiled by the emperor and then recalled for trial. He refused to leave the city, insisting that his people should have the witness of his martyrdom.

Cyprian was a mixture of kindness and courage, vigor and steadiness. He was cheerful and serious, so that people did not know whether to love or respect him more. He waxed warm during the baptismal controversy; his feelings must have concerned him, for it was at this time that he wrote his treatise on patience. St. Augustine remarks that Cyprian atoned for his anger by his glorious martyrdom.

COMMENT: The controversies about Baptism and Penance in the third century remind us that the early Church had no ready-made solutions from the Holy Spirit. The leaders and members of the Church of that day had to move painfully through the best series of judgments they could make in an attempt to follow the entire teaching of Christ and not be diverted by exaggerations to right or left.

QUOTE: "You cannot have God for your Father if you do not have the Church for your mother....God is one and Christ is one, and his Church is one; one is the faith, and one is the people cemented together by harmony into the strong unity of a body....If we are the heirs of Christ, let us abide in the peace of Christ; if we are the sons of God, let us be lovers of peace" (St. Cyprian, *The Unity of the Catholic Church*).

Robert Bellarmine

Bishop and Doctor (1542-1621)

When Robert Bellarmine was ordained in 1570, the study of Church history and the Fathers of the Church was in a sad state of neglect. A promising scholar from his youth in Tuscany, he devoted his energy to these two subjects, as well as to Scripture, in order to systematize Church doctrine against the attacks of the Reformers. He was the first Jesuit to become a professor at Louvain.

His most famous work is his three-volume *Disputations on the Controversies* of the Christian faith. Particularly noteworthy are the sections on the temporal power of the pope and the role of the laity. He incurred the anger of both England and France by showing the divine-right-of-kings theory untenable. He developed the theory of the indirect power of the pope in temporal affairs; although he was defending the pope against the Scottish philosopher Barclay, he also incurred the ire of Pope Sixtus V.

Bellarmine was made a cardinal by Pope Clement VIII on the grounds that "he had not his equal for learning." While he occupied apartments in the Vatican, Bellarmine relaxed none of his former austerities. He limited his household expenses to what was barely essential, eating only the food available to the poor.

He was known to have ransomed a soldier who had deserted from the army and he used the hangings of his rooms to clothe poor people, remarking, "The walls won't catch cold."

Among many activities, he became theologian to Pope Clement VIII, preparing two catechisms which have had great influence in the Church.

The last major controversy of Bellarmine's life came in 1616 when he had to admonish his friend Galileo, whom he admired. Bellarmine delivered the admonition on behalf of the Holy Office, which had decided that the heliocentric theory of Copernicus was contrary to Scripture. The admonition amounted to a caution against putting forward—other than as a hypothesis— theories not yet fully proved. It was an example of the fact that saints are not infallible.

Bellarmine died on September 17, 1621. The process for his canonization was begun in 1627 but was delayed for political reasons, stemming from his writings, until 1930. In 1931 Pius XI declared him a doctor of the Church.

COMMENT: The renewal in the Church sought by Vatican II was difficult for many Catholics. In the course of change, many felt a lack of firm guidance from those in authority. They yearned for the stone columns of orthodoxy and an iron command with clearly defined lines of authority.

Vatican II assures us in *The Church in the Modern World*, "There are many realities which do not change and which have their ultimate foundation in Christ, who is the same yesterday and today, yes, and forever."

Robert Bellarmine devoted his life to the study of Scripture and Catholic doctrine. His writings help us understand that not only is the content of our faith important, it is Jesus' living person—as revealed by his life, death and resurrection—that is the source of revelation.

The real source of our faith is not merely a set of doctrines but rather the person of Christ still living in the Church today.

When he left his apostles, Jesus assured them of his living presence: "When the Spirit of truth comes, he will lead you to the complete truth" (see John 16:30).

QUOTE: "Sharing in solicitude for all the churches, bishops exercise this episcopal office of theirs, received through episcopal consecration, in communion with and under the authority of the Supreme Pontiff. All are united in a college or body with respect to teaching the universal Church of God and governing her as shepherds" (*Decree on the Bishops' Pastoral Office*, 3).

SEPTEMBER 19   OPTIONAL

Januarius

Bishop and Martyr (d. 305?)

Nothing is known of Januarius's life. He is believed to have been martyred in the persecution of Diocletian of 305. Legend has it that after he was thrown to the bears in the amphitheater of Pozzuoli, he was beheaded, and his blood ultimately brought to Naples.

COMMENT: It is defined Catholic doctrine that miracles can happen and can be recognized—hardly a mind-boggling statement to anyone who believes in God. Problems arise, however, when we must decide whether an occurrence is *unexplainable* in natural terms, or only *unexplained*. We do well to avoid an excessive credulity, which may be a sign of insecurity. On the other hand, when even scientists speak about "probabilities" rather than "laws" of nature, it is something less than imaginative for Christians to think that God is too "scientific" to work *extraordinary* miracles to wake us up to the

241

everyday miracles of sparrows and dandelions, raindrops and snowflakes.

QUOTE: "A dark mass that half fills a hermetically sealed four-inch glass container, and is preserved in a double reliquary in the Naples cathedral as the blood of St. January, liquefies 18 times during the year....This phenomenon goes back to the 14th century....Tradition connects it with a certain Eusebia, who had allegedly collected the blood after the martyrdom....The ceremony accompanying the liquefaction is performed by holding the reliquary close to the altar on which is located what is believed to be the martyr's head. While the people pray, often tumultuously, the priest turns the reliquary up and down in the full sight of the onlookers until the liquefaction takes place....Various experiments have been applied, but the phenomenon eludes natural explanation. There are, however, similar miraculous claims made for the blood of John the Baptist, Stephen, Pantaleon, Patricia, Nicholas of Tolentino and Aloysius Gonzaga—nearly all in the neighborhood of Naples" (*Catholic Encyclopedia*).

Andrew Kim Taegon; Paul Chong Hasang and Companions

Priest and Martyr; Martyrs (1821-1846)

This first native Korean priest was the son of Korean converts. His father, Ignatius Kim, was martyred during the persecution of 1839 and was beatified in 1925. After baptism at the age of 15, Andrew traveled 1,300 miles to the seminary in Macao, China.

After six years he managed to return to his country through Manchuria. That same year he crossed the Yellow Sea to Shanghai and was ordained priest. Back home again, he was assigned to arrange for more missionaries to enter by a water route that would elude the border patrol. He was arrested, tortured and finally beheaded at the Han River near Seoul, the capital.

Paul Chong Hasang was a seminarian, aged 45.

Christianity came to Korea during the Japanese invasion in 1592 when some Koreans were baptized, probably by Christian Japanese soldiers. Evangelization was difficult because Korea refused all contact with the outside world except for an annual journey to Peking to pay taxes. On one of these occasions, around 1777, Christian literature obtained from Jesuits in China led educated Korean Christians to study. A home Church began. When a Chinese priest managed to enter secretly a dozen years later, he found 4,000 Catholics, none of whom had ever seen a priest. Seven years later there were 10,000 Catholics. Religious freedom came in 1883.

When Pope John Paul visited Korea in 1984 he canonized, besides Andrew and Paul, 98 Koreans and three French missionaries who had been martyred between 1839 and 1867. Among them were bishops and priests, but for the most part they were laypersons: 47 women, 45 men.

Among the martyrs in 1839 was Columba Kim, an unmarried woman of 26. She was put in prison, pierced with hot awls and seared with burning coals. She and her sister Agnes were disrobed and kept for two days in a cell with condemned criminals, but were not molested. After Columba complained about the indignity, no more women were subjected to it. The two were beheaded. A boy of 13, Peter Ryou, had his flesh so badly torn that he could pull off pieces and throw them at the judges. He was killed by strangulation. Protase Chong, a 41-year-old noble, apostatized under torture and was freed. Later he came back, confessed his faith and was tortured to death.

Today there are 1.7 million Catholics in Korea.

COMMENT: We marvel at the fact that the Korean Church was strictly a lay Church for a dozen years after its birth. How did they survive without the Eucharist? It is no belittling of this and other sacraments to realize that there must be a living faith before there can be a truly beneficial celebration of the Eucharist. The sacraments are signs of God's initiative and response to faith already present. The sacraments increase grace and faith, but only if there is something ready to be increased.

QUOTE: "The Korean Church is unique because it was founded entirely by laypeople. This fledgling Church, so young and yet so strong in faith, withstood wave after wave of fierce persecution. Thus, in less than a century, it could boast of 10,000 martyrs. The death of these martyrs became the leaven of the Church and led to today's splendid flowering of the Church in Korea. Even today their undying spirit sustains the Christians in the Church of silence in the north of this tragically divided land" (Pope John Paul II, speaking at the canonization).

SEPTEMBER 21   FEAST

Matthew

Apostle and Evangelist

Matthew was a Jew who worked for the occupying Roman forces, collecting taxes from other Jews. Though the Romans probably did not allow extremes of extortion, their main concern was their own purses. They were not scrupulous about what the "tax-farmers" got for themselves. Hence the latter, known as "publicans," were generally hated as traitors by their fellow Jews. The Pharisees lumped them with "sinners." So it was shocking to them to hear Jesus call such a man to be one of his intimate followers.

Matthew got Jesus in further trouble by having a sort of going-away party at his house. The Gospel tells us that "many" tax collectors and "those known as sinners" came to the dinner. The Pharisees were still more badly shocked. What business did the supposedly great teacher have associating with such immoral people? Jesus' answer was, "Those who are well do not need a physician, but the sick do. Go and learn the meaning of the words, 'I desire mercy, not sacrifice.' I did not come to call the righteous but sinners" (Matthew 9:12b-13). Jesus is not setting aside ritual and worship; he is saying that loving others is even more important.

No other particular incidents about Matthew are found in the New Testament.

COMMENT: From such an unlikely situation, Jesus chose one of the foundations of the Church, a man others, judging from his job, thought was not holy enough for the position. But he was honest enough to admit that he was one of the sinners Jesus came to call. He was open enough to recognize truth when he saw him. "And he got up and followed him" (Matthew 9:9b).

STORY: We imagine Matthew, after the terrible events surrounding the death of Jesus, going to the mountain to which the risen Lord had summoned them. "When they saw him, they worshiped, but they doubted. Then Jesus approached and said to them [we think of him looking at each one in turn, Matthew listening and excited with the rest], 'All power in heaven and on earth has been given to me. Go, therefore, and make disciples of all nations, baptizing them in the name of the Father, and of the Son, and of the holy Spirit, teaching them to observe all that I have commanded you. And behold, I am with you always, until the end of the age' " (Matthew 28:17-20).

Matthew would never forget that day. He proclaimed the

Good News by his life and by his word. Our faith rests upon his witness and that of his fellow apostles.

Cosmas and Damian

Martyrs (d. 303?)

Nothing is known of their lives except that they suffered martyrdom in Syria during the persecution of Diocletian.

A church erected on the site of their burial place was enlarged by the emperor Justinian. Devotion to the two saints spread rapidly in both East and West. A famous basilica was erected in their honor in Constantinople. Their names were placed in the canon of the Mass, probably in the sixth century.

Legend says that they were twin brothers born in Arabia, who became skilled doctors. They were among those who are venerated in the East as the "moneyless ones" because they did not charge a fee for their services. It was impossible that such prominent persons would escape unnoticed in time of persecution: they were arrested and beheaded.

COMMENT: For a long time, it seems, we have been very conscious of Jesus' miracles as proofs of his divinity. What we sometimes overlook is Jesus' consuming interest in simply *healing* people's sickness, whatever other meaning his actions had. The power that "went out from him" was indeed a sign that God was definitively breaking into human history in final fulfillment of his promises; but the love of God was also concrete in a very human heart that was concerned about the suffering of his brothers and sisters. It is a reminder to Christians that salvation is for the whole *person*, the unique body-spirit unity.

QUOTE: "Do you not know that your body is a temple of the holy Spirit within you, whom you have from God, and that you are not your own? For you have been purchased at a price. Therefore glorify God in your body" (1 Corinthians 6:19-20).

SEPTEMBER 27   MEMORIAL

Vincent de Paul
Priest (1580?-1660)

The deathbed confession of a dying servant opened Vincent's eyes to the crying spiritual needs of the peasantry of France. This seems to have been a crucial moment in the life of the man from a small farm in Gascony, France, who had become a priest with little more ambition than to have a comfortable life.

It was the Countess de Gondi (whose servant he had helped) who persuaded her husband to endow and support a group of able and zealous missionaries who would work among the poor, the vassals and tenants and the country people in general. Vincent was too humble to accept leadership at first, but after working for some time in Paris among imprisoned galley-slaves, he returned to be the leader of what is now known as the Congregation of the Mission, or the Vincentians. These priests, with vows of poverty, chastity, obedience and stability, were to devote themselves entirely to the people in smaller towns and villages.

Later Vincent established confraternities of charity for the spiritual and physical relief of the poor and sick of each parish. From these, with the help of St. Louise de Marillac, came the Sisters of Charity, "whose convent is the sickroom, whose chapel is the parish church, whose cloister is the streets of the city." He organized the rich women of Paris to collect funds for his missionary projects, founded several hospitals, collected relief funds for the victims of war and ransomed over 1200 galley slaves from North Africa. He was zealous in conducting retreats for clergy at a time when there was great laxity, abuse and ignorance among them. He was a pioneer in clerical training and was instrumental in establishing seminaries.

Most remarkably, Vincent was by temperament a very irascible person—even his friends admitted it. He said that except for the grace of God he would have been "hard and repulsive, rough and cross." But he became a tender and affectionate man, very sensitive to the needs of others.

Pope Leo XIII made him the patron of all charitable societies. Outstanding among these, of course, is the Society of St. Vincent de Paul, founded in 1833 by his admirer Frederic Ozanam.

COMMENT: The Church is for all God's children, rich and poor, peasants and scholars, the sophisticated and the simple. But obviously the greatest concern of the Church must be for those who need the most help—those made helpless by sickness, poverty, ignorance or cruelty. Vincent de Paul is a particularly appropriate patron for all Christians today, when hunger has become starvation, and the high living of the rich stands in more and more glaring contrast to the physical and moral degradation in which many of God's children are forced to live.

QUOTE: "Strive to live content in the midst of those things that cause your discontent.

"Free your mind from all that troubles you, God will take care of things. You will be unable to make haste in this [choice] without, so to speak, grieving the heart of God, because he sees that you do not honor him sufficiently with holy trust. Trust in him, I beg you, and you will have the fulfillment of what your heart desires" (St. Vincent de Paul, Letters).

Lawrence Ruiz and Companions

Martyrs (1600?-1637)

Lawrence (Lorenzo) was born in Manila of a Chinese father and a Filipino mother, both Christians. Thus he learned Chinese and Tagalog from them and Spanish from the Dominicans whom he served as altar boy and sacristan. He became a professional calligrapher, transcribing documents in beautiful penmanship. He was a full member of the Confraternity of the Holy Rosary under Dominican auspices. He married and had two sons and a daughter.

His life took an abrupt turn when he was accused of murder. Nothing further is known except the statement of two Dominicans that "he was sought by the authorities on account of a homicide to which he was present or which was attributed to him."

At that time three Dominican priests, Antonio Gonzalez, Guillermo Courtet and Miguel de Aozaraza, were about to sail to Japan in spite of a violent persecution there. With them was a Japanese priest, Vicente Shiwozuka de la Cruz, and a layman named Lazaro, a leper. Lorenzo, having taken asylum with them, was allowed to accompany them. But only when they were at sea did he learn that they were going to Japan.

They landed at Okinawa. Lorenzo could have gone on to Formosa, but "I decided to stay with the Fathers, because the Spaniards would hang me there." In Japan they were soon found out, arrested and taken to Nagasaki. The site of wholesale bloodshed when the first atomic bomb was dropped had known tragedy before. The 50,000 Catholics who once lived there were dispersed or killed by persecution.

They were subjected to an unspeakable kind of torture: After huge quantities of water were forced down their throats, they

249

were made to lie down. Long boards were placed on their stomachs and guards then stepped on the ends of the boards, forcing the water to spurt violently from mouth, nose and ears.

The superior, Antonio, died after some days. Both the Japanese priest and Lazaro broke under torture, which included the insertion of bamboo needles under their fingernails. But both were brought back to courage by their companions.

In Lorenzo's moment of crisis, he asked the interpreter, "I would like to know if, by apostatizing, they will spare my life." The interpreter was noncommittal, but Lorenzo, in the ensuing hours, felt his faith grow strong. He became bold, even audacious, with his interrogators.

The five were put to death by being hanged upside down in pits. Boards fitted with semicircular holes were fitted around their waists and stones put on top to increase the pressure. They were tightly bound, to slow circulation and prevent a speedy death. They were allowed to hang for three days. By that time Lorenzo and Lazaro were dead. The three Dominican priests, still alive, were beheaded.

Pope John Paul II canonized these six and 10 others, Asians and Europeans, men and women, who spread the faith in the Philippines, Formosa and Japan. Lorenzo Ruiz is the first canonized Filipino martyr.

COMMENT: We ordinary Christians of today—how would we stand up in the circumstances these martyrs faced? We sympathize with the two who temporarily denied the faith. We understand Lorenzo's terrible moment of temptation. But we see also the courage—unexplainable in human terms—which surged from their store of faith. Martyrdom, like ordinary life, is a miracle of grace.

QUOTE: The Governors: "If we grant you life, will you renounce your faith?"

Lorenzo: "That I will never do, because I am a Christian, and

I shall die for God, and for him I will give many thousands of lives if I had them. And so, do with me as you please."

Wenceslaus

Martyr (907?-929)

If saints have been falsely characterized as "otherworldly," the life of Wenceslaus stands as an example to the contrary: he stood for Christian values in the midst of the political intrigues which characterized 10th-century Bohemia.

He was born in 907 near Prague, son of the Duke of Bohemia. His saintly grandmother, Ludmilla, raised him and sought to promote him as ruler of Bohemia in place of his mother, who favored the anti-Christian factions. Ludmilla was eventually murdered, but rival Christian forces were victorious, and Wenceslaus was able to assume leadership of the government.

His rule was marked by efforts toward unification within Bohemia, support of the Church and peace-making negotiations with Germany, a policy which caused him trouble with the anti-Christian opposition. His brother Boleslav joined in the plotting, and in September of 929 invited Wenceslaus to Alt-Bunglou for the celebration of the feast of Sts. Cosmas and Damian. On the way to Mass, Boleslav attacked his brother, and in the struggle, Wenceslaus was killed by supporters of Boleslav.

Although his death resulted primarily from political upheaval, Wenceslaus was hailed as a martyr for the faith, and his tomb became a pilgrimage shrine. He is hailed as the patron of the Bohemian people and of modern Czechoslovakia.

COMMENT: "Good King Wenceslaus" was able to incarnate his

Christianity in a world filled with political unrest. While we are often victims of violence of a different sort, we can easily identify with his struggle to bring harmony to society. The call to become involved in social change and in political activity is addressed to Christians; the values of the gospel are sorely needed today.

QUOTE: "While recognizing the autonomy of the reality of politics, Christians who are invited to take up political activity should try to make their choices consistent with the Gospel and, in the framework of a legitimate plurality, to give both personal and collective witness to the seriousness of their faith by effective and disinterested service of men" (Pope Paul VI, "A Call to Action," 46).

SEPTEMBER 29   FEAST

Michael, Gabriel and Raphael
Archangels

Angels—messengers from God—appear frequently in Scripture, but only these three are named.

Michael appears in Daniel's vision as "the great prince" who defends Israel against its enemies; in the Book of Revelation, he leads God's armies to final victory over the forces of evil. Devotion to Michael is the oldest angelic devotion, rising in the East in the fourth century. The Church in the West began to observe a feast honoring Michael and the angels in the fifth century.

Gabriel also makes an appearance in Daniel's visions, announcing Michael's role in God's plan. His best-known appearance is an encounter with a young Jewish girl named Mary, who consents to bear the Messiah.

Raphael's activity is confined to the Old Testament story of Tobit. There he appears to guide Tobit's son Tobiah through a series of fantastic adventures which lead to a threefold happy ending: Tobiah's marriage to Sarah, the healing of Tobit's blindness and the restoration of the family fortune.

The memorials of Gabriel (March 24) and Raphael (October 24) were added to the Roman calendar in 1921. The 1970 revision of the calendar joined their feasts to Michael's.

COMMENT: Each of these archangels performs a different mission in Scripture: Michael protects; Gabriel announces; Raphael guides. Earlier belief that inexplicable events were due to the actions of spiritual beings has given way to a scientific world-view and a different sense of cause and effect. Yet believers still experience God's protection, communication and guidance in ways which defy description. We cannot dismiss angels too lightly.

QUOTE: "The question of how many angels could dance on the point of a pin no longer is absurd in molecular physics, with its discovery of how broad that point actually is, and what part invisible electronic 'messengers' play in the dance of life" (Lewis Mumford).

Jerome

Priest and Doctor (345-420)

Most of the saints are remembered for some outstanding virtue or devotion which they practiced, but Jerome is remembered too frequently for his bad temper! It is true that he had a very bad temper and could use a vitriolic pen, but his love for God and his Son Jesus Christ was extraordinarily intense; anyone who taught error was an enemy of God and truth, and St. Jerome went after him or her with his mighty and sometimes sarcastic pen.

He was above all a Scripture scholar, translating the Old Testament from the Greek. He also wrote commentaries which are a great source of scriptural inspiration for us today. He was an avid student, a thorough scholar, a prodigious letter-writer and a consultant to monk, bishop and pope. St. Augustine said of him, "What Jerome is ignorant of, no mortal has ever known."

St. Jerome is particularly important for having made a translation of the Bible which came to be called the Vulgate. It is not the most critical edition of the Bible, but its acceptance by the Church was fortunate. As a modern scholar says, "No man before Jerome or among his contemporaries and very few men for many centuries afterwards were so well qualified to do the work." The Council of Trent called for a new and corrected edition of the Vulgate, and declared it the authentic text to be used in the Church.

In order to be able to do such work, Jerome prepared himself well. He was a master of Latin, Greek, Hebrew and Chaldaic. He began his studies at his birthplace, Stridon in Dalmatia (now Yugoslavia). After his preliminary education he went to Rome, the center of learning at that time, and thence to Trier, Germany, where the scholar was very much in evidence. He spent several years in each place trying always to find the very best teachers.

After these preparatory studies he traveled extensively in Palestine, marking each spot of Christ's life with an outpouring of devotion. Mystic that he was, he spent five years in the desert of Chalcis so that he might give himself up to prayer, penance and study. Finally he settled in Bethlehem where he lived in the cave believed to have been the birthplace of Christ. On September 30, 420, Jerome died in Bethlehem. The remains of his body now lie buried in the Basilica of St. Mary Major in Rome.

COMMENT: Jerome was a strong, outspoken man. He had the virtues and the unpleasant fruits of being a fearless critic and all the usual moral problems of a man. He was, as someone has said, no admirer of moderation whether in virtue or against evil. He was swift to anger, but also swift to feel remorse, even more severe on his own shortcomings than on those of others. A pope is said to have remarked, on seeing a picture of Jerome striking his breast with a stone, "You do well to carry that stone, for without it the Church would never have canonized you" (*Butler's Lives of the Saints*).

QUOTE: "In the remotest part of a wild and stony desert, burnt up with the heat of the scorching sun so that it frightens even the monks that inhabit it, I seemed to myself to be in the midst of the delights and crowds of Rome. In this exile and prison to which for the fear of hell I had voluntarily condemned myself, I many times imagined myself witnessing the dancing of the Roman maidens as if I had been in the midst of them: in my cold body and in my parched-up flesh, which seemed dead before its death, passion was able to live. Alone with this enemy, I threw myself in spirit at the feet of Jesus, watering them with my tears, and I tamed my flesh by fasting whole weeks. I am not ashamed to disclose my temptations, but I grieve that I am not now what I then was" ("Letter to St. Eustochium").

Theresa of the Child Jesus
Virgin (1873-1897)

"I prefer the monotony of obscure sacrifice to all ecstasies. To pick up a pin for love can convert a soul." These are the words of Theresa of the Child Jesus, a Carmelite nun who lived a cloistered life of obscurity in the convent of Lisieux, France. And her preference for hidden sacrifice did indeed convert souls. Few saints of God are more popular than this young nun. Her autobiography, *The Story of a Soul*, is read and loved throughout the world. Therese Martin entered the convent at the age of 15 and died in 1897 at the age of 24.

Life in a Carmelite convent is indeed uneventful and consists mainly of prayer and hard domestic work. But Theresa possessed that holy insight that redeems the time, however dull that time may be. She saw in quiet suffering *redemptive* suffering, suffering that was indeed her apostolate. Theresa said she came to the Carmel convent "to save souls and pray for priests." And shortly before she died, she wrote: "I want to spend my heaven doing good on earth."

COMMENT: Theresa has much to teach our age of the image, the appearance, the "sell." We have become a dangerously self-conscious people, painfully aware of the need to be fulfilled, yet knowing we are not. Theresa, like so many saints, sought to serve others, to do something outside herself, to forget herself in quiet acts of love. She is one of the great examples of the gospel paradox that we gain our life by losing it, and that the seed that falls to the ground must die in order to live (see John 12).

Preoccupation with self separates modern men and women from God, from their fellow human beings, and ultimately from themselves. We must relearn to forget ourselves, to contemplate a God who draws us out of ourselves, and to serve others as the ultimate expression of selfhood. These are the insights of St. Theresa of Lisieux, and they are more valid today than ever.

QUOTE: All her life long St. Theresa suffered from illness. As a young girl she underwent a three-month malady characterized by violent crises, extended delirium and prolonged fainting spells. Afterwards she was ever frail and yet she worked hard in the laundry and refectory of the convent. Psychologically, she endured prolonged periods of darkness when the light of faith seemed all but extinguished. The last year of her life she slowly wasted away from tuberculosis. And yet shortly before her death on September 30 she murmured, "I would not suffer less."

Truly she was a valiant woman who did not whimper about her illnesses and anxieties. Here was a person who saw the power of love, that divine alchemy which can change everything, including weakness and illness, into service and redemptive power for others. Is it any wonder that she is patroness of the missions? Who else but those who embrace suffering with their love really convert the world?

OCTOBER 2   MEMORIAL

Guardian Angels

Perhaps no aspect of Catholic piety is as comforting to parents as the belief that an angel protects their little ones from dangers real and imagined. Yet guardian angels are not just for children. Their role is to represent individuals before God, to watch over them always, to aid their prayer and to present their souls to God at death.

The concept of an angel assigned to guide and nurture each

human being is a development of Catholic doctrine and piety based on Scripture but not directly drawn from it. Jesus' words in Matthew 18:10 best support the belief: "See that you do not despise one of these little ones, for I say to you that their angels in heaven always look upon the face of my heavenly Father."

Devotion to the angels began to develop with the birth of the monastic tradition. St. Benedict gave it impetus and Bernard of Clairvaux, the great 12th-century reformer, was such an eloquent spokesman for the guardian angels that angelic devotion assumed its current form in his day.

A feast in honor of the guardian angels was first observed in the 16th century. In 1615 Pope Paul V added it to the Roman calendar.

COMMENT: The concept of an unseen companion has given rise to many childish titters about leaving room for an angel in a crowded seat and teacher-induced terrors about the danger of sudden death for a child who fails to honor the angel with prayer. But devotion to the angels is, at base, an expression of faith in God's enduring love and providential care extended to each person day-in and day-out until life's end.

QUOTE: "May the angels lead you into paradise;
may the martyrs come to welcome you
and take you to the holy city,
the new and eternal Jerusalem."

(*Rite for Christian Burial*)

Francis of Assisi

(1181?-1226)

Francis of Assisi was a poor little man who astounded and inspired the Church by taking the Gospel literally—not in a narrow fundamentalist sense, but by actually following all that Jesus said and did, joyfully, without limit and without a mite of self-importance.

Serious illness brought the young Francis to see the emptiness of his frolicking life as leader of Assisi's youth. Prayer—lengthy and difficult—led him to a self-emptying like that of Christ, climaxed by embracing a leper he met on the road. It symbolized his complete obedience to what he had heard in prayer: "Francis! Everything you have loved and desired in the flesh it is your duty to despise and hate, if you wish to know my will. And when you have begun this, all that now seems sweet and lovely to you will become intolerable and bitter, but all that you used to avoid will turn itself to great sweetness and exceeding joy."

From the cross in the neglected field-chapel of San Damiano, Christ told him, "Francis, go out and build up my house, for it is nearly falling down." Francis became the totally poor and humble workman.

He must have suspected a deeper meaning to "build up my house." But he would have been content to be for the rest of his life the poor "nothing" man actually putting brick on brick in abandoned chapels. He gave up every material thing he had, piling even his clothes before his earthly father (who was demanding restitution for Francis' "gifts" to the poor) so that he would be totally free to say, "Our Father in heaven." He was, for a time, considered to be a religious "nut," begging from door to door when he could not get money for his work, bringing sadness or disgust to the hearts of his former friends, ridicule from the unthinking.

But genuineness will tell. A few people began to realize that this man was actually trying to be Christian. He really believed what Jesus said: "Announce the kingdom! Possess no gold or silver or copper in your purses, no traveling bag, no sandals, no staff" (see Luke 9:1-3).

Francis' first rule for his followers was a collection of texts from the Gospels. He had no idea of founding an order, but once it began he protected it and accepted all the legal structures needed to support it. His devotion and loyalty to the Church were absolute and highly exemplary at a time when various movements of reform tended to break the Church's unity.

He was torn between a life devoted entirely to prayer and a life of active preaching of the Good News. He decided in favor of the latter, but always returned to solitude when he could. He wanted to be a missionary in Syria or in Africa, but was prevented by shipwreck and illness in both cases. He did manage to try to convert the sultan of Egypt during the Fifth Crusade.

During the last years of his relatively short life (he died at 44) he was half blind and seriously ill. Two years before his death, he received the stigmata, the real and painful wounds of Christ in his hands, feet and side.

On his deathbed, he said over and over again the last addition to his Canticle of the Sun, "Be praised, O Lord, for our Sister Death." He sang Psalm 141, and at the end asked his superior to have his clothes removed when the last hour came and for permission to expire lying naked on the earth, in imitation of his Lord.

COMMENT: Francis of Assisi was poor only that he might be Christ-like. He loved nature because it was another manifestation of the beauty of God. He did great penance (apologizing to "Brother Body" later in life) that he might be totally disciplined for the will of God. His poverty had a sister, humility, by which he meant total dependence on the good God. But all this was, as it were, preliminary to the heart of his spirituality: living the gospel life, summed up in the charity of Jesus and perfectly expressed in the Eucharist.

QUOTE: "We adore you and we bless you, Lord Jesus Christ, here and in all the churches which are in the whole world, because by your holy cross you have redeemed the world" (St. Francis).

Bruno
Priest (1030?-1101)

This saint has the honor of having founded a religious order which, as the saying goes, has never had to be *re*formed because it was never *de*formed. No doubt both the founder and the members would reject such high praise, but it is an indication of the saint's intense love of a penitential life in solitude.

He was born in Cologne, became a famous teacher at Rheims and was appointed chancellor of the archdiocese at the age of 45. He supported Pope Gregory VII in his fight against the decadence of the clergy, and took part in the removal of his own scandalous archbishop Manasses. Bruno suffered the plundering of his house for his pains.

He had a dream of living in solitude and prayer, and persuaded a few friends to join him in a hermitage. After a while he felt the place unsuitable and, through a friend, was given some land which was to become famous for his foundation "in the Chartreuse" (from which comes the word *Carthusians*). The climate, desert, mountainous terrain and inaccessibility guaranteed silence, poverty and small numbers.

Bruno and his friends built an oratory with small individual cells at a distance from each other. They met for Matins and Vespers each day, and spent the rest of the time in solitude, eating together only on great feasts. Their chief work was copying manuscripts.

The pope, hearing of Bruno's holiness, called for his assistance in Rome. When the pope had to flee Rome, Bruno pulled up stakes again, and spent his last years (after refusing a bishopric) in the wilderness of Calabria.

He was never formally canonized, because the Carthusians were averse to all occasions of publicity. Pope Clement extended his feast to the whole Church in 1674.

COMMENT: If there is always a certain uneasy questioning of the contemplative life, there is an even greater puzzlement about the extremely penitential combination of community and hermit life lived by the Carthusians.

QUOTE: "Members of those communities which are totally dedicated to contemplation give themselves to God alone in solitude and silence and through constant prayer and ready penance. No matter how urgent may be the needs of the active apostolate, such communities will always have a distinguished part to play in Christ's Mystical Body..." (*Decree on the Renewal of Religious Life*, 7).

Marie-Rose Durocher
Virgin (1811-1849)

Canada was one diocese from coast to coast during the first eight years of Marie-Rose Durocher's life. Its half-million Catholics had received civil and religious liberty from the English only 44 years before. When Marie-Rose was 29, Bishop Ignace Bourget became bishop of Montreal. He would be a decisive influence in her life.

He faced a shortage of priests and sisters and a rural population that had been largely deprived of education. Like his counterparts in the United States, he scoured Europe for help and himself founded four communities, one of which was the Sisters of the Holy Names of Jesus and Mary. Its first sister and reluctant foundress was Marie-Rose.

She was born in a little village near Montreal in 1811, the 10th of 11 children. She had a good education, was something of a tomboy, rode a horse named Caesar and could have married well. At 16 she felt the desire to become a religious but was forced to abandon the idea because of her weak constitution. At 18, when her mother died, her priest brother invited her and her father to come to his parish in Beloeil, not far from Montreal. For 13 years she served as housekeeper, hostess and parish worker. She became well known for her graciousness, courtesy, leadership and tact; she was, in fact, called "the saint of Beloeil." Perhaps she was too tactful during two years when her brother treated her coldly.

As a young woman she had hoped there would someday be a community of teaching sisters in every parish, never thinking she would found one. But her spiritual director, Father Pierre Telmon, O.M.I., after thoroughly (and severely) leading her in the spiritual life, urged her to found a community herself. Bishop Bourget concurred, but she shrank from the prospect. No

Canadian woman had ever done anything of the kind. She was in poor health and her father and her brother needed her.

She finally agreed and, with two friends, Melodie Dufresne and Henriette Cere, entered a little home in Longueuil, across the St. Lawrence river from Montreal. With them were 13 young girls already assembled for boarding school. Longueuil became successively her Bethlehem, Nazareth and Gethsemane. She was 32 and would live only six more years—years filled with poverty, trials, sickness and slander. The qualities she had nurtured in her "hidden" life came forward—a strong will, intelligence and common sense, a total lack of human respect and yet a great deference to directors. Thus was born an international congregation of women religious dedicated to education in the faith.

She was severe with herself and by today's standards quite strict with her sisters. Beneath it all, of course, was what is common to all saints: an unshakable love of her crucified Savior.

On her deathbed the prayers most frequently on her lips were "Jesus, Mary, Joseph! Sweet Jesus, I love you. Jesus, be to me *Jesus*!" Before she died, she smiled and said to the sister with her, "Your prayers are keeping me here—let me go."

COMMENT: The Christian triad has always been and will always be prayer, penance and charity. In our day we have seen a great burst of charity, a genuine interest in the poor. Countless Christians have experienced a deep form of prayer. But penance? We squirm when we read of terrible physical penance done by saints like Marie-Rose. That is not for most people, of course. But the pull of a materialistic consumer culture oriented to pleasure and entertainment is not impossible to resist with some form of deliberate and Christ-conscious abstinence. That is part of the way to answer Jesus' call to repent and turn completely to God.

QUOTE: To a novice leaving religious life: "Do not imitate those persons who, after having spent a few months as postulant or novice in a community, dress differently, even ludicrously. You are returning to the secular state. My advice is, follow the styles of the day, but from afar, as it were."

Our Lady of the Rosary

Pope St. Pius V established this feast in 1573. The purpose was to thank God for the victory of Christians over the Turks at Lepanto—a victory attributed to the praying of the rosary. Clement XI extended the feast to the universal Church in 1716.

The development of the rosary has a long history. First, a practice developed of praying 150 Our Fathers in imitation of the 150 Psalms. Then there was a parallel practice of praying 150 Hail Marys. Soon a mystery of Jesus' life was attached to each Hail Mary. Though Mary's giving the rosary to St. Dominic is recognized as unhistorical, the development of this prayer-form owes much to the followers of St. Dominic. One of them, Alan de la Roche, was known as "the apostle of the rosary." He founded the first Confraternity of the Rosary in the 15th century. In the 16th century the rosary was developed to its present form—with the 15 joyful, sorrowful and glorious mysteries.

COMMENT: The purpose of the rosary is to help us meditate on the great mysteries of our salvation. Pius XII called it a compendium of the gospel. The main focus is on Jesus—his birth, life, death and resurrection. The Our Fathers remind us that Jesus' Father is the initiator of salvation. The Hail Marys remind us to join with Mary in contemplating these mysteries. They also make us aware that Mary was and is intimately joined with her Son in all the mysteries of his earthly and heavenly existence. The Glorys remind us that the purpose of all life is the glory of the Trinity.

The rosary appeals to many. It is simple. The constant repetition of words helps create an atmosphere in which to contemplate the mysteries of God. We sense that Jesus and Mary are with us in the joys and sorrows of life. We grow in hope that God will bring us to share in the glory of Jesus and Mary forever.

QUOTE: "[The Rosary] sets forth the mystery of Christ in the very way in which it is seen by St. Paul in the celebrated 'hymn' of the Epistle to the Philippians—kenosis [self-emptying], death and exaltation (2:6-11)....By its nature the recitation of the Rosary calls for a quiet rhythm and a lingering pace, helping the individual to meditate on the mysteries of the Lord's life as grasped by the heart of her who was closer to the Lord than all others" (Paul VI, *Devotion to the Blessed Virgin Mary*, 45, 47).

Denis and Companions

Bishop and Martyr; Martyrs (d. 258?)

This martyr and patron of France is traditionally held to have been the first bishop of Paris. His popularity is due to a series of legends, especially those connecting him with the great abbey church of St. Denis in Paris. He was for a time confused with the writer now called Pseudo-Dionysius.

The best hypothesis contends that Denis was sent to Gaul from Rome in the third century and beheaded in the persecution under Valerius in 258.

According to one of the legends, after he was martyred on Montmartre (literally, "mountain of martyrs") in Paris, he carried his head to a village northeast of the city. St. Genevieve built a basilica over his tomb at the beginning of the sixth century.

COMMENT: Again we have the case of a saint about whom almost nothing is known, yet one whose cult has been a vigorous part of the Church's history for centuries. We can only conclude that the deep impression the saint made on the people of his day must have resulted from a life of unusual holiness. In all such cases, there are two fundamental facts: A great man gave his life for Christ, and the Church has never forgotten him—a human symbol of God's eternal mindfulness.

QUOTE: "Martyrdom is part of the Church's nature since it manifests Christian death in its pure form, as the death of unrestrained faith, which is otherwise hidden in the ambivalence of all human events. Through martyrdom the Church's holiness, instead of remaining purely subjective, achieves by God's grace the visible expression it needs. As early as the second century one who accepted death for the sake of Christian faith or Christian morals was looked on and revered as a 'martus' (witness). The term is scriptural in that Jesus Christ is the 'faithful witness' absolutely (Revelations 1:5; 3:14)" (Karl Rahner, *Theological Dictionary*).

John Leonardi

Priest (1541?-1609)

"I am only one person! Why should I do anything? What good would it do?" Today, as in any age, people seem plagued with the dilemma of getting involved. In his own way John Leonardi answered these questions. He chose to become a priest.

After his ordination, he became very active in the works of the ministry, especially in hospitals and prisons. The example and dedication of his work attracted several young laymen who began to assist him. They later became priests themselves.

John lived in a time of reform after the Reformation and the Council of Trent. He and his followers projected a new congregation of diocesan priests. For some reason the plan, which was ultimately approved, provoked great political opposition and he was an exile from his home town of Lucca, Italy, for almost the entire remainder of his life. He received encouragement and help from St. Philip Neri (May 26) who gave him his quarters—along with the care of his cat!

In 1579 he formed the Confraternity of Christian Doctrine, and published a compendium of Christian doctrine that remained in use until the 19th century.

Father Leonardi and his priests became a great power for good in Italy, and their congregation was confirmed by Pope Clement in 1595. He died at the age of 68 from a disease caught when tending those stricken by the plague.

By the deliberate policy of the founder, the Clerks Regular of the Mother of God have never had more than 15 churches and today form only a very small congregation.

COMMENT: What can one person do? If you ever glanced through a *Christopher Notes* pamphlet you know—plenty! In the life of each saint one thing stands clear: God and one are a majority! What one person, following God's will and plan for his or her life, can do is more than our mind could ever hope for or imagine. Each of us, like John Leonardi, has a mission to fulfill in God's plan for the world. Each one of us is unique and has been given talent to use for the service of our brothers and sisters for the building up of God's Kingdom.

QUOTE: "Do not be afraid any longer, little flock, for your Father is pleased to give you the kingdom. Sell your belongings and give alms. Provide money bags for yourselves that do not wear out, an inexhaustible treasure in heaven that no thief can reach nor moth destroy" (Luke 12:32-33).

Callistus I
Pope and Martyr (d. 223?)

The most reliable information about this saint comes from his enemy St. Hippolytus (August 13), the first antipope, later a martyr for the Church. A negative principle is used: If some worse things had happened, Hippolytus would surely have mentioned them.

Callistus was a slave in the imperial Roman household. Put in charge of the bank by his master, he lost the money deposited, fled and was caught. After serving time for a while, he was released to make some attempt to recover the money. Apparently he carried his zeal too far, being arrested for brawling in a Jewish synagogue. This time he was condemned to work in the mines of Sardinia. He was released through the influence of the emperor's mistress and lived at Anzio (site of a famous World War II beachhead).

He won his freedom, was made superintendent of the public Christian burial ground in Rome (still called the cemetery of St. Callistus), probably the first land owned by the Church. The pope ordained him a deacon and made him his friend and adviser.

He was himself elected pope by a majority vote of the clergy and laity of Rome, and thereafter was bitterly attacked by the losing candidate, St. Hippolytus, who let himself be set up as the first antipope in the history of the Church. The schism lasted about 18 years.

Hippolytus is venerated as a saint. He was banished during the persecution of 235 and was reconciled to the Church. He died from his sufferings in Sardinia. He attacked Callistus on two fronts—doctrine and discipline. Hippolytus seems to have exaggerated the distinction between Father and Son (almost making two gods) possibly because theological language had not yet been refined. He also accused Callistus of being too lenient, for reasons we may find surprising: (1) Callistus admitted to Communion those who had already done public penance for murder, adultery, fornication; (2) he held marriages between free women and slaves to be valid—contrary to Roman law; (3) he authorized the ordination of men who had been married two or three times; (4) he held that mortal sin was not a sufficient reason to depose a bishop; (5) he held to a policy of leniency toward those who had temporarily apostatized during persecution.

Callistus was martyred during a local disturbance in Trastevere, Rome, and is the first pope (except for Peter) to be commemorated as a martyr in the earliest martyrology of the Church.

Some are of the opinion that, even from the little we know about him, Callistus may rank among the greatest popes.

COMMENT: The life of this man is another reminder that the course of Church history, like that of true love, never did run smooth. The Church had to (and still must) go through the agonizing struggle to state the mysteries of the faith in language that, at the very least, sets up definite barriers to error. On the disciplinary side, the Church had to preserve the mercy of Christ against rigorism while still upholding the gospel ideal of radical conversion and self-discipline. Every pope—indeed every Christian—must walk the difficult path between "reasonable" indulgence and "reasonable" rigorism.

QUOTE: His contemporaries, Jesus said, were "like children who sit in marketplaces and call to one another, 'We played the flute for you, but you did not dance, we sang a dirge but you did not mourn.' For John [the Baptist] came neither eating nor drinking, and they said, 'He is possessed by a demon.' The Son of Man came eating and drinking and they said, 'Look, he is a glutton and a drunkard, a friend of tax collectors and sinners' " (Matthew 11:16b-19a).

Teresa of Jesus
Virgin and Doctor (1515-1582)

Teresa lived in an age of exploration as well as political, social and religious upheaval. It was the 16th century, an age of turmoil and reform. Her life began with the culmination of Protestant reform, and ended shortly after the Council of Trent.

The gift of God to Teresa in and through which she became holy and left her mark on the Church and the world is threefold: She was a woman; she was a contemplative; she was an active reformer.

As a woman, Teresa stood on her own two feet, even in the man's world of her time. She was "her own woman," entering the Carmelites despite strong opposition from her father. She is a person wrapped not so much in silence as in mystery. Beautiful, talented, outgoing, adaptable, affectionate, courageous, enthusiastic, she was totally human. Like Jesus, she was a mystery of paradoxes: wise, yet practical; intelligent, yet much in tune with her experience; mystic, yet an energetic reformer. A holy woman, a womanly woman.

Teresa was a woman "for God," a woman of prayer, discipline and compassion. Her heart belonged to God. Her own conversion was no overnight affair; it was an arduous lifelong struggle, involving ongoing purification and suffering. She was misunderstood, misjudged, opposed in her efforts at reform. Yet she struggled on, courageous and faithful; she struggled with her own mediocrity, her illness, her opposition. And in the midst of all this she clung to God in life and in prayer. Her writings on prayer and contemplation are drawn from her experience: powerful, practical and graceful. A woman of prayer; a woman for God.

Teresa was a woman "for others." Though a contemplative she spent much of her time and energy seeking to reform herself and the Carmelites, to lead them back to the full observance of the primitive rule. She founded over a half-dozen new monasteries. She traveled, wrote, fought—always to renew, to reform. In her self, in her prayer, in her life, in her efforts to reform, in all the people she touched, she was a woman for others, a woman who inspired and gave life.

In 1970 the Church gave her the title she had long held in the popular mind: doctor of the Church. She was the first woman so honored.

COMMENT: Today we live in a time of turmoil, a time of reform and a time of liberation. Modern women have in Teresa a challenging example. Promoters of renewal, promoters of prayer, all have in Teresa a woman to reckon with, one whom they can admire and imitate.

QUOTE: Teresa knew well the continued presence and value of suffering (physical illness, opposition to reform, difficulties in prayer), but she grew to be able to embrace suffering, even desire it: "Lord, either to suffer or to die." Toward the end of her life she exclaimed: "Oh, my Lord! How true it is that whoever works for you is paid in troubles! And what a precious price to those who love you if we understand its value."

Hedwig

Religious (1174?-1243)

Far too rarely do humans realize the possibilities of the wise use of earthly power and worldly wealth. Hedwig was one of the few. Born to nobility toward the close of the 12th century, she was given in marriage at an early age to Henry, Duke of Silesia. Through her persuasion and personal efforts, a large number of monastic institutions of both men and women were established in Silesia. Several hospitals, one for lepers, were likewise founded. She was personally a great force in establishing peace in the surrounding areas in those troubled times of power struggles. To her great sorrow, she was unable to prevent a pitched battle between the forces of two of her sons, one of whom was dissatisfied over the partition of estates that Henry had made between them.

After she and her husband had made a mutual vow of continence, she lived, for the most part, at the monastery at Trebnitz where, although not a formal member of the religious institute, she nevertheless participated in the religious exercises of the community. She died in 1243 and was buried at Trebnitz.

COMMENT: Whatever possessions we may be blessed with are not for our own needs or personal comfort alone, but are also to be used in the assistance of others. To whatever use these goods may be put, they should always promote, never impede, progress in God's love. It is true that earthly things of themselves in no way contradict God's love, but rather are evidences of it; still, we can become so interested in and enticed by what we sense that we become forgetful of the God from whom these blessings come.

STORY: Hedwig sacrificed her wish to become a religious in later life in order that she might use earthly goods to help the poor. For herself, she chose poverty, distrusting the comforts her means might have afforded her and denying herself even such basic necessities as shoes in winter. She wore the religious habit, lived the life of a religious, but would not give up the administration of her possessions because she wanted these goods to help the poor. She lived her life and used whatever goods were hers so that she and those she was able to help might better appreciate the supernatural life of God's grace.

Margaret Mary Alacoque
Virgin (1647-1690)

Margaret Mary was chosen by Christ to arouse the Church to a realization of the love of God symbolized by the heart of Jesus.

Her early years were marked by sickness and a painful home situation. "The heaviest of my crosses was that I could do nothing to lighten the cross my mother was suffering." After considering marriage for some time, she entered the Order of Visitation nuns at the age of 24.

A Visitation nun was "*not* to be extraordinary except by being ordinary," but the young nun was not to enjoy this anonymity. A fellow novice (shrewdest of critics) termed Margaret humble, simple and frank, but above all kind and patient under sharp criticism and correction. She could not meditate in the formal way expected, though she tried her best to give up her "prayer of simplicity." Slow, quiet and clumsy, she was assigned to help an infirmarian who was a bundle of energy.

On December 27, 1674, three years a nun, she received the first of her revelations. She felt "invested" with the presence of

God, though always afraid of deceiving herself in such matters. The request of Christ was that his love for humankind be made evident through her. During the next 13 months, he appeared to her at intervals. His human heart was to be the symbol of his divine-human love. By her own love she was to make up for the coldness and ingratitude of the world—by frequent and loving Holy Communion, especially on the first Friday of each month, and by an hour's vigil of prayer every Thursday night in memory of his agony and isolation in Gethsemane. He also asked that a feast of reparation be instituted.

Like all saints, Margaret had to pay for her gift of holiness. Some of her own sisters were hostile. Theologians who were called in declared her visions delusions and suggested that she eat more heartily. Later, parents of children she taught called her an imposter, an unorthodox innovator. A new confessor, Blessed Claude de la Colombiere, a Jesuit, recognized her genuineness and supported her. Against her great resistance, Christ called her to be a sacrificial victim for the shortcomings of her own sisters, and to make this known.

After serving as novice mistress and assistant superior, she died at the age of 43 while being anointed. "I need nothing but God, and to lose myself in the heart of Jesus."

COMMENT: Our scientific-materialistic age cannot "prove" private revelations. Theologians, if pressed, admit that we do not *have* to believe in them. But it is impossible to deny the message Margaret Mary heralded: that God loves us with a passionate love. Her insistence on reparation and prayer and the reminder of final judgment should be sufficient to ward off superstition and superficiality in devotion to the Sacred Heart while preserving its deep Christian meaning.

QUOTE: Christ speaks to St. Margaret Mary: "Behold this Heart which has so loved men that it has spared nothing, even to exhausting and consuming itself, in order to testify its love. In

275

return, I receive from the greater part only ingratitude, by their irreverence and sacrileges, and by the coldness and contempt they have for me in this Sacrament of love....I come into the heart I have given you in order that through your fervor you may atone for the offences which I have received from lukewarm and slothful hearts that dishonor me in the Blessed Sacrament" (Third apparition).

Ignatius of Antioch

Bishop and Martyr (d. 107?)

Born in Syria, Ignatius converted to Christianity and eventually became bishop of Antioch. In the year 107 the emperor Trajan visited Antioch and forced the Christians there to choose between death and apostasy. Ignatius would not deny Christ and thus was condemned to be put to death in Rome.

Ignatius is well known for the seven letters he wrote on the long journey from Antioch to Rome. Five of these letters are to Churches in Asia Minor; they urge the Christians there to remain faithful to God and to obey their superiors. He warns them against heretical doctrines, providing them with the solid truths of the Christian faith.

The sixth letter was to Polycarp, bishop of Smyrna, who was later martyred for the faith. The final letter begs the Christians in Rome not to try to stop his martyrdom. "The only thing I ask of you is to allow me to offer the libation of my blood to God. I am the wheat of the Lord, may I be ground by the teeth of the beasts to become the immaculate bread of Christ."

In the year 107 Ignatius bravely met the lions in the Coliseum.

COMMENT: Ignatius's great concern was for the unity and order of the Church. Even greater was his willingness to suffer martyrdom rather than deny his Lord Jesus Christ. Not to his own suffering did Ignatius draw attention, but to the love of God which strengthened him. He knew the price of commitment and would not deny Christ, even to save his own life.

QUOTE: "I greet you from Smyrna together with the Churches of God present here with me. They comfort me in every way, both in body and in soul. My chains, which I carry about on me for Jesus Christ, begging that I may happily make my way to God, exhort you: persevere in your concord and in your community prayers" (Ignatius of Antioch, *Letter to the Church at Tralles*).

Luke

Evangelist

Luke wrote one of the major portions of the New Testament, a two-volume work comprising the third Gospel and the Acts of the Apostles. In the two books he shows the parallel between the life of Christ and that of the Church. He is the only Gentile Christian among the Gospel writers. Tradition holds him to be a native of Antioch, and Paul calls him "our beloved physician" (Colossians 4:14). His Gospel was probably written between A.D. 70 and 85.

He appears in Acts during Paul's second journey, remains at Philippi for several years until Paul returns from his third journey, accompanies Paul to Jerusalem and remains near him when he is imprisoned in Caesarea. During these two years, Luke had time to seek information and interview persons who had known Jesus. He accompanied Paul on the dangerous journey to Rome where he was a faithful companion. "Only Luke is with me," Paul writes (2 Timothy 4:11).

COMMENT: Luke wrote as a Gentile for Gentile Christians. The Gospel reveals Luke's expertise in classic Greek style as well as his knowledge of Jewish sources.

The character of Luke may best be seen by the emphases of his Gospel, which has been given a number of subtitles: (1) The Gospel of Mercy: Luke emphasizes Jesus' compassion and patience with the sinners and the suffering. He has a broadminded openness to all, showing concern for Samaritans, lepers, publicans, soldiers, public sinners, unlettered shepherds, the poor. Luke alone records the stories of the sinful woman, the lost sheep and coin, the prodigal son, the good thief. (2) The Gospel of Universal Salvation: Jesus died for all. He is the son of Adam, not just of David, and Gentiles are his friends too. (3) The Gospel of the Poor: "Little people" are prominent— Zechariah and Elizabeth, Mary and Joseph, shepherds, Simeon and the elderly widow, Anna. He is also concerned with what we now call "evangelical poverty." (4) The Gospel of Absolute Renunciation: He stresses the need for total dedication to Christ. (5) The Gospel of Prayer and the Holy Spirit: He shows Jesus at prayer before every important step of his ministry. The Spirit is bringing the Church to its final perfection. (6) The Gospel of Joy: Luke succeeds in portraying the joy of salvation that permeated the primitive Church.

QUOTE: The end of Luke's Gospel: "Then [Jesus] led them [out] as far as Bethany, raised his hands, and blessed them. As he blessed them he parted from them and was taken up to heaven. They did him homage and then returned to Jerusalem with great joy, and they were continually in the temple praising God" (Luke 24:50-53).

Isaac Jogues and John de Brébeuf and Companions

Priests and Martyrs; Martyrs

Isaac Jogues (1607-1646). Isaac Jogues and his companions were the first martyrs of the North American continent. As a young Jesuit, Isaac Jogues, a man of learning and culture, taught literature in France. He gave up that career to work among the Huron Indians in the New World, and in 1636 he and his companions, under the leadership of John de Brébeuf, arrived in Quebec. The Hurons were constantly warred upon by the Iroquois, and in a few years Father Jogues was captured by the Iroquois and imprisoned for 13 months. His letters and journals tell how he and his companions were led from village to village, how they were beaten, tortured and forced to watch as their Huron converts were mangled and killed.

An unexpected chance for escape came to Isaac Jogues through the Dutch, and he returned to France, bearing the marks of his sufferings. Several fingers had been cut, chewed or burnt off. Pope Urban VIII gave him permission to offer Mass with his mutilated hands: "It would be shameful that a martyr of Christ be not allowed to drink the Blood of Christ." Welcomed home as a hero, Father Jogues might have sat back, thanked God for his safe return and died peacefully in his homeland. But his zeal led him back once more to the fulfillment of his dreams. In a few months he sailed for his missions among the Hurons.

In 1646 he and Jean de Lalande, who had offered his services to the missioners, set out for Iroquois country in the belief that a recently signed peace treaty would be observed. They were captured by a Mohawk war party, and on October 18 Father Jogues was tomahawked and beheaded. Jean de Lalande was killed the next day at Ossernenon, a village near Albany, New York.

The first of the Jesuit missionaries to be martyred was Rene Goupil who, with Lalande, had offered his services as an oblate. He was tortured along with Isaac Jogues in 1642, and was tomahawked for having made the Sign of the Cross on the brow of some children.

John de Brébeuf (1593-1649). Jean de Brébeuf was a French Jesuit who came to Canada at the age of 32 and labored there for 24 years. He returned to France when the English captured Quebec in 1629 and expelled the Jesuits, but returned to his missions four years later. An epidemic of smallpox among the Hurons was blamed on the Jesuits by the medicine men, but Jean remained with them.

He composed catechisms and a dictionary in Huron, and saw 7,000 converted before his death. He was captured by the Iroquois and died after four hours of extreme torture at Sainte Marie, near Georgian Bay, Canada.

Father Anthony Daniel, working among Hurons who were gradually becoming Christian, was killed by Iroquois on July 4, 1648. His body was thrown into his chapel, which was set on fire.

Gabriel Lalemant had taken a fourth vow—to sacrifice his life to the Indians. He was horribly tortured to death along with Father Brébeuf.

Father Charles Garnier was shot to death as he baptized children and catechumens during an Iroquois attack.

Father Noel Chabanel was killed before he could answer his recall to France. He had found it exceedingly hard to adapt to mission life. He could not learn the language, the food and life of the Indians revolted him and he suffered spiritual dryness during his whole stay in Canada. Yet he made a vow to remain until death in his mission.

These eight Jesuit martyrs of North America were canonized in 1930.

COMMENT: Faith and heroism planted belief in Christ's cross deep in our land. The Church in North America sprang from the blood of martyrs. Are we as eager to keep that cross standing in our midst? Do we bear witness to deep-seated faith in us, the Good News of the cross (redemption) into our home, our work, our social world?

QUOTE: "My confidence is placed in God who does not need our help for accomplishing his designs. Our single endeavor should be to give ourselves to the work and to be faithful to him, and not to spoil his work by our shortcomings" (From a letter of Isaac Jogues to a Jesuit friend in France, September 12, 1646, a month before he died).

OCTOBER 23   OPTIONAL

John of Capistrano
Priest (1386-1456)

It has been said the Christian saints are the world's greatest optimists. Not blind to the existence and consequences of evil, they base their confidence on the power of Christ's redemption. The power of conversion through Christ extends not only to sinful people but also to calamitous events.

Imagine being born in the 14th century. One-third of the population and nearly 40 percent of the clergy were wiped out by the Black Death. The Western Schism split the Church with two or three claimants to the Holy See at one time. England and France were at war. The city-states of Italy were constantly in conflict. No wonder that gloom dominated the spirit of the culture and the times.

John Capistrano was born in 1386. His education was thorough. His talents and success were great. When he was 26 he was made governor of Perugia. Imprisoned after a battle against the Malatestas, he resolved to change his way of life completely. At the age of 30 he entered the Franciscan novitiate and was ordained priest in four years.

His preaching attracted great throngs at a time of religious apathy and confusion. He and 12 Franciscan brethren were received in the countries of central Europe as angels of God. They were instrumental in reviving a dying faith and devotion.

The Franciscan Order itself was in turmoil over the interpretation and observance of the Rule of St. Francis. Through John's tireless efforts and his expertise in law, the heretical Fraticelli were suppressed and the "Spirituals" were freed from interference in their stricter observance.

He helped bring about a reunion with the Greek and Armenian Churches, unfortunately only a brief arrangement.

When the Turks captured Constantinople, he was commissioned to preach a Crusade for the defense of Europe. Gaining little response in Bavaria and Austria, he decided to concentrate his efforts in Hungary. He himself led the army to Belgrade. Under the great general John Junyadi they gained an overwhelming victory, and the siege of Belgrade was lifted. Worn out by his superhuman efforts Capistrano was an easy prey to the infection bred by the refuse of battle. He died October 23, 1456.

COMMENT: John Hofer, a biographer of John Capistrano, recalls a Brussels organization named after the saint which aimed at solving life problems in a fully Christian spirit. Its motto was: "Initiative, Organization, Activity." These three words truly are most characteristic of John's life. He was not one to sit around, ever. His deep Christian optimism drove him to battle problems at all levels with the confidence engendered by a deep faith in Christ.

QUOTE: On the saint's tomb in the Hungarian town of Villach, the governor had this message inscribed: "This tomb holds John, by birth of Capistrano, a man worthy of all praise, defender and promoter of the faith, guardian of the Church, zealous protector of his order, an ornament to all the world, lover of truth and justice, mirror of life, surest guide in doctrine; praised by countless tongues, he reigns blessed in heaven." That is a fitting epitaph for a real and successful optimist.

OCTOBER 24   OPTIONAL

Anthony Claret
Bishop (1807-1870)

The "spiritual father of Cuba" was a missionary, religious founder, social reformer, queen's chaplain, writer and publisher, archbishop and refugee. He was a Spaniard whose work took him to the Canary Islands, Cuba, Madrid, Paris and to the First Vatican Council.

In his spare time as weaver and designer in the textile mills of Barcelona, he learned Latin and printing: the future priest and publisher was preparing. Ordained at 28, he was prevented by ill health from entering religious life as a Carthusian or as a Jesuit, but went on to become one of Spain's most popular preachers. He spent 10 years giving popular missions and retreats, always placing great emphasis on the Eucharist and devotion to the Immaculate Heart of Mary. Her rosary, it was said, was never out of his hand. At 42, beginning with five young priests, he founded a religious institute of missionaries, known today as the Claretians.

He was appointed to head the much-neglected archdiocese of Santiago in Cuba. He began its reform by almost ceaseless preaching and hearing of confessions, and suffered bitter opposition—mainly for stamping out concubinage and giving instruction to black slaves. A hired assassin (whose release from prison Anthony had obtained) slashed open his face and wrist. Anthony succeeded in getting the would-be assassin's death sentence commuted to a prison term. His solution for the misery of Cubans was family-owned farms producing a variety of foods for the family's own needs and for the market. This invited the enmity of the vested interests who wanted everyone to work on a single cash crop—sugar. Among all his religious writings, it is interesting to note the titles of two books he wrote in Cuba: *Reflections on Agriculture* and *Country Delights*.

He was called back to Spain for a job he did not relish—being chaplain for the queen. He went on three conditions: He would reside away from the palace, he would come only to hear the queen's confession and instruct the children and he would be exempt from court functions. In the revolution of 1868, he fled with the queen's party to Paris, where he preached to the Spanish colony.

All his life Anthony was interested in the Catholic Press. He founded the Religious Publishing House, a major Catholic publishing venture in Spain, and wrote or published 200 books and pamphlets.

At Vatican I, where he was a staunch defender of the doctrine of infallibility, he won the admiration of his fellow bishops. Cardinal Gibbons of Baltimore remarked of him, "There goes a true saint." He died in exile near the border of Spain at the age of 63.

COMMENT: Jesus foretold that those who are truly representative of him would suffer the same persecution as he did. Besides 14 attempts on his life, Anthony had to undergo such a barrage of the ugliest slander that the very name *Claret* became a byword for humiliation and misfortune. The powers of evil do not easily give up their prey.

No one needs to go looking for persecution. All we need to

do is be sure we suffer because of our genuine faith in Christ, not for our own whims and imprudences.

STORY: Queen Isabella II once said to Anthony, "No one tells me things as clearly and frankly as you do." Later she told her chaplain, "Everybody is always asking me for favors, but you never do. Isn't there something you would like for yourself?" He replied, "Yes, that you let me resign." The queen made no more offers.

Simon and Jude

Apostles

Jude is so named by Luke and Acts. Matthew and Mark call him Thaddeus. He is not mentioned elsewhere in the Gospels, except, of course, where all the apostles are referred to. Scholars hold that he is not the author of the epistle of Jude. Actually, Jude had the same name as Judas Iscariot. Evidently because of the disgrace of that name, it was shortened to "Jude" in English.

Simon is mentioned on all four lists of the apostles. On two of them he is called "the Zealot." The Zealots were a Jewish sect which represented an extreme of Jewish nationalism. For them, the messianic promise of the Old Testament meant that the Jews were to be a free and independent nation. God alone was their king, and any payment of taxes to the Romans—the very domination of the Romans—was a blasphemy against God. No doubt some of the Zealots were the spiritual heirs of the Maccabees, carrying on their ideals of religion and independence. But many were the counterparts of modern terrorists. They raided and killed, attacking both foreigners and "collaborating" Jews. They were chiefly responsible for the rebellion against Rome which ended in the destruction of Jerusalem in A.D. 70.

COMMENT: As in the case of all the apostles except for Peter, James and John, we are faced with men who are really unknown, and we are struck by the fact that their holiness is simply taken to be a gift of Christ. He chose some unlikely people: a former Zealot, a former (crooked) tax collector, an impetuous fisherman, two "sons of thunder" and a man named Judas Iscariot.

It is a reminder that we cannot receive too often. Holiness does not depend on human merit, culture, personality, effort or achievement. It is entirely God's creation and gift.

God needs no Zealots to bring about the kingdom by force. Jude, like all the saints, is the saint of the impossible: only God can create his divine life in human beings. And God wills to do so, for all of us.

QUOTE: "Just as Christ was sent by the Father, so also he sent the apostles, filled with the Holy Spirit. This he did so that, by preaching the gospel to every creature (cf. Mark 16:15), they might proclaim that the Son of God, by his death and resurrection, had freed us from the power of Satan (cf. Acts 26:18) and from death, and brought us into the kingdom of his Father" (*Constitution on the Liturgy*, 6).

All Saints

The earliest certain observance of a feast in honor of all the saints is an early fourth-century commemoration of "all the martyrs." In the early seventh century, after successive waves of invaders plundered the catacombs, Pope Boniface IV gathered up some 28 wagon-loads of bones and reinterred them beneath the Pantheon, a Roman temple dedicated to all the gods, and rededicated the shrine as a Christian church. According to Bede, the pope intended "that the memory of all the saints might in the future be honored in the place which had formerly been dedicated to the worship not of gods but of demons" (*On the Calculation of Time*).

But the rededication of the Pantheon, like the earlier commemoration of all the martyrs, occurred in May. Many Eastern Rite Churches still honor all the saints in the spring, either during the Easter season or immediately after Pentecost.

How the Western Church came to celebrate this feast in November is a puzzle to historians. The Anglo-Saxon theologian Alcuin observed the feast on November 1 in 800, as did his friend Arno, Bishop of Salzburg. Rome finally adopted that date in the ninth century.

COMMENT: This feast first honored martyrs. Later, when Christians were free to worship according to their conscience, the Church gave homage to other evidence of sanctity. In the early centuries the only criterion was popular acclaim, even when the bishop's approval became the final step in placing a commemoration on the calendar. The first papal canonization occurred in 973; the lengthy process now required to prove extraordinary sanctity took form in the last 500 years. Today's feast honors the obscure as well as the famous—the saints each of us have known.

QUOTE: "After this I had a vision of a great multitude, which no one could count, from every nation, race, people, and tongue. They stood before the throne and before the Lamb, wearing white robes and holding palm branches in their hands....[One of the elders] said to me, 'These are the ones who have survived the time of great distress; they have washed their robes and made them white in the blood of the Lamb' " (Revelation 7:9, 14).

NOVEMBER 2

All Souls

The Church has encouraged prayer for the dead from the earliest times as an act of Christian charity. "If we had no care for the dead," Augustine noted, "we would not be in the habit of praying for them." Yet pre-Christian rites for the deceased kept such a strong hold on the superstitious imagination that a liturgical commemoration was not observed until the early Middle Ages, when monastic communities began to mark an annual day of prayer for the departed members.

In the middle of the eleventh century, St. Odilo, Abbot of Cluny, decreed that all Cluniac monasteries offer special prayers and sing the Office for the Dead on November 2, the day after the feast of All Saints. The custom spread from Cluny and was finally adopted throughout the Roman Church.

The theological underpinning of the feast is the acknowledgment of human frailty. Since few people achieve perfection in this life but, rather, go to the grave still scarred with traces of sinfulness, some period of purification seems necessary before a soul comes face-to-face with God. The Council of Trent affirmed this purgatory state and insisted that the prayers of the living can speed the process of purification.

Superstition still clung to the observance. Medieval popular belief held that the souls in purgatory could appear on this day in the form of witches, toads or will-o'-the-wisps. Graveside food offerings supposedly eased the dead's rest.

Observances of a more religious nature have survived. These include public processions or private visits to cemeteries and decorating graves with flowers and lights.

COMMENT: Whether or not one should pray for the dead is one of the great arguments which divide Christians. Appalled by the abuse of indulgences in the Church of his day, Luther rejected the concept of purgatory. Yet prayer for a loved one is, for the believer, a way of erasing any distance, even death. In prayer we stand in God's presence in the company of someone we love, even if that person has gone before us into death.

QUOTE: "We must not make purgatory into a flaming concentration camp on the brink of hell—or even a 'hell for a short time.' It is blasphemous to think of it as a place where a petty God exacts the last pound—or ounce—of flesh....St. Catherine of Genoa, a mystic of the 15th century, wrote that the 'fire' of purgatory is God's love 'burning' the soul so that, at last, the soul is wholly aflame. It is the pain of wanting to be made totally worthy of One who is seen as infinitely lovable, the pain of desire for union that is now absolutely assured, but not yet fully tasted" (Leonard Foley, O.F.M., *Believing in Jesus*).

Martin de Porres

Religious (1579-1639)

"Father unknown" is the cold legal phrase for it on baptismal records. "Half-breed" or "war souvenir" is the cruel name inflicted by those of "pure" blood. Like many others, Martin might have grown to be a bitter man, but he did not. It was said that even as a child he gave his heart and his goods to the poor and despised.

He was the illegitimate son of a freedwoman of Panama, probably black but also possibly of Native American stock, and a Spanish grandee of Lima, Peru. He inherited the features and dark complexion of his mother and, though this irked his father, he finally acknowledged his son after eight years. After the birth of a sister, the father abandoned the family. Martin was reared in poverty, locked into a low level of Lima's society.

At 12 his mother apprenticed him to a barber-surgeon. He learned how to cut hair and also how to draw blood (a standard medical treatment then), care for wounds and prepare and administer medicines.

After a few years in this medical apostolate, Martin applied to the Dominicans to be a "lay helper," not feeling himself worthy to be a religious brother. After nine years, the example of his prayer and penance, charity and humility led the community to request him to make full religious profession. Many of his nights were spent in prayer and penitential practices; his days were filled with nursing the sick and caring for the poor. It was particularly impressive that he treated all people regardless of their color, race or status. He was instrumental in founding an orphanage, took care of slaves brought from Africa and managed the daily alms of the priory with practicality as well as generosity. He became the procurator for both priory and city, whether it was a matter of "blankets, shirts, candles, candy, miracles or prayers!" When his priory was in debt, he said, "I am only a poor mulatto. Sell me. I am the property of the order. Sell me."

Side by side with his daily work in the kitchen, laundry and infirmary, God chose to fill Martin's life with extraordinary gifts: ecstasies that lifted him into the air, light filling the room where he prayed, bilocation, miraculous knowledge, instantaneous cures and a remarkable control over animals. His charity extended to beasts of the field and even to the vermin of the kitchen. He would excuse the raids of mice and rats on the grounds that they were underfed, and kept stray cats and dogs at his sister's house.

He became a formidable fund-raiser, obtaining thousands of dollars for dowries for poor girls so that they could marry or enter a convent.

Many of his fellow religious took him as their spiritual director, but he continued to call himself a "poor slave." He was a good friend of another Dominican saint of Peru, Rose of Lima.

COMMENT: Racism is a sin almost nobody confesses. Like pollution, it is a "sin of the world" that is everybody's responsibility but apparently nobody's fault. One could hardly imagine a more fitting patron of Christian forgiveness (on the part of those discriminated against) and Christian justice (on the part of reformed racists) than Martin de Porres.

QUOTE: Pope John XXIII remarked at the canonization of Martin (May 6, 1962), "He excused the faults of others. He forgave the bitterest injuries, convinced that he deserved much severer punishments on account of his own sins. He tried with all his might to redeem the guilty; lovingly he comforted the sick; he provided food, clothing and medicine for the poor; he helped, as best he could, farm laborers and Negroes, as well as mulattoes, who were looked upon at that time as akin to slaves: thus he deserved to be called by the name the people gave him: 'Martin of Charity.' "

Charles Borromeo
Bishop (1538-1584)

The name of St. Charles Borromeo is associated with reform. He lived during the time of the Protestant Reformation, and had a hand in the reform of the whole Church during the final years of the Council of Trent.

Although he belonged to a noble Milanese family and was related to the powerful Medici family, he desired to devote himself to the Church. When his uncle, Cardinal de Medici, was elected pope in 1559 as Pius IV, he made Charles cardinal-deacon and administrator of the archdiocese of Milan while he was still a layman and a young student. Because of his intellectual qualities he was entrusted with several important offices connected with the Vatican and later appointed secretary of state with full charge of the administration of the papal states. The untimely death of his elder brother brought Charles to a definite decision to be ordained a priest, despite relatives' insistence that he marry. He was ordained a priest at the age of 25, and soon afterward he was consecrated bishop of Milan.

Because of his work at the Council of Trent he was not allowed to take up residence in Milan until the Council was over. It had been Charles who encouraged the pope to renew the Council in 1562 after it had been suspended 10 years before. Working behind the scenes, St. Charles deserves the credit for keeping the Council in session when at several points it was on the verge of breaking up. He took upon himself the task of the entire correspondence during the final phase. Eventually Charles was allowed to devote his time to the archdiocese of Milan, where the religious and moral picture was far from bright. The reform needed in every phase of Catholic life among both clergy and laity was initiated at the provincial council of all his suffragan bishops. Specific regulations were drawn up for bishops and other clergy: If the people were to be converted to a better life, these had to be the first to give a good example and renew their apostolic spirit.

Charles himself took the initiative in giving good example. He allotted most of his income to charity, forbade himself all luxury and imposed severe penances upon himself. He sacrificed wealth, high honors, esteem and influence to become poor. During the plague and famine of 1576 he tried to feed 60,000 to 70,000 people daily. To do this he borrowed large sums of money that required years to repay. When the civil authorities fled at the height of the plague, he stayed in the city, where he ministered to the sick and the dying and helped those in want.

Work and the heavy burdens of his high office began to affect his health. He died at the age of 46.

COMMENT: St. Charles made his own the words of Christ: "...I was hungry and you gave me food, I was thirsty and you gave me drink, a stranger and you welcomed me, naked and you clothed me, ill and you cared for me, in prison and you visited me" (Matthew 25:35-36). Charles saw Christ in his neighbor and knew that charity done for the least of his flock was charity done for Christ.

QUOTE: "Christ summons the Church, as she goes her pilgrim way, to that continual reformation of which she always has need, insofar as she is an institution of men here on earth. Therefore, if the influence of events or of the times has led to deficiencies in conduct, in Church discipline, or even in the formulation of doctrine (which must be carefully distinguished from the deposit of faith itself), these should be appropriately rectified at the proper moment" (*Decree on Ecumenism*, 6).

Dedication of St. John Lateran

Most Catholics think of St. Peter's as the pope's church, but they are wrong. St. John Lateran is the pope's church, the cathedral of the diocese of Rome where the Bishop of Rome presides.

The first basilica on the site was built in the fourth century when Constantine donated land he had received from the wealthy Lateran family. That structure and its successors suffered fire, earthquake and the ravages of war, but the Lateran remained the church where popes were consecrated until the popes returned from Avignon in the 15th century to find the church and the adjoining palace in ruins.

Pope Innocent X commissioned the present structure in 1646. One of Rome's most imposing churches, the Lateran's towering facade is crowned with 15 colossal statues of Christ, John the Baptist, John the Evangelist and 12 doctors of the Church. Beneath its high altar rests the remains of the small wooden table on which tradition holds St. Peter himself celebrated Mass.

COMMENT: Unlike the commemorations of other Roman churches (St. Mary Major, August 5, Sts. Peter and Paul, November 18), this anniversary is a feast. The dedication of a church is a feast for all its parishioners. St. John Lateran is, in a sense, the parish church of all Catholics, for it is the pope's parish, the cathedral church of the Bishop of Rome. This church is the spiritual home of the people who are the Church.

QUOTE: "What was done here, as these walls were rising, is reproduced when we bring together those who believe in Christ. For, by believing they are hewn out, as it were, from mountains and forests, like stones and timber; but by catechizing, baptism and instruction they are, as it were, shaped, squared and planed by the hands of the workers and artisans. Nevertheless, they do not make a house for the Lord until they are fitted together through love" (St. Augustine, *Sermon 36*).

Leo the Great
Pope and Doctor (d. 461)

With apparent strong conviction of the importance of the bishop of Rome in the Church, and of the Church as the ongoing sign of Christ's presence in the world, Leo the Great displayed endless dedication in his role as pope. Elected in 440, he worked tirelessly as "Peter's successor," guiding his fellow bishops as "equals in the episcopacy and infirmities."

Leo is known as one of the best administrative popes of the ancient Church. His work branched into four main areas, indicative of his notion of the pope's total responsibility for the flock of Christ. He worked at length to control the heresies of Pelagianism, Manichaeism and others, placing demands on their followers so as to secure true Christian beliefs. A second major area of his concern was doctrinal controversy in the Church in the East, to which he responded with a classic letter setting down the Church's teaching on the nature of Christ. With strong faith, he also led the defense of Rome against barbarian attack, taking the role of peacemaker.

In these three areas, Leo's work has been highly regarded. His growth to sainthood has its basis in the spiritual depth with which he approached the pastoral care of his people, which was a fourth focus of his work. He is known for his spiritually profound sermons. An instrument of the call to holiness, well-versed in

Scripture and ecclesiastical awareness, Leo had the ability to reach the everyday needs and interests of his people. One of his Christmas sermons is still famous today.

COMMENT: At a time when there is widespread criticism of structure in the Church, we also hear criticism that bishops and priests—indeed, all of us—are too preoccupied with administration of temporal matters. Pope Leo is an example of a great administrator who used his talents in areas where spirit and structure are inseparably combined: doctrine, peace and pastoral care. He avoided an "angelism" that tries to live without the body, as well as the "practicality" that deals only in externals.

STORY: It is said of Leo that his true significance rests in his doctrinal insistence on the mysteries of Christ and the Church and in the supernatural charisms of the spiritual life given to humanity in Christ and in his Body, the Church. Thus Leo held firmly that everything he did and said as pope for the administration of the Church was participated in by Christ, the head of the Mystical Body, and by St. Peter, in whose place Leo acted.

Martin of Tours

Bishop (316?-397)

A conscientious objector who wanted to be a monk; a monk who was maneuvered into being a bishop; a bishop who fought paganism as well as pleaded for mercy to heretics—such was Martin of Tours, one of the most popular of saints.

He was born of pagan parents in what is now Hungary and

raised in Italy. The son of a veteran, he was forced to serve in the army against his will at the age of 15. He became a Christian catechumen and was baptized at 18. It was said that he lived more like a monk than a soldier. At 23 he refused a war bounty from Julian Caesar with the words, "I have served you as a soldier; now let me serve Christ. Give the bounty to those who are going to fight. But I am a soldier of Christ and it is not lawful for me to fight." After great difficulties, he was discharged and went to be a disciple of Hilary of Poitiers.

He was ordained an exorcist and worked with great zeal against the Arians. He became a monk, living first at Milan and later on a small island. When Hilary (January 13) was restored to his see after exile, Martin returned to France and established what may have been the first French monastery near Poitiers. He lived there for 10 years, forming his disciples and preaching throughout the countryside.

The people of Tours demanded that he become their bishop. He was drawn to that city by a ruse—the need of a sick person—and was brought to the church, where he reluctantly allowed himself to be consecrated bishop. Some of the consecrating bishops thought his rumpled appearance and unkempt hair indicated that he was not dignified enough for the office.

Along with St. Ambrose, Martin rejected Bishop Ithacius's principle of putting heretics to death—as well as the intrusion of the emperor into such matters. He prevailed upon the emperor to spare the life of the heretic Priscillian. For his efforts, Martin was accused of the same heresy, and Priscillian was executed after all. Martin then pleaded for a cessation of the persecution of Priscillian's followers in Spain. He still felt he could cooperate with Ithacius in other areas, but afterwards his conscience troubled him about this decision.

As death approached, his followers begged him not to leave them. He prayed, "Lord, if your people still need me, I do not refuse the work. Your will be done."

COMMENT: Martin's worry about cooperation reminds us that almost nothing is either all black or all white. The saints are not creatures of another world: they face the same perplexing decisions that we do. Any decision of conscience always involves some risk. If we choose to go north, we may never know what would have happened had we gone east, west or south. A hypercautious withdrawal from all perplexing situations is not the virtue of prudence; it is, in fact, a bad decision, for "not to decide is to decide."

STORY: On a bitterly cold day, the famous legend goes, Martin met a poor man, almost naked, trembling in the cold and begging from passersby at the city gate. Martin had nothing but his weapons and his clothes. He drew his sword, cut his cloak into two pieces, gave one to the beggar and wrapped himself in the other half. Some of the bystanders laughed at his now odd appearance; others were ashamed at not having relieved the man's misery. That night in his sleep Martin saw Christ dressed in the half of the garment he had given away, and heard him say: "Martin, still a catechumen, has covered me with this garment."

Josaphat
Bishop and Martyr (1580?-1623)

In 1967, newspaper photos of Pope Paul VI embracing Athenagoras I, the Orthodox patriarch of Constantinople, marked a significant step toward the healing of a division in Christendom that has spanned nine centuries.

In 1595, when today's saint was a boy, the Orthodox bishop

of Brest-Litovsk (famous in World War I) in Lithuania and five other bishops representing millions of Ruthenians, sought reunion with Rome. John Kunsevich (Josaphat became his name in religious life) was to dedicate his life and suffer his death in the same cause. Born in what was then Poland, he went to work in Wilno and was influenced by clergy adhering to the Union of Brest. He became a Basilian monk, then a priest, and soon was well known as a preacher and as an ascetic.

He became bishop of Vitebsk (now in Russia) at a relatively young age, and faced a difficult situation. Most religious, fearing interference in liturgy and customs, did not want union with Rome. By synods, catechetical instruction, reform of the clergy and personal example, however, Josaphat was successful in winning the greater part of the Orthodox in Lithuania to the union.

But the next year a dissident hierarchy was set up, and his opposite number spread the accusation that Josaphat had "gone Latin" and that all his people would have to do the same. He was not enthusiastically supported by the Latin bishops of Poland.

Despite warnings, he went to Vitebsk, still a hotbed of trouble. Attempts were made to foment trouble and drive him from the diocese: A priest was sent to shout insults to him from his own courtyard. When Josaphat had him removed and shut up in his house, the opposition rang the town hall bell, and a mob assembled. The priest was released, but members of the mob broke into the bishop's home. He was brained with a halberd, then shot and his body thrown into the river. It was later recovered and is now buried at Biala, Poland. He was the first saint of the Eastern Church to be canonized by Rome.

His death brought a movement toward Catholicism and unity, but the controversy continued, and the dissidents, too, had their martyr. After the partition of Poland, the Russians forcibly joined a majority of the Ruthenians to the Orthodox Church of Russia.

COMMENT: The seeds of separation were sown in the fourth century when the Roman Empire was divided into East and West. The actual split came over relatively unimportant customs (unleavened bread, Saturday fasting, celibacy). No doubt the political involvement of religious leaders on both sides was a large factor, and doctrinal disagreement was present. But no reason was enough to justify the present tragic division in Christendom, which is 64 percent Roman Catholic, 13 percent separated Eastern Churches (mostly Orthodox) and 23 percent Protestant, and this when the 71 percent of the world that is not Christian should be getting the witness of unity and Christlike charity from Christians!

STORY: Surrounded by an angry mob shortly before his death, Josaphat said, "You people of Vitebsk want to put me to death. You make ambushes for me everywhere, in the streets, on the bridges, on the highways and in the marketplace. I am here among you as your shepherd and you ought to know that I should be happy to give my life for you. I am ready to die for the holy union, for the supremacy of St. Peter and of his successor the Supreme Pontiff."

NOVEMBER 13   MEMORIAL (U.S.A.)

Frances Xavier Cabrini
Virgin (1850-1917)

Frances Xavier Cabrini was the first United States citizen to be canonized. Her deep trust in the loving care of her God gave her the strength to be a valiant woman doing the work of Christ.

Refused admission to the religious order which had educated her to be a teacher, she began charitable work at the House of

Providence Orphanage in Cadogno, Italy. In September 1877, she made her vows there and took the religious habit.

When the bishop closed the orphanage in 1880, he named Frances prioress of the Missionary Sisters of the Sacred Heart. Seven young women from the orphanage joined with her.

Since her early childhood in Italy, Frances had wanted to be a missionary in China but, at the urging of Pope Leo XIII, Frances went west instead of east. She traveled with six sisters to New York City to work with the thousands of Italian immigrants living there.

She found disappointment and difficulties with every step. When she arrived in New York City, the house that was to be her first orphanage in the United States was not available. The archbishop advised her to return to Italy. But Frances, truly a valiant woman, departed from the archbishop's residence all the more determined to establish the orphanage. And she succeeded.

In 35 years Frances Xavier Cabrini founded 67 institutions dedicated to caring for the poor, the abandoned, the uneducated and the sick. Seeing great need among Italian immigrants who were losing their faith, she organized schools and adult education classes.

As a child, she was always frightened of water, unable to overcome her fear of drowning. Yet, despite this fear, she traveled across the seas more than 30 times. She died of malaria in her own Columbus Hospital in Chicago.

COMMENT: The compassion and dedication of Mother Cabrini is still seen in hundreds of thousands of her fellow citizens, not yet canonized, who care for the sick in hospitals, nursing homes and state institutions. We complain of increased medical costs in an affluent society, but the daily news shows us millions who have little or no medical care, and who are calling for new Mother Cabrinis to become citizen-servants of their land.

QUOTE: At her canonization on July 7, 1946, Pius XII said,

"Although her constitution was very frail, her spirit was endowed with such singular strength that, knowing the will of God in her regard, she permitted nothing to impede her from accomplishing what seemed beyond the strength of a woman."

Albert the Great

Bishop and Doctor (1206-1280)

Albert the Great was a 13th-century German Dominican who influenced decisively the stance of the Church toward Aristotelian philosophy brought to Europe by the spread of Islam.

Students of philosophy know him as the master of Thomas Aquinas. Albert's attempt to understand Aristotle's works established the climate in which Thomas Aquinas developed his synthesis of Greek wisdom and Christian theology. But Albert deserves recognition on his own merits as a curious, honest and diligent scholar.

He was the eldest son of a powerful and wealthy German lord of military rank. He was educated in the liberal arts. Despite fierce family opposition, he entered the Dominican novitiate.

His boundless interests prompted him to write a compendium of all knowledge: natural science, logic, rhetoric, mathematics, astronomy, ethics, economics, politics and metaphysics. His explanation of learning took 20 years to complete. "Our intention," he said, "is to make all the aforesaid parts of knowledge intelligible to the Latins."

He achieved his goal while serving as an educator at Paris and Cologne, as Dominican provincial and even as bishop of Regensburg for a time. He defended the mendicant orders and preached the Crusade to Germany and Bohemia.

Albert is a doctor of the Church and the patron of scientists and philosophers.

COMMENT: An information glut faces us Christians today in all branches of learning. One needs only to read current Catholic periodicals to experience the varied reactions to the findings of the social sciences, for example, in regard to Christian institutions, Christian life-styles and Christian theology. Ultimately, in canonizing Albert, the Church seems to point to his openness to truth, wherever it may be found, as his claim to holiness. His characteristic curiosity prompted Albert to mine deeply for wisdom within a philosophy his Church warmed to with great difficulty.

QUOTE: "There are some who desire knowledge merely for its own sake; and that is shameful curiosity. And there are others who desire to know, in order that they may themselves be known; and that is vanity, disgraceful too. Others again, desire knowledge in order to acquire money or preferment by it; that too is a discreditable quest. But there are also some who desire knowledge, that they may build up the souls of others with it; and that is charity. Others, again, desire it that they may themselves be built up thereby; and that is prudence. Of all these types, only the last two put knowledge to the right use" (St. Bernard, *Sermon on the Canticle of Canticles*).

Margaret of Scotland

(1050?-1093)

Margaret of Scotland was a truly liberated woman in the sense that she was free to be herself. For her, that meant freedom to love God and serve others.

Margaret was not Scottish by birth. She was the daughter of Princess Agatha of Hungary and the Anglo-Saxon Prince Edward Atheling. She spent much of her youth in the court of her great-uncle, the English king, Edward the Confessor. Her family fled from William the Conqueror and was shipwrecked off the coast of Scotland. King Malcolm befriended them and was captivated by the beautiful, gracious Margaret. They were married at the castle of Dunfermline in 1070.

Malcolm was good-hearted, but rough and uncultured, as was his country. Because of Malcolm's love for Margaret, she was able to soften his temper, polish his manners and help him become a virtuous king. He left all domestic affairs to her and often consulted her in state matters.

Margaret tried to improve her adopted country by promoting the arts and education. For religious reform, she instigated synods and was present for the discussions which tried to correct religious abuses common among priests and people, such as simony, usury and incestuous marriages. With her husband, she founded several churches.

Margaret was not only a queen, but a mother. She and Malcolm had six sons and two daughters. Margaret personally supervised their religious instruction and their other studies.

Although she was very much caught up in the affairs of the household and country, she remained detached from the world. Her private life was austere. She had certain times for prayer and reading Scripture. She ate sparingly and slept little in order to have time for devotions. She and Malcolm kept two Lents, one before Easter and one before Christmas. During these times she always rose at midnight for Mass. On the way home she would wash the feet of six poor persons and give them alms. She was always surrounded by beggars in public and never refused them. It is recorded that she never sat down to eat without first feeding nine orphans and 24 adults.

In 1093, King William Rufus made a surprise attack on Alnwick castle. King Malcolm and his oldest son, Edward, were killed. Margaret, already on her deathbed, died four days after her husband.

COMMENT: There are two ways to be charitable: the "clean way" and the "messy way." The "clean way" is to give money or clothing to organizations which serve the poor. The "messy way" is dirtying your own hands in personal service to the poor. Margaret's outstanding virtue was her love of the poor. Although very generous with material gifts, Margaret also visited the sick and nursed them with her own hands. She and her husband served orphans and the poor on their knees during Advent and Lent. Like Christ, she was charitable the "messy way."

QUOTE: "When [Margaret] spoke, her conversation was seasoned with the salt of wisdom. When she was silent, her silence was filled with good thoughts. So thoroughly did her outward bearing correspond with the staidness of her character that it seemed as if she has been born the pattern of a virtuous life" (Turgot, St. Margaret's confessor).

Gertrude

Virgin (1256?-1302)

St. Gertrude was one of the great mystics of the 13th century. Together with St. Mechtild, she practiced a spirituality called "nuptial mysticism," that is, she came to see herself as the bride of Christ. Her spiritual life was a deep personal union with Jesus and his Sacred Heart, leading her into the very life of the Trinity.

But this was no individualistic piety. Gertrude lived the rhythm of the liturgy, where she found Christ. In the liturgy and Scripture, she found the themes and images to enrich and express her piety. There was no clash between her personal prayer life and the liturgy.

COMMENT: Gertrude's life is another reminder that the heart of the Christian life is prayer: private and liturgical, ordinary or mystical, always personal.

QUOTE: "Lord, you have granted me your secret friendship by opening the sacred ark of your divinity, your deified heart, to me in so many ways as to be the source of all my happiness; sometimes imparting it freely, sometimes as a special mark of our mutual friendship. You have so often melted my soul with your loving caresses that, if I did not know the abyss of your overflowing condescensions, I should be amazed were I told that even your Blessed Mother had been chosen to receive such extraordinary marks of tenderness and affection" (Adapted from *The Life and Revelations of Saint Gertrude*).

Elizabeth of Hungary

Religious (1207-1231)

In her short life Elizabeth manifested such great love for the poor and suffering that she has become the patroness of Catholic charities and of the Franciscan Third Order. The daughter of the king of Hungary, Elizabeth chose a life of penance and asceticism when a life of leisure and luxury could easily have been hers. This choice endeared her in the hearts of the common people throughout Europe.

At the age of 14 Elizabeth was married to Louis of Thuringia (a German principality), whom she deeply loved; she bore three children. Under the spiritual direction of a Franciscan friar, she led a life of prayer, sacrifice and service to the poor and sick. Seeking to become one with the poor, she wore simple clothing. Daily she would take bread to hundreds of the poorest in the land, who came to her gate.

After six years of marriage, her husband died in the Crusades, and she was grief-stricken. Her husband's family looked upon her as squandering the royal purse, and mistreated her, finally throwing her out of the palace. The return of her husband's allies from the Crusades resulted in her being reinstated, since her son was legal heir to the throne.

In 1228 Elizabeth joined the Third Order of St. Francis, spending the remaining few years of her life caring for the poor in a hospital which she founded in honor of St. Francis. Elizabeth's health declined, and she died before her 24th birthday in 1231. Her great popularity resulted in her canonization four years later.

COMMENT: Elizabeth understood well the lesson Jesus taught when he washed his disciples' feet at the Last Supper: The Christian must be one who serves the humblest needs of others, even if one serves from an exalted position. Of royal blood, Elizabeth could have lorded it over her subjects. Yet she served them with such a loving heart that her brief life won for her a special place in the hearts of many. Elizabeth is also an example to us in her following the guidance of a spiritual director. Growth in the spiritual life is a difficult process. We can play games very easily if we don't have someone to challenge us or to share experiences so as to help us avoid pitfalls.

QUOTE: "In our times a special obligation binds us to make ourselves the neighbor of absolutely every person, and of actively helping him when he comes across our path, whether he be an old person abandoned by all, a foreign laborer unjustly looked down upon, a refugee, a child born of an unlawful union and wrongly suffering for a sin he did not commit, or a hungry person who disturbs our conscience by recalling the voice of the Lord: 'As long as you did it for one of these, the least of my brethren, you did it for me' (Matthew 15:40)" (*The Church in the Modern World*, 27).

Rose Philippine Duchesne
Virgin (1769-1852)

Born in Grenoble, France, of a family that was among the new rich, Philippine learned political skills from her father and a love of the poor from her mother. The dominant feature of her temperament was a strong and dauntless will, which became the material—and the battlefield—of her holiness. She entered the convent at 19 without telling her parents and remained despite their opposition. As the French Revolution broke, the convent was closed, and she began taking care of the poor and sick, opened a school for street urchins and risked her life helping priests in the underground.

When the situation cooled, she personally rented her old convent, now a shambles, and tried to revive its religious life. The spirit was gone, and soon there were only four nuns left. They joined the infant Society of the Sacred Heart, whose young superior, St. Madeleine Sophie Barat, would be her lifelong friend. In a short time Philippine was a superior and supervisor of the novitiate and a school. But her ambition since hearing tales of missionary work in Louisiana as a little girl was to go to America and work among the Indians. At 49, she thought this would be her work. With four nuns, she spent 11 weeks at sea en route to New Orleans, and seven weeks more on the Mississippi to St. Louis. She then met one of the many disappointments of her life. The bishop had no place for them to live and work among Native Americans. Instead, he sent her to what she sadly called "the remotest village in the U.S.," St. Charles, Missouri. With characteristic drive and courage, she founded the first free school for girls west of the Mississippi.

It was a mistake. Though she was as hardy as any of the pioneer women in the wagons rolling west, cold and hunger drove them out—to Florissant, Missouri, where she founded the first Catholic Indian school, adding others in the territory. "In her first decade in America Mother Duchesne suffered practically every hardship the frontier had to offer, except the threat of Indian massacre—poor lodging, shortages of food, drinking water, fuel and money, forest fires and blazing chimneys, the vagaries of the Missouri climate, cramped living quarters and the privation of all privacy, and the crude manners of children reared in rough surroundings and with only the slightest training in courtesy" (Louis E. Callan, R.S.C.J., *Philippine Duchesne*).

Finally, at 72, in poor health and retired, she got her lifelong wish. A mission was founded at Sugar Creek, Kansas, among the Potawatomi. She was taken along. Though she could not learn

309

their language, they soon named her "Woman-Who-Prays-Always." While others taught, she prayed. Legend has it that Native American children sneaked behind her as she knelt and sprinkled bits of paper on her habit, and came back hours later to find them undisturbed. She died in 1852 at the age of 83.

COMMENT: Divine grace channeled her iron will and determination into humility and selflessness, and to a desire not to be made superior. Still, even saints can get involved in silly situations. In an argument with a priest over a minor change in the sanctuary, he threatened to remove *her* tabernacle. She patiently let herself be criticized by younger nuns for not being progressive enough. Through it all, 31 years, she hewed to the line of a dauntless love and an unshakable observance of her religious vows.

QUOTE: "We cultivate a very small field for Christ, but we love it, knowing that God does not require great achievements but a heart that holds back nothing for self....The truest crosses are those we do not choose ourselves....He who has Jesus has everything."

NOVEMBER 18   OPTIONAL

Dedication of the Churches of Peter and Paul

St. Peter's is probably the most famous church in Christendom. Massive in scale and a veritable museum of art and architecture, it began on a much humbler scale. Vatican Hill was a simple cemetery where believers gathered at St. Peter's tomb to pray. In 319 Constantine built on the site a basilica which stood for more than a thousand years until, despite numerous restorations, it threatened to collapse. In 1506 Pope Julius II ordered it razed and reconstructed, but the new basilica was not completed and dedicated for more than two centuries.

St. Paul's Outside the Walls stands near the Abbazia delle Tre Fontane, where St. Paul is believed to have been beheaded. The largest church in Rome until St. Peter's was rebuilt, it also rises over the traditional site of its namesake's grave. The most recent edifice dates only to the last century, when it was rebuilt after a fire in 1823. The first basilica was also Constantine's doing.

Constantine's building projects enticed the first of a centuries-long parade of pilgrims to Rome. From the time the basilicas were first built until the empire crumbled under "barbarian" invasions, the two churches, although miles apart, were linked by a roofed colonnade of marble columns.

COMMENT: Peter, the rough fisherman whom Jesus named the rock on which the Church is built, and the educated Paul, reformed persecuter of Christians, Roman citizen and missionary to the Gentiles, are the original odd couple. The major similarity in their faith-journeys is the journey's end: Both, according to tradition, died a martyr's death in Rome, Peter on a cross and Paul beneath the sword. Their combined gifts shaped the early Church and believers have prayed at their tombs from the earliest days.

QUOTE: "It is extraordinarily interesting that Roman pilgrimage began at an...early time. Pilgrims did not wait for the Peace of the Church [Constantine's edict of toleration] before they visited the tombs of the Apostles. They went to Rome a century before there were any public churches and when the Church was confined to the *tituli* [private homes] and the catacombs. The two great pilgrimage sites were exactly as today—the tombs, or memorials, of St. Peter upon the Vatican Hill and the tomb of St. Paul off the Ostian Way" (H. V. Morton, *This Is Rome*).

Presentation of Mary

Mary's presentation was celebrated in Jerusalem in the sixth century. A church was built there in honor of this mystery. The Eastern Church was more interested in the feast, but it does appear in the West in the 11th century. Although the feast at times disappeared from the calendar, in the 16th century it became a feast of the universal Church.

As with Mary's birth, we read of Mary's presentation in the temple only in apocryphal literature. In what is recognized as an unhistorical account, the *Protoevangelium of James* tells us that Anna and Joachim offered Mary to God in the temple when she was three years old. This was to carry out a promise made to God when Anna was still childless.

Though unhistorical, Mary's presentation has an important theological purpose. It continues the impact of the feasts of the Immaculate Conception and of the birth of Mary. It emphasizes that the holiness conferred on Mary from the beginning of her life on earth continued through her early childhood and beyond.

COMMENT: It is sometimes difficult for modern Westerners to appreciate a feast like this. The Eastern Church, however, was quite open to this feast and even somewhat insistent about celebrating it. Even though the feast has no basis in history, it stresses an important truth about Mary: From the beginning of her life, she was dedicated to God. She herself became a greater temple than any made by hands. God came to dwell in her in a marvelous manner and sanctified her for her unique role in God's saving work. At the same time, the magnificence of Mary rebounds upon her children. They, too, are temples of God and sanctified in order that they might enjoy and share in God's saving work.

"Hail, holy throne of God, divine sanctuary, house of glory, jewel most fair, chosen treasure house, and mercy seat for the whole world, heaven showing forth the glory of God. Purest Virgin, worthy of all praise, sanctuary dedicated to God and raised above all human condition, virgin soil, unplowed field, flourishing vine, fountain pouring out waters, virgin bearing a child, mother without knowing man, hidden treasure of innocence, ornament of sanctity, by your most acceptable prayers, strong with the authority of motherhood, to our Lord and God, Creator of all, your Son who was born of you without a father, steer the ship of the Church and bring it to a quiet harbor" (adapted from a homily by St. Germanus on the Presentation of the Mother of God).

Cecilia

Virgin and Martyr

Although Cecilia is one of the most famous of the Roman martyrs, the familiar stories about her are apparently not founded on authentic material. There is no trace of honor being paid her in early times. A fragmentary inscription of the late fourth century refers to a church named after her, and her feast was celebrated at least in 545.

According to legend, Cecilia was a young Christian of high rank betrothed to a Roman named Valerian. Through her influence Valerian was converted, and was martyred along with his brother. The legend about Cecilia's death says that after being struck three times on the neck with a sword, she lived for three days, and asked the pope to convert her home into a church.

Since the time of the Renaissance she has usually been portrayed with a viola or a small organ.

COMMENT: Like any good Christian, Cecilia sang in her heart, and sometimes with her voice. She has become a symbol of the Church's conviction that good music is an integral part of the liturgy, of greater value to the Church than any other art. In the present confused state of church music, it may be useful to recall some words of Vatican II (see below).

QUOTE: "Liturgical action is given a more noble form when sacred rites are solemnized in song, with the assistance of sacred ministers and the active participation of the people....Choirs must be diligently promoted, but bishops and other pastors must ensure that, whenever the sacred action is to be celebrated with song, the whole body of the faithful may be able to contribute that active participation which is rightfully theirs....Gregorian chant, other things being equal, should be given pride of place in liturgical services. But other kinds of sacred music, especially polyphony, are by no means excluded....Religious singing by the people is to be skillfully fostered, so that in devotions and sacred exercises, as also during liturgical services, the voices of the faithful may ring out" (*Constitution on the Liturgy*, 112-118).

Clement I

Pope and Martyr

Clement of Rome was the third successor of St. Peter and reigned as pope during the last decade of the first century. History tells us that he died a martyr in 101. However, the accounts of his martyrdom are legendary, composed about the fourth or fifth century. Probably the Basilica of St. Clement in Rome, one of the earliest parish churches of that city, is built on the site of Clement's home. Clement's First Epistle to the Corinthians was preserved and widely read in the early Church. It is a letter from the Church of Rome, authored by Clement (not to be confused with the writer now called Pseudo-Clement), to the Church in Corinth, concerning a split that alienated a large number of the laity from the clergy. Clement deplores the unauthorized and unjustifiable division in the Corinthian Church and urges unity. He cites the cause of the quarrel as "envy and jealousy."

COMMENT: Clement urged charity to heal the division in the Church of Corinth, for "without charity, nothing is pleasing to God." After Vatican II the entire Church experienced a polarization between the *old* and *new*. May we modern Christians take to heart the exhortation of Clement, implementing these words of St. Paul: "And over all these put on love, that is, the bond of perfection" (Colossians 3:14).

QUOTE: "Charity unites us to God....There is nothing mean in charity, nothing arrogant. Charity knows no schism, does not rebel, does all things in concord. In charity all the elect of God have been made perfect" (*First Epistle to the Corinthians*).

Columban
Abbot (543?-615)

Columban was the greatest of the Irish missionaries who worked on the European continent. As a young man he was greatly tormented by temptations of the flesh, and sought the advice of a religious woman who had lived a hermit's life for years. He saw in her answer a call to leave the world. He went first to a monk on an island in Lough Erne, then to the great monastic seat of learning at Bangor.

After many years of seclusion and prayer, he traveled to Gaul with 12 companion missionaries. They won wide respect for the rigor of their discipline, their preaching, and their commitment to charity and religious life in a time characterized by clerical slackness and civil strife. Columban established several monasteries in Europe which became centers of religion and culture.

Like all saints, he met opposition. Ultimately he had to appeal to the pope against complaints of Frankish bishops, for vindication of his orthodoxy and approval of Irish customs. He reproved the king for his licentious life, insisting that he marry. Since this threatened the power of the queen mother, Columban was ordered deported back to Ireland. His ship ran aground in a storm, and he continued his work in Europe, ultimately arriving in Italy, where he found favor with the king of the Lombards. In his last years he established the famous monastery of Bobbio, where he died. His writings include a treatise on penance and against Arianism, sermons, poetry and his monastic rule.

COMMENT: Now that public sexual license is approaching the extreme, we need the Church's jolting memory of a young man as concerned about chastity as Columban. And now that the comfort-captured Western world stands in tragic contrast to starving millions, we need the challenge to austerity and discipline of a group of Irish monks. They were too strict, we say; they went too far. How far shall *we* go?

QUOTE: Writing to the pope about a doctrinal controversy in Lombardy, Columban said: "We Irish, living in the farthest parts of the earth, are followers of St. Peter and St. Paul and of the disciples who wrote down the sacred canon under the Holy Spirit. We accept nothing outside this evangelical and apostolic teaching....I confess I am grieved by the bad repute of the chair of St. Peter in this country....Though Rome is great and known afar, she is great and honored with us only because of this chair....Look after the peace of the Church, stand between your sheep and the wolves."

Andrew Dung-Lac and Companions

Priest and Martyr; Martyrs

St. Andrew was one of 117 martyrs who met death in Vietnam between 1820 and 1862. Members of this group were beatified on four different occasions between 1900 and 1951. Now all have been canonized by Pope John Paul II.

Christianity came to Vietnam (then three separate kingdoms) through the Portuguese. Jesuits opened the first permanent mission at Da Nang in 1615. They ministered to Japanese Catholics who had been driven from Japan.

The king of one of the kingdoms banned all foreign

317

missionaries and tried to make all Vietnamese apostatize by trampling on a crucifix. Like the priest-holes in Ireland during English persecution, many hiding places were offered in homes of the faithful.

Severe persecutions were again launched three times in the 19th century. During the six decades after 1820, between 100,000 and 300,000 Catholics were killed or subjected to great hardship. Foreign missionaries martyred in the first wave included priests of the Parish Mission Society, and Spanish Dominican priests and tertiaries.

Persecution broke out again in 1847 when the emperor suspected foreign missionaries and Vietnamese Christians of sympathizing with the rebellion of one of his sons.

The last of the martyrs were 17 laypersons, one of them a 9-year-old, executed in 1862. That year a treaty with France guaranteed religious freedom to Catholics, but it did not stop all persecution.

By 1954 there were over a million and a half Catholics— about seven percent of the population—in the north. Buddhists represented about 60 percent. Persistent persecution forced some 670,000 Catholics to abandon lands, homes and possessions and flee to the south. In 1964, there were still 833,000 Catholics in the north, but many were in prison. In the south, Catholics were enjoying the first decade of religious freedom in centuries, their numbers swelled by refugees.

During the Vietnamese war, Catholics again suffered in the north, and again moved to the south in great numbers. Now the whole country is under Communist rule.

COMMENT: It may help a people who associate Vietnam only with a recent war to realize that the cross has long been a part of the lives of the people of that country. Even as we ask again the unanswered questions about United States involvement and disengagement, the faith rooted in Vietnam's soil proves hardier than the forces which would destroy it.

QUOTE: "The Church in Vietnam is alive and vigorous, blessed with strong and faithful bishops, dedicated religious, and courageous and committed laypeople....The Church in Vietnam is living out the gospel in a difficult and complex situation with remarkable persistence and strength" (statement of three U.S. archbishops returning from Vietnam in January 1989).

NOVEMBER 30   FEAST

Andrew

Apostle

Andrew was St. Peter's brother, and was called with him. "As [Jesus] was walking by the sea of Galilee, he saw two brothers, Simon who is now called Peter, and his brother Andrew, casting a net into the sea; they were fishermen. He said to them, 'Come after me, and I will make you fishers of men.' At once they left their nets and followed him" (Matthew 4:18-20).

John the Evangelist presents Andrew as a disciple of John the Baptist. When Jesus walked by one day, John said, "Behold, the Lamb of God." Andrew and another disciple followed Jesus. "Jesus turned and saw them following him and said to them, 'What are you looking for?' They said to him, 'Rabbi' (which translated means Teacher), 'where are you staying?' He said to them, 'Come, and you will see.' So they went and saw where he was staying, and they stayed with him that day" (John 1:38-39a).

Little else is said about Andrew in the Gospels. Before the multiplication of the loaves, it was Andrew who spoke up about the boy who had the barley loaves and fishes (see John 6:8-9). When the Gentiles went to see Jesus, they came to Philip, but Philip then had recourse to Andrew (see John 12:20-22).

Legend has it that Andrew preached the Good News in what

is now modern Greece and Turkey and was crucified at Patras.

COMMENT: As in the case of all the apostles except Peter and John, the Gospels give us little about the holiness of Andrew. He was an apostle. That is enough. He was called personally by Jesus to proclaim the Good News, to heal with Jesus' power and to share his life and death. Holiness today is no different. It is a gift that includes a call to be concerned about the Kingdom, an outgoing attitude that wants nothing more than to share the riches of Christ with all people.

STORY: "...[T]he Twelve called together the community of the disciples and said, 'It is not right for us to neglect the word of God to serve at table. Brothers, select from among you seven reputable men, filled with the Spirit and wisdom, whom we shall appoint to this task, whereas we shall devote ourselves to prayer and to the ministry of the word' " (Acts 6:2-4).

Francis Xavier

Priest (1506-1552)

Jesus asked, "What profit would there be for one to gain the whole world and forfeit his life?" (Matthew 16:26a). The words were repeated to a young teacher of philosophy who had a highly promising career in academics, with success and a life of prestige and honor before him.

Francis Xavier, 24 at the time, and living and teaching in Paris, did not heed these words at once. They came from a good friend, Ignatius of Loyola, whose tireless persuasion finally won the young man to Christ. Francis then made the spiritual exercises under the direction of Ignatius, and in 1534 joined his little community (the infant Society of Jesus). Together at Montmartre they vowed poverty, chastity and apostolic service according to the directions of the pope.

From Venice, where he was ordained priest in 1537, he went on to Lisbon and from there sailed to the East Indies, landing at Goa, on the west coast of India. For the next 10 years he labored to bring the faith to such widely scattered peoples as the Hindus, the Malayans and the Japanese.

Wherever he went, he lived with the poorest people, sharing their food and rough accommodations. He spent countless hours ministering to the sick and the poor, particularly to lepers. Very often he had no time to sleep or even to say his breviary but, as we know from his letters, he was filled always with joy.

Francis went through the islands of Malaysia, then up to Japan. He learned enough Japanese to preach to simple folk, to instruct and to baptize, and to establish missions for those who were to follow him. From Japan he had dreams of going to China, but this plan was never realized. Before reaching the mainland he died.

COMMENT: All of us are called to "go and preach to all nations" (see Matthew 28:19). Our preaching is not necessarily on distant shores but to our families, our children, our husband or wife, our coworkers. And we are called to preach not with words, but by our everyday lives. Only by sacrifice, the giving up of all selfish gain, could Francis be free to bear the Good News to the world. Sacrifice is leaving yourself behind at times for a greater good, the good of prayer, the good of helping someone in need, the good of just listening to another. The greatest gift we have is our time. Francis gave his to others.

STORY: Francis died on the island of Sancian, a hundred miles southwest of Hong Kong. In his final sickness he had to be removed from the ship because the Portuguese sailors feared that kindness to him would offend their master. They were forced to leave him on the sands of the shore, exposed to a bitter wind, but a Portuguese merchant led him into a ramshackle hut. He prayed continually, between spasms of delirium and the doubtful therapy of bleeding. He grew weaker and weaker. "I [Anthony, his friend] could see that he was dying, and put a lighted candle in his hand. Then, with the name of Jesus on his lips, he gave his spirit to his Creator and Lord with great peace and repose."

John Damascene

Priest and Doctor (676?-749)

John spent most of his life in the monastery of St. Sabas, near Jerusalem, and all of his life under Moslem rule, indeed, protected by it. He was born in Damascus, received a classical and theological education, and followed his father in a government position under the Arabs. After a few years he resigned and went to the monastery of St. Sabas.

He is famous in three areas. First, he is known for his writings against the iconoclasts, who opposed the veneration of images. Paradoxically, it was the Eastern Christian emperor Leo who forbade the practice, and it was because John lived in Moslem territory that his enemies could not injure him. Second, he is famous for his treatise, *Exposition of the Orthodox Faith*, a summary of the Greek Fathers (of which he became the last). It is said that this book is to Eastern schools what the *Summa* of Aquinas became to the West. Thirdly, he is known as a poet, one of the two greatest of the Eastern Church, the other being Romanus the Melodist. His devotion to the Blessed Mother and his sermons on her feasts are well known.

COMMENT: John defended the Church's understanding of the veneration of images and explained the faith of the Church in several other controversies. For over 30 years he combined a life of prayer with these defenses and his other writings. His holiness expressed itself in putting his literary and preaching talents at the service of the Lord.

QUOTE: "The saints must be honored as friends of Christ and children and heirs of God, as John the theologian and evangelist says: 'But as many as received him, he gave them the power to be made the sons of God....' Let us carefully observe the manner of life of all the apostles, martyrs, ascetics and just men who announced the coming of the Lord. And let us emulate their faith, charity, hope, zeal, life, patience under suffering, and perseverance unto death, so that we may also share their crowns of glory" (*Exposition of the Orthodox Faith*).

Nicholas

Bishop (d. 350?)

The absence of the "hard facts" of history is not necessarily an obstacle to the popularity of saints, as the devotion to St. Nicholas shows. Both the Eastern and Western Churches honor him, and it is claimed that, after the Blessed Virgin, he is the saint most pictured by Christian artists. And yet, historically, we can pinpoint only the fact that Nicholas was the fourth-century bishop of Myra, a city in Lycia, a province of Asia Minor.

As with many of the saints, however, we are able to capture the relationship which Nicholas had with God through the admiration which Christians have had for him—an admiration expressed in the colorful stories which have been told and retold through the centuries.

Perhaps the best-known story about Nicholas concerns his charity toward a poor man who was unable to provide dowries for his three daughters of marriageable age. Rather than see them forced to prostitution, Nicholas secretly tossed a bag of gold through the poor man's window on three separate occasions, thus enabling the daughters to be married. Over the centuries, this particular legend evolved into the custom of gift-giving on the saint's feast. In the English-speaking countries, St. Nicholas became, by a twist of the tongue, Santa Claus—further expanding the example of generosity portrayed by this holy bishop.

COMMENT: The critical eye of modern history makes us take a deeper look at the legends surrounding St. Nicholas. But perhaps we can utilize the lesson taught by his legendary charity, look deeper at our approach to material goods in the Christmas season and seek ways to extend our sharing to those in real need.

QUOTE: "In order to be able to consult more suitably the welfare of the faithful according to the condition of each one, a bishop should strive to become duly acquainted with their needs in the social circumstances in which they live....He should manifest his concern for all, no matter what their age, condition, or nationality, be they natives, strangers, or foreigners" (*Decree on the Bishops' Pastoral Office*, 16).

Ambrose

Bishop and Doctor (340?-397)

One of Ambrose's biographers observed that at the Last Judgment people would still be divided between those who admired Ambrose and those who heartily disliked him. He emerges as the man of action who cut a furrow through the lives of his contemporaries. Even royal personages were numbered among those who were to suffer crushing divine punishments for standing in Ambrose's way.

When the Empress Justina attempted to wrest two basilicas from Ambrose's Catholics and give them to the Arians, he dared the eunuchs of the court to execute him. His own people rallied behind him in the face of imperial troops. In the midst of riots he both spurred and calmed his people with bewitching new hymns set to exciting Eastern melodies.

In his disputes with the Emperor Auxentius, he coined the principle: "The emperor is in the Church, not above the Church." He publicly admonished Emperor Theodosius for the massacre of seven thousand innocent people. The emperor did public penance for his crime. This was Ambrose, the fighter, sent to Milan as Roman governor and chosen while yet a catechumen to be the people's bishop.

There is yet another side of Ambrose—one which influenced Augustine, whom Ambrose converted. Ambrose was a passionate little man with a high forehead, a long melancholy face and great eyes. We can picture him as a frail figure clasping the codex of sacred Scripture. This was the Ambrose of aristocratic heritage and learning.

Augustine found the oratory of Ambrose less soothing and entertaining but far more learned than that of other contemporaries. Ambrose's sermons were often modeled on Cicero and his ideas betrayed the influence of contemporary thinkers and philosophers. He had no scruples in borrowing at length from pagan authors. He gloried in the pulpit in his ability to parade his spoils—"gold of the Egyptians"—taken over from the pagan philosophers.

His sermons, his writings and his personal life reveal him as an "other-worldly" man involved in the great issues of his day. Humankind, for Ambrose, was, above all, spirit. In order to think rightly of God and the human soul, the closest thing to God, no material reality at all was to be dwelt upon. He was an enthusiastic champion of consecrated virginity.

The influence of Ambrose on Augustine will always be open for discussion. The *Confessions* reveal some manly brusque encounters between Ambrose and Augustine, but there can be no doubt of Augustine's profound esteem for the learned bishop.

Neither is there any doubt that Monica loved Ambrose as an

angel of God who uprooted her son from his former ways and led him to his convictions about Christ. It was Ambrose, after all, who placed his hands on the shoulders of the naked Augustine as he descended into the baptismal fountain to put on Christ.

COMMENT: Ambrose exemplifies for us the truly catholic character of Christianity. He is a man steeped in the learning, law and culture of the ancients and of his contemporaries. Yet, in the midst of active involvement in this world, this thought runs through Ambrose's life and preaching: The hidden meaning of the Scriptures calls our spirit to rise to another world.

QUOTE: "Now, man is not wrong when he regards himself as superior to bodily concerns, and as more than a speck of nature or a nameless constituent of the city of man. For by his interior qualities he outstrips the whole sum of mere things....Steeped in wisdom, man passes through visible realities to those which are unseen" (*The Church in the Modern World*, 14-15).

Immaculate Conception

A feast called the Conception of Mary arose in the Eastern Church in the seventh century. It came to the West in the eighth century. In the 11th century it received its present name, the Immaculate Conception. In the 18th century it became a feast of the universal Church.

In 1854 Pius IX gave the infallible statement: "The most Blessed Virgin Mary, in the first instant of her conception, by a singular grace and privilege granted by almighty God, in view of the merits of Jesus Christ, the savior of the human race, was preserved free from all stain of original sin."

It took a long time for this doctrine to develop. While many Fathers and Doctors of the Church considered Mary the greatest and holiest of the saints, they often had difficulty in seeing Mary as sinless—either at her conception or throughout her life. This is one of the Church teachings that arose more from the piety of the faithful than from the insights of brilliant theologians. Even such champions of Mary as Bernard and Thomas Aquinas could not see theological justification for this teaching.

Two Franciscans, William of Ware and John Duns Scotus, helped develop the theology. They point out that Mary's Immaculate Conception enhances Jesus' redemptive work. Other members of the human race are cleansed from original sin after birth. In Mary Jesus' work was so powerful as to prevent original sin at the outset.

COMMENT: In Luke 1:28 the angel Gabriel, speaking on God's behalf, addresses Mary as "full of grace" (or "highly favored"). In that context this phrase means that Mary is receiving all the special divine help necessary for the task ahead. However, the Church grows in understanding with the help of the Holy Spirit. The Spirit led the Church, especially non-theologians, to the insight that Mary had to be the most perfect work of God next to the Incarnation. Or rather, Mary's intimate association with the Incarnation called for the special involvement of God in Mary's whole life. The logic of piety helped God's people to believe that Mary was full of grace and free of sin from the first moment of her existence. Moreover, this great privilege of Mary is the highlight of all that God has done in Jesus. Rightly understood, the incomparable holiness of Mary shows forth the incomparable goodness of God.

QUOTE: "[Mary] gave to the world the Life that renews all things, and she was enriched by God with gifts appropriate to such a role.

"It is no wonder, then, that the usage prevailed among the

holy Fathers whereby they called the mother of God entirely holy and free from all stain of sin, fashioned by the Holy Spirit into a kind of new substance and new creature. Adorned from the first instant of her conception with the splendors of an entirely unique holiness, the Virgin of Nazareth is, on God's command, greeted by an angel messenger as 'full of grace' (cf. Luke 1:28). To the heavenly messenger she replies: 'Behold the handmaid of the Lord, be it done to me according to thy word' (Luke 1:38)" (*Constitution on the Church*, 56).

Damasus I
Pope (305?-384)

To his secretary St. Jerome, Damasus was "an incomparable person, learned in the Scriptures, a virgin doctor of the virgin Church, who loved chastity and heard its praises with pleasure."

Damasus seldom heard such unrestrained praise. Internal political struggles, doctrinal heresies, uneasy relations with his fellow bishops and those of the Eastern Church marred the peace of his pontificate.

The son of a Roman priest, possibly of Spanish extraction, Damasus started as a deacon in his father's church, and rose to priest of what later became the basilica of San Lorenzo in Rome. He served Pope Liberius (352-366) and followed him into exile.

When Liberius died, Damasus was elected bishop of Rome; but a minority elected and consecrated another deacon, Ursinus, as pope. The controversy between Damasus and the antipope resulted in violent battles in two basilicas, scandalizing the bishops of Italy. At the synod Damasus called on the occasion of his birthday, he asked them to approve his actions. The bishops' reply was curt: "We assembled for a birthday, not to condemn a man unheard." Supporters of the antipope even managed to get Damasus accused of a grave crime—probably sexual—as late as A.D. 378. He had to clear himself before both a civil court and a Church synod.

As pope his life-style was simple in contrast to other ecclesiastics of Rome, and he was fierce in his denunciation of Arianism and other heresies. A misunderstanding of the Trinitarian terminology used by Rome threatened amicable relations with the Eastern Church, and Damasus was only moderately successful in dealing with the situation.

It was during his pontificate (380) that Christianity was declared the official religion of the Roman state, and Latin became the principal liturgical language as part of the pope's reforms. His encouragement of St. Jerome's biblical studies led to the Vulgate, the Latin translation of Scripture which the Council of Trent (11 centuries later) declared to be "authentic in public readings, disputations, preachings."

Comments: The history of the papacy and the Church is inextricably mixed with the personal biography of Damasus. In a troubled and pivotal period of Church history, he stands forth as a zealous defender of the faith who knew when to be progressive and when to entrench.

Damasus makes us aware of two qualities of good leadership: alertness to the promptings of the Spirit and service. His struggles are a reminder that Jesus never promised his Rock protection from hurricane winds nor his followers immunity from difficulties. His only guarantee is final victory.

QUOTE: "He who walking on the sea could calm the bitter waves, who gives life to the dying seeds of the earth; he who was able to loose the mortal chains of death, and after three days' darkness could bring again to the upper world the brother for his sister Martha: he, I believe, will make Damasus rise again from the dust" (epitaph Damasus wrote for himself).

Our Lady of Guadalupe

The Mass in honor of Our Lady of Guadalupe goes back to the 16th century. Chronicles of that period tell us the story.

A poor Indian named Cuatitlatoatzin was baptized and given the name Juan Diego. He was a 57-year-old widower and lived in a small village near Mexico City. On Saturday morning, December 9, 1531, he was on his way to a nearby barrio to attend Mass in honor of Our Lady.

He was walking by a hill called Tepeyac when he heard beautiful music like the warbling of birds. A radiant cloud appeared and within it a young Native American maiden dressed like an Aztec princess. The lady spoke to him in his own language and sent him to the bishop of Mexico, a Franciscan named Juan de Zumarraga. The bishop was to build a chapel in the place where the lady appeared.

Eventually the bishop told Juan Diego to have the lady give him a sign. About this same time Juan Diego's uncle became seriously ill. This led poor Diego to try to avoid the lady. The lady found Diego, nevertheless, assured him that his uncle would recover and provided roses for Juan to carry to the bishop in his cape or tilma.

Juan Diego opened his tilma in the bishop's presence, the roses fell to the ground and the bishop sank to his knees. On Juan Diego's tilma appeared a painting of Mary as she had appeared at the hill of Tepeyac. It was December 12, 1531.

COMMENT: Mary's appearance to Juan Diego as one of his people is a powerful reminder that Mary and the God who sent her accept all peoples. In the context of the sometimes rude and cruel treatment of the Indians by the Spaniards, the apparition was a rebuke to the Spaniards and an event of vast significance for

Native Americans. While a number of them had converted before this incident, they now came in droves. According to a contemporary chronicler nine million Indians became Catholic in a very short time. In these days when we hear so much about God's preferential option for the poor, Our Lady of Guadalupe cries out to us that God's love for and identification with the poor is an age-old truth that stems from the gospel itself.

QUOTE: Mary to Juan Diego: "My dearest son, I am the eternal Virgin Mary, Mother of the true God, Author of Life, Creator of all and Lord of the Heavens and of the Earth...and it is my desire that a church be built here in this place for me, where, as your most merciful Mother and that of all your people, I may show my loving clemency and the compassion that I bear to the Indians, and to those who love and seek me..." (from an ancient chronicle).

Lucy

Virgin and Martyr (d. 304)

Every little girl named Lucy must bite her tongue in disappointment when she first tries to find out what there is to know about her patron saint. The older books will have a lengthy paragraph detailing a small number of traditions. Newer books will have a lengthy paragraph showing that there is little basis in history for these traditions. The single fact survives that a disappointed suitor accused Lucy of being a Christian and she was executed in Syracuse of Sicily in the year 304. But it is also true that her name is mentioned in the First Eucharistic Prayer, geographical places are named after her, a popular song has her name as its title and down through the centuries many thousands of little girls were proud of the name *Lucy*.

One can easily imagine what a young Christian woman had to contend with in pagan Sicily in the year 300. If you have trouble imagining, just glance at the pagan world around you today and the barriers it presents against leading a good Christian life.

Her friends must have wondered aloud about this hero of Lucy's, an obscure itinerant preacher in a far-off captive nation that had been destroyed more than 200 years before. Once a carpenter, he had been crucified by the Roman soldiers after his own people sentenced him to death. Lucy believed with her whole soul that this man had risen from the dead. Heaven had put a stamp on all he said and did. To give witness to her faith she had made a vow of virginity.

What a hubbub this caused among her pagan friends! The kindlier ones just thought her a little strange. To be pure before marriage was an ancient Roman ideal, rarely found but not to be condemned. To exclude marriage altogether, however, was too much. She must have something sinister to hide, the tongues wagged.

Lucy knew of the heroism of earlier virgin martyrs. She remained faithful to their example and to the example of the carpenter, whom she knew to be the Son of God.

COMMENT: If you are a little girl named Lucy, you need not bite your tongue in disappointment. Your patron is a genuine, authentic heroine, first class, an abiding inspiration for you and for all Christians. The moral courage of the young Sicilian martyr shines forth as a guiding light, just as bright for today's youth as it was in A.D. 304.

QUOTE: "The Gospel tells us of all that Jesus suffered, of the insults that fell upon him. But, from Bethlehem to Calvary, the brilliance that radiates from his divine purity spread more and more and won over the crowds. So great was the austerity and the enchantment of his conduct.

"So may it be with you, beloved daughters. Blessed be the discretion, the mortifications and the renouncements with which you seek to render this virtue more brilliant....May your conduct prove to all that chastity is not only a possible virtue but a social virtue, which must be strongly defended through prayer, vigilance and the mortification of the senses" (Pope John XXIII, *Letter to Women Religious*).

John of the Cross
Priest and Doctor (1541-1591)

John is a saint because his life was a heroic effort to live up to his name: "of the Cross." The folly of the cross came to full realization in time. "Whoever wishes to come after me must deny himself, take up his cross, and follow me" (Mark 8:34b) is the story of John's life. The Paschal Mystery—through death to life—strongly marks John as reformer, mystic-poet and theologian-priest.

Ordained a Carmelite priest at 25 (1567), John met Teresa of Jesus (Avila) and like her vowed himself to the primitive rule of the Carmelites. As partner with Teresa and in his own right John engaged in the work to reform, and came to experience the price of reform: increasing opposition, misunderstanding, persecution, imprisonment. He came to know the cross acutely—to experience the dying of Jesus—as he sat month after month in his dark, damp, narrow cell with only his God!

Yet, the paradox! In this dying of imprisonment John came to life, uttering poetry. In the darkness of the dungeon, John's spirit came into the Light. There are many mystics, many poets; John is unique as mystic-poet, expressing in his prison-cross the ecstasy of mystical union with God in the *Spiritual Canticle*.

But as agony leads to ecstasy, so John had his *Ascent to Mt. Carmel*, as he named it in his prose masterpiece. As man-Christian-Carmelite, he experienced in himself this purifying ascent; as spiritual director, he sensed it in others; as psychologist-theologian, he described and analyzed it in his prose writings. His prose works are outstanding in underscoring the cost of discipleship, the path of union with God: rigorous discipline, abandonment, purification. Uniquely and strongly John underlines the gospel paradox: The cross leads to resurrection, agony to ecstasy, darkness to light, abandonment to possession, denial of self to union with God. If you want to save your life, you must lose it. John is truly "of the Cross." He died at 49—a life short, but full.

COMMENT: John in his life and writings has a crucial word for us today. We tend to be rich, soft, comfortable. We shrink even from words like *self-denial, mortification, purification, asceticism, discipline.* We run from the cross. John's message—like the gospel—is loud and clear: *Don't*—if you really want to live!

QUOTE: Thomas Merton said of John: "Just as we can never separate asceticism from mysticism, so in St. John of the Cross we find darkness and light, suffering and joy, sacrifice and love united together so closely that they seem at times to be identified."

In John's words:
> "Never was fount so clear,
> undimmed and bright;
> From it alone, I know proceeds all light,
> although 'tis night."

Peter Canisius

Priest and Doctor (1521-1597)

The energetic life of Peter Canisius should demolish any stereotypes we may have of the life of a saint as dull or routine. Peter lived in his 76 years at a pace which cannot but be considered heroic, even in our time of rapid change. A man blessed with many talents, Peter is an excellent example of the scriptural man who develops his talents for the sake of the Lord's work.

He was one of the most important figures in the Catholic Counter-Reformation in Germany. His was such a key role that he has often been called the "second apostle of Germany" in that his life parallels the earlier work of Boniface.

Although Peter once accused himself of idleness in his youth, he could not have been idle too long, for at the age of 19 he received a master's degree from the university at Cologne. Soon afterwards he met Peter Faber, the first disciple of Ignatius Loyola, who influenced him so much that he joined the recently formed Society of Jesus.

At this early age Peter had already taken up a practice he continued throughout his life—a process of study, reflection, prayer and writing. After his ordination in 1546, he became widely known for his editions of the works of St. Cyril of Alexandria and St. Leo the Great. Besides this reflective literary bent, Peter had a zeal for the apostolate. He could often be found visiting the sick or prisoners, even when his assigned duties in other areas were more than enough to keep most people fully occupied.

In 1547 Peter attended several sessions of the Council of Trent, whose decrees he was later assigned to implement. After a brief teaching assignment at the Jesuit college at Messina, Peter was entrusted with the mission to Germany—from that point on his life's work. He taught in several universities and was instrumental in establishing many colleges and seminaries. He wrote a catechism which explained the Catholic faith in a way which common people could understand—a great need of that age.

Renowned as a popular preacher, Peter packed churches with those eager to hear his eloquent proclamation of the gospel. He had great diplomatic ability, often serving as a reconciler between disputing factions. In his letters (filling eight volumes) one finds words of wisdom and counsel to people in all walks of life. At times he wrote unprecedented letters of criticism to leaders of the Church—yet always in the context of a loving, sympathetic concern.

At 70 Peter suffered a paralytic seizure, but he continued to preach and write with the aid of a secretary until his death on December 21, 1597.

COMMENT: Peter's untiring efforts are an apt example for those involved in the renewal of the Church or the growth of moral consciousness in business or government. He is regarded as one of the creators of the Catholic press, and can easily be a model for the Christian author or journalist. Teachers can see in his life a passion for the transmission of truth. Whether we have much to give, as Peter Canisius did, or whether we have only a little to give, as did the poor widow in the Gospel (see Luke 21:1-4), the important thing is to give our all. It is in this way that Peter is so exemplary for Christians in an age of rapid change when we are called to be in the world but not of the world.

QUOTE: When asked if he felt overworked, Peter replied, "If you have too much to do, with God's help you will find time to do it all."

John of Kanty

Priest (1390?-1473)

John was a country lad who made good in the big city and the big university of Kraków, Poland. After brilliant studies he was ordained a priest and became a professor of theology. The inevitable opposition which saints encounter led to his being ousted by rivals and sent to be a parish priest at Olkusz. An extremely humble man, he did his best, but his best was not to the liking of his parishioners. Besides, he was afraid of the responsibilities of his position. But in the end he won his people's hearts. After some time he returned to Kraków and taught Scripture for the remainder of his life.

He was a serious man, and humble, but known to all the poor of Kraków for his kindness. His goods and his money were always at their disposal, and time and again they took advantage of him. He kept only the money and clothes absolutely needed to support himself. He slept little, and then on the floor, ate sparingly, and took no meat. He made a pilgrimage to Jerusalem, hoping to be martyred by the Turks. He made four pilgrimages to Rome, carrying his luggage on his back. When he was warned to look after his health, he was quick to point out that, for all their austerity, the fathers of the desert lived remarkably long lives.

COMMENT: John of Kanty is a typical saint: He was kind, humble and generous, he suffered opposition and led an austere, penitential life. Most Christians in an affluent society can understand all the ingredients but the last: Anything more than mild self-discipline seems reserved for athletes and ballet dancers. Christmas is a good time at least to reject self-indulgence.

STORY: The old breviary included this story: John of Kanty was once accosted by robbers, who took his money. They asked if he had any more, and he replied in the negative. When they had gone, he discovered some coins sewn in his cloak, ran after the robbers, shouted for them to stop and gave them the coins. They were so amazed that they gave back what they had taken.

Stephen

First Martyr (d. 36?)

All we know of Stephen is found in Acts 6 and 7. It is enough to tell us what kind of man he was.

> At that time, as the number of disciples continued to grow, the Hellenists complained against the Hebrews because their widows were being neglected in the daily distribution. So the Twelve called together the community of the disciples and said, "It is not right for us to neglect the word of God to serve at table. Brothers, select from among you seven reputable men, filled with the Spirit and wisdom, whom we shall appoint to this task, whereas we shall devote ourselves to prayer and to the ministry of the word." The proposal was acceptable to the whole community, so they chose Stephen, a man filled with faith and the holy Spirit....(Acts 6:1-5)

Acts says that Stephen was a man filled with grace and power, who worked great wonders among the people. Certain Jews, members of the Synagogue of Roman Freedmen, debated with Stephen but proved no match for the wisdom and spirit with which he spoke. They persuaded others to make the charge of blasphemy against him. He was seized and carried before the Sanhedrin.

In his speech, Stephen recalled God's guidance through Israel's history, as well as Israel's idolatry and disobedience. He then claimed that his persecutors were showing this same spirit. "[Y]ou always oppose the holy Spirit; you are just like your ancestors" (Acts 7:51b).

His speech brought anger from the crowd. "But [Stephen], filled with the holy Spirit, looked up intently to heaven and saw the glory of God and Jesus standing at the right hand of God, and he said, 'Behold, I see the heavens opened and the Son of Man standing at the right hand of God.'...They threw him out of the city, and began to stone him.... As they were stoning Stephen, he called out, 'Lord Jesus, receive my spirit....Lord, do not hold this sin against them'" (Acts 7:55-56, 58a, 59, 60b).

COMMENT: Stephen died as Jesus did: falsely accused, brought to unjust condemnation because he spoke the truth fearlessly. He died with his eyes trustfully fixed on God, and with a prayer of forgiveness on his lips. A "happy" death is one that finds us in the same spirit, whether our dying is as quiet as Joseph's or as violent as Stephen's: dying with courage, total trust and forgiving love.

STORY: "The witnesses laid down their cloaks at the feet of a young man named Saul....

"Now Saul was consenting to his execution. On that day there broke out a severe persecution of the church in Jerusalem....Saul, meanwhile, was trying to destroy the church; entering house after house and dragging out men and women, he handed them over for imprisonment....

"...[S]till breathing murderous threats against the disciples of the Lord...as he was nearing Damascus, a light from the sky suddenly flashed around [Saul]. He fell to the ground and heard a voice saying to him, 'Saul, Saul, why are you persecuting me?' He said, 'Who are you, sir?' The reply came, 'I am Jesus, whom you are persecuting' " (Acts 7:58b; 8:1, 3; 9:1a, 3-5).

John

Apostle and Evangelist

It is God who calls; human beings answer. The vocation of John
and his brother James is stated very simply in the Gospels, along
with that of Peter and his brother Andrew: Jesus called them;
they followed. The absoluteness of their response is indicated by
the account. James and John "were in a boat, with their father
Zebedee, mending their nets. He called them, and immediately
they left their boat and their father and followed him" (Matthew
4:21b-22).

For the three former fishermen—Peter, James and John—
that faith was to be rewarded by a special friendship with Jesus.
They alone were privileged to be present at the Transfiguration,
the raising of the daughter of Jairus and the agony in
Gethsemane. But John's friendship was even more special.
Tradition assigns to him the Fourth Gospel, although most
modern Scripture scholars think it unlikely that the apostle and
the evangelist are the same person.

John's own Gospel refers to him as "the disciple whom Jesus
loved" (see John 13:23; 19:26; 20:2), the one who reclined next
to Jesus at the Last Supper, and the one to whom he gave the
exquisite honor, as he stood beneath the cross, of caring for his
mother. "Woman, behold your son....Behold, your mother" (John
19:26b, 27b).

Because of the depth of his Gospel, John is usually thought
of as the eagle of theology, soaring in high regions that other
writers did not enter. But the ever-frank Gospels reveal some very

human traits. Jesus gave James and John the nickname, "sons of thunder." While it is difficult to know exactly what this meant, a clue is given in two incidents.

In the first, as Matthew tells it, they (Mark says their mother) asked that they might sit in the places of honor in Jesus' kingdom—one on his right hand, one on his left. When Jesus asked them if they could drink the cup he would drink and be baptized with his baptism of pain, they blithely answered, "We can!" Jesus said that they would indeed share his cup, but that sitting at his right hand was not his to give. It was for those to whom it had been reserved by the Father. The other apostles were indignant at the mistaken ambition of the brothers, and Jesus took the occasion to teach them the true nature of authority: "...[W]hoever wishes to be first among you shall be your slave. Just so, the Son of Man did not come to be served but to serve and to give his life as a ransom for many" (Matthew 20:27-28).

On another occasion the "sons of thunder" asked Jesus if they should not call down fire from heaven upon the inhospitable Samaritans, who would not welcome Jesus because he was on his way to Jerusalem. But Jesus "turned and rebuked them" (see Luke 9:51-55).

On the first Easter, Magdalene "ran and went to Simon Peter and to the other disciple whom Jesus loved, and told them, 'They have taken the Lord from the tomb, and we don't know where they put him' " (John 20:2). John recalls, perhaps with a smile, that he and Peter ran side by side, but then "the other disciple ran faster than Peter and arrived at the tomb first" (John 20:4b). He did not enter, but waited for Peter and let him go in first. "Then the other disciple also went in, the one who had arrived at the tomb first, and he saw and believed" (John 20:8).

John was with Peter when the first great miracle after the Resurrection took place—the cure of the man crippled from birth—which led to their spending the night in jail together. The mysterious experience of the Resurrection is perhaps best contained in the words of Acts: "Observing the boldness of Peter and John and perceiving them to be uneducated, ordinary men, they [the questioners] were amazed, and they recognized them as the companions of Jesus" (Acts 4:13).

The evangelist wrote the great Gospel, the letters and the Book of Revelation. His Gospel is a very personal account. He sees the glorious and divine Jesus already in the incidents of his mortal life. At the Last Supper, John's Jesus speaks as if he were already in heaven. It is the Gospel of Jesus' glory.

COMMENT: It is a long way from being eager to sit on a throne of power or to call down fire from heaven to becoming the man who could write: "The way we came to know love was that he laid down his life for us; so we ought to lay down our lives for our brothers" (1 John 3:16).

QUOTE: A persistent story has it that John's "parishioners" grew tired of his one sermon, which relentlessly emphasized: "Love one another." Whether the story is true or not, it has basis in John's writing. He wrote what may be called a summary of the Bible: "We have come to know and to believe in the love God has for us. God is love, and whoever remains in love remains in God and God in him" (1 John 4:16).

Holy Innocents

Martyrs

Herod "the Great," king of Judea, was unpopular with his people because of his connections with the Romans and his religious indifference. Hence he was insecure and fearful of any threat to his throne. He was a master politician and a tyrant capable of extreme brutality. He killed his wife, his brother and his sister's two husbands, to name only a few.

Matthew 2:1-18 tells this story: Herod was "greatly troubled" when astrologers from the east came asking the whereabouts of "the newborn king of the Jews," whose star they had seen. They were told that the Jewish Scriptures named Bethlehem as the place where the Messiah would be born. Herod cunningly told them to report back to him so that he could also "do him homage." They found Jesus, offered him their gifts and, warned by an angel, avoided Herod on their way home. Jesus escaped to Egypt.

Herod became furious and "ordered the massacre of all the boys in Bethlehem and its vicinity two years old and under." Since Bethlehem was a small town, the number of babies killed was perhaps 20 or 25. The horror of the massacre and the devastation of the mothers and fathers led Matthew to quote Jeremiah: "A voice was heard in Ramah,/sobbing and loud lamentation;/Rachel weeping for her children..." (Matthew 2:18). Rachel was the wife of Jacob/Israel. She is pictured as weeping at the place where the Israelites were herded together by the conquering Assyrians for their march into captivity.

COMMENT: Twenty babies are few, in comparison to the genocide and abortion of our day. But even if there had been only one, we recognize the greatest treasure God put on the earth—a human person, destined for eternity and graced by Jesus' death and resurrection.

QUOTE: "Lord, you give us life even before we understand" (Prayer Over the Gifts, Feast of the Holy Innocents).

Thomas Becket

Bishop and Martyr (1118-1170)

A strong man who wavered for a moment, but then learned one
cannot come to terms with evil and so became a strong
churchman, a martyr and a saint—that was Thomas Becket,
Archbishop of Canterbury, murdered in his cathedral December
29, 1170.

His career had been a stormy one. While archdeacon of
Canterbury, he was made chancellor of England at the age of 36
by his friend King Henry II. When Henry felt it advantageous to
raise his chancellor to the archbishopric of Canterbury, Thomas
gave him fair warning: he might not accept all of Henry's
intrusions into Church affairs. Nevertheless, he was made
archbishop (1162), resigned his chancellorship and reformed his
whole way of life!

Troubles began. Henry insisted upon usurping Church
rights. At one time, supposing some conciliatory action possible,
Thomas came close to compromise. He momentarily approved
the Constitutions of Clarendon, which would have denied the
clergy the right of trial by a Church court and prevented them
from making direct appeal to Rome. But Thomas rejected the
Constitutions, fled to France for safety and remained in exile for
seven years. When he returned to England he suspected it would
mean certain death. Because Thomas refused to remit censures he
had placed upon bishops favored by the king, Henry cried out in
a rage, "Will no one rid me of this troublesome priest!" Four
knights, taking his words as his wish, slew Thomas in the
Canterbury cathedral.

Within three years Thomas was a saint of the Church and
his tomb a shrine of pilgrimage. Henry II himself did penance at
Thomas's tomb, but a later Henry (VIII) despoiled that tomb and

scattered the saint's relics. Thomas Becket, however, remains a hero-saint down to our own times.

COMMENT: No one becomes a saint without struggle, especially with himself. Thomas knew he must stand firm in defense of truth and right, even at the cost of his life. We also must take a stand in the face of pressures—against dishonesty, deceit, destruction of life—at the cost of popularity, convenience, promotion and even greater goods.

QUOTE: In T.S. Eliot's drama, *Murder in the Cathedral*, Becket faces a final temptation to seek martyrdom for earthly glory and revenge. With real insight into his life situation, Thomas responds:
"The last temptation is the greatest treason:
To do the right deed for the wrong reason."

Sylvester I

Pope (d. 335)

When you think of this pope, you think of the Edict of Milan, the emergence of the Church from the catacombs, the building of the great basilicas, Saint John Lateran, Saint Peter's and others, the Council of Nicaea and other critical events. But for the most part, these events were planned or brought about by the Emperor Constantine.

A great store of legends has grown up around the man who was pope at this most important time, but very little can be established historically. We know for sure that his papacy lasted from 314 until his death in 335. Reading between the lines of history, we are assured that no one but a very strong and wise man could have preserved the essential independence of the Church in the face of the overpowering figure of the Emperor Constantine. The bishops in general remained loyal to the Holy See and at times expressed apologies to Sylvester for undertaking important ecclesiastical projects at the urging of Constantine.

COMMENT: It takes deep humility and courage in the face of criticism for a leader to stand aside and let events take their course, when asserting one's authority would only lead to useless tension and strife. Sylvester teaches a valuable lesson for Church leaders, politicians, parents and others in authority.

QUOTE: To emphasize the continuity of Holy Orders, the recent Roman breviary in its biographies of popes ends with important statistics. On the feast of Saint Sylvester it recounts: "He presided at seven December ordinations at which he created 42 priests, 25 deacons and 65 bishops for various sees." The Holy Father is indeed the heart of the Church's sacramental system, an essential element of its unity.

Index